KU-239-485

HARRY BENSON
SCRAM!

The Gripping First-hand Account of the
Helicopter War in the Falklands

arrow books

Published by Arrow 2012

10 9 8 7 6 5 4 3 2 1

First published in Great Britain in 2012 by Preface Publishing

20 Vauxhall Bridge Road
London, SW1V 2SA

An imprint of The Random House Group Limited

www.randomhouse.co.uk

Addresses for companies within The Random House Group Limited
can be found at www.randomhouse.co.uk

The Random House Group Limited Reg. No. 954009

A CIP catalogue record for this book is available from the British Library

ISBN 978 0 09956 882 7

The Random House Group Limited supports The Forest Stewardship Council
(FSC®), the leading international forest certification organisation. Our books
carrying the FSC label are printed on FSC® certified paper. FSC is the only
forest certification scheme endorsed by the leading environmental organisations,
including Greenpeace. Our paper procurement policy can be found at
ronment

k Production Limited

UK) Ltd, Croydon CR0 4YY

Contents

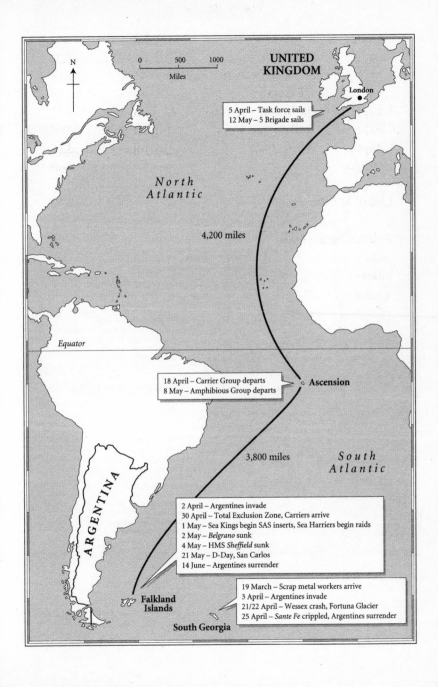

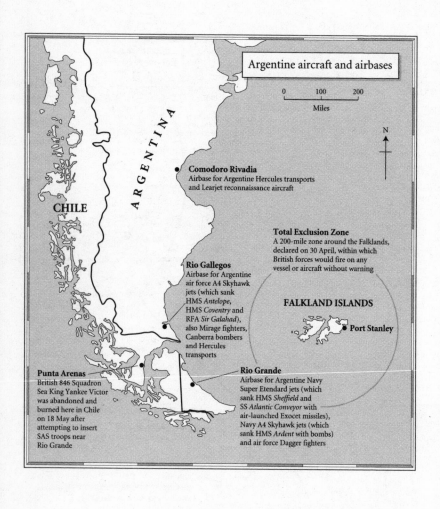

Argentine aircraft and airbases

0   100   200

Miles

N

C H I L E

A R G E N T I N A

Comodoro Rivadia
Airbase for Argentine Hercules transports
and Learjet reconnaissance aircraft

Total Exclusion Zone
A 200-mile zone around the Falklands,
declared on 30 April, within which
British forces would fire on any
vessel or aircraft without warning

Rio Gallegos
Airbase for Argentine
air force A4 Skyhawk
jets (which sank
HMS *Antelope*,
HMS *Coventry* and
RFA *Sir Galahad*),
also Mirage fighters,
Canberra bombers
and Hercules
transports

FALKLAND ISLANDS

● Port Stanley

Punta Arenas
British 846 Squadron
Sea King Yankee Victor
was abandoned and
burned here in Chile
on 18 May after
attempting to insert
SAS troops near
Rio Grande

Rio Grande
Airbase for Argentine Navy
Super Etendard jets (which
sank HMS *Sheffield* and
SS *Atlantic Conveyor* with
air-launched Exocet missiles),
Navy A4 Skyhawk jets (which
sank HMS *Ardent* with bombs)
and air force Dagger fighters

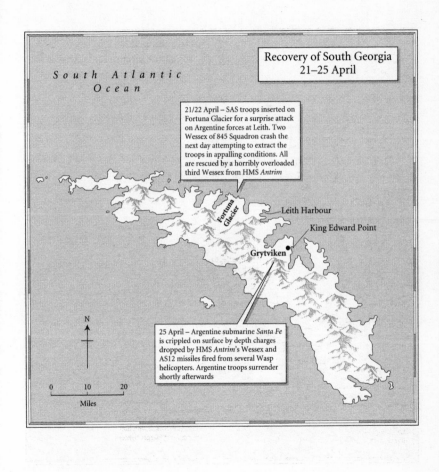

**Recovery of South Georgia
21–25 April**

*South Atlantic
Ocean*

21/22 April – SAS troops inserted on
Fortuna Glacier for a surprise attack
on Argentine forces at Leith. Two
Wessex of 845 Squadron crash the
next day attempting to extract the
troops in appalling conditions. All
are rescued by a horribly overloaded
third Wessex from HMS *Antrim*

*Fortuna
Glacier*

Leith Harbour

King Edward Point

Grytviken

N

25 April – Argentine submarine *Santa Fe*
is crippled on surface by depth charges
dropped by HMS *Antrim*'s Wessex and
AS12 missiles fired from several Wasp
helicopters. Argentine troops surrender
shortly afterwards

0   10   20

Miles

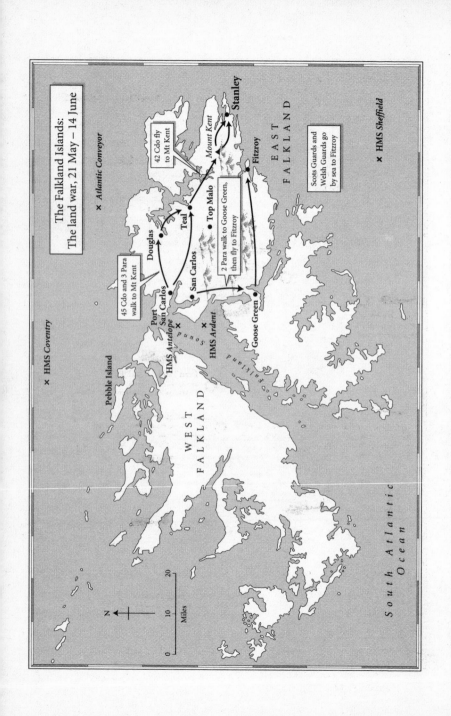

The Falkland Islands:
The land war, 21 May – 14 June

× *Atlantic Conveyor*

× HMS *Coventry*

× HMS *Sheffield*

Pebble Island

WEST FALKLAND

EAST FALKLAND

South Atlantic Ocean

N

0   10   20
Miles

Port San Carlos
San Carlos
× HMS *Antelope*
× HMS *Ardent*

Sound
Falkland Sound

Goose Green

Douglas
Teal
Top Malo
Mount Kent
Fitzroy
Stanley

45 Cdo and 3 Para walk to Mt Kent

42 Cdo fly to Mt Kent

2 Para walk to Goose Green, then fly to Fitzroy

Scots Guards and Welsh Guards go by sea to Fitzroy

San Carlos helicopter bases
21 May – 14 June

Port San Carlos settlement
All 845 Wessex and the Chinook
moved here on 30 May. 847 Wessex
arrived on 1 June and 9 June

San Carlos Water

Old House Creek FOB
846 Sea King day flyers and
845 Wessex spent first week
here. Chinook arrived 26 May

Pollock's Passage
846 Sea King night flyers
based here for a week
from 29 May

Fern Valley Creek FOB
846 Sea King day flyers moved here
27 May, joined by the night flyers 8 June

San Carlos settlement
825 Sea Kings based here from 29 May,
joined by rest from overcrowded
Port San Carlos 3 June

Ajax Bay
Two 845 Wessex started
here then moved to
Old House Creek FOB

N

'Teeny Weeny' Gazelles and Scouts spread
out through the southern end of the bay

0   1   2

Miles

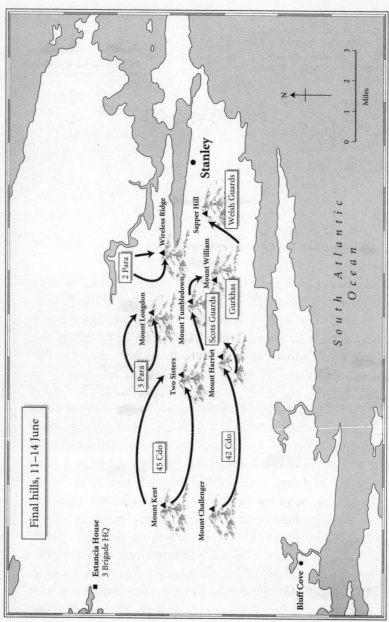

The final land battles of the Falklands war took place in two distinct phases. Night of 11/12 June: Longdon, Two Sisters, Harriet. Night of 13/14 June: Tumbledown, Wireless Ridge and Sapper Hill.

Foreword

Julian Thompson
Commander 3rd Commando Brigade in 1982

Harry Benson's aptly named *Scram!* is the first account to be written about the *junglies* part in the Falklands War of 1982. The *junglies* being the name for the Royal Navy troop lift helicopters, dating back to the campaign in the jungles of Borneo in the 1960s. Back then, the Fleet Air Arm helicopter aircrews made a name for themselves as 'can do' people – a reputation that they more than upheld in the Falklands War. 'Scram', broadcast over the helicopter control radio net during the Falklands War meant take cover from Argentine fighters. This call was a regular feature of life down south, especially during the first six days after we landed while the Royal Navy fought and won the Battle of San Carlos Water; arguably the toughest fight by British ships against enemy air attack since Crete in 1941. As the Argentine fighter/bombers came barrelling in I would watch heart in mouth as the *junglies* headed for folds in the ground, remaining burning and turning until the enemy had left. Sometimes there was nothing for it but for them to keep on flying, especially if the helicopter in question was carrying an underslung load; or had just lifted from a ship well out in San Carlos Water, with nowhere handy to hide.

Today there is a road network in East Falkland. In 1982 there were no roads outside Stanley and a rough track from Fitzroy to Stanley. Every single bean, bullet, and weapon had to be flown forward from where it had been offloaded from ships – unless it was carried on the back of a marine or soldier, or by the handful of tracked vehicles capable of negotiating the ubiquitous peat bog that along with stone runs and dinosaur-like spine backed hills constituted the Falklands landscape. Likewise every casualty had to be flown back. Without the *junglies* there would have been no point in us going south to retake the Falklands; we would have got nowhere.

I am glad that Harry Benson has given space to tell of some of the activities of the non *junglie* choppers. He relates in some detail the story of the epic rescue of the SAS from the Fortuna Glacier in South Georgia by HMS *Antrim*'s anti-submarine helicopter; a *pinger* to the *junglies*. What the SAS thought they were doing up there is another matter, and my opinions on the matter are best left unsaid. Harry Benson also devotes space to the activities of the 3rd Commando Brigade Air Squadron; the gallant 3 BAS, or to some TWA (standing for Teeny Weeny Airways) – 3 BAS suffered the highest casualty rate and was awarded the most decorations in proportion to its numbers of any organisation on the British side in that War. The outstanding support given to the land forces by the only RAF Chinook to survive the sinking of the *Atlantic Conveyor* is also given due recognition.

We went south with far too few helicopters initially. Those we had were flown every hour they could be; often with bullet holes in fuselages, red warning lights on in cockpits denoting malfunctioning equipment; breaking every peacetime rule. One of the 3 BAS Scout helicopters had a bullet hole in the tail section patched with the lid from a Kiwi boot polish tin. Today's health and safety nerds would have an apoplectic fit. The aircrews worked themselves into the ground. In wartime you should have at least one and a half times the number of aircrew as you have aircraft. Aircrew fatigue will strike long before the aircraft wear out. We did not have this ratio of crews to aircraft. The imperatives of warfighting had long been forgotten. While the rats in the shape of politicians and civil servants had gnawed away at the manpower of the Fleet Air Arm along with everything else connected with defence. Fighting 8,000 miles from home was not the war we had prepared for in the long years of the cold war. But you rarely fight the war you think you are going to fight; this had been forgotten too. Fortunately for those of us fighting the land campaign, none of this fazed the *junglie* aircrew; our lifeline. They got on with the job, often flying in appalling weather, in snow blizzards both by day and night, with low cloud concealing high ground, and often along routes easily predictable to the enemy, with the ever-present threat of being bounced by enemy fighters in daylight; most deadly of all being the turbo-prop Pucara which with its low speed was far more dangerous to a helicopter than a jet.

The story of the deeds of the *junglies* in the Falklands War is well overdue. I am delighted that it has been written at last.

Introduction

A great deal has been said and written about the Falklands War: the task force, the Sea Harriers, the Exocets, the Paras, the Marines, the amphibious landings. But what is so extraordinary is how little is known of the exploits of the young helicopter crews, my friends and colleagues – the *junglies* – who made much of the war happen. *Junglies* are Royal Navy commando pilots, a throwback to the 1960s when British helicopters flew over the jungles of Borneo. Days after the Argentine invasion of the Falkland Islands in April 1982, a British task force was deployed with *junglie* crews spread throughout the fleet. These squadrons, with their Sea King and Wessex helicopters, flew most of the land-based missions in the war. Yet almost nothing has been written about our exploits.

It wasn't until an informal reunion in June 2007 that I realised this. A bunch of us former *junglies* had arranged to meet in a pub in Whitehall the night before we were to parade down the Mall for the formal twenty-fifth anniversary celebrations. I hadn't seen many of these guys in years. Seeing old friends was an emotional moment at first. But then the beer did its work and we were off, armed with a licence to tell each other our war stories.

What was so amazing that evening was not just that there were so many fantastic stories, but that none of us knew what the others had done during the war. In many cases, the stories were coming out for the first time. I sat transfixed as I heard about the helicopter missile strike on Port Stanley. And although I knew about the helicopter crashes, I had never heard any of the detail first hand. I knew little of the dramatic rescues from burning ships and even less of the harrowing story of being on the wrong end of an Exocet strike. I had absolutely no idea that anybody had gone head to head with an Argentine A-4 Skyhawk or the dreaded Pucara, or been strafed by a Mirage and survived. None of us had spoken about it. Until now.

As helicopter crews, we'd been so busy doing our own thing, flying our own missions, very often unaware of what else was going on. We only ever saw our little piece of the jigsaw, our own personal adventure. But between the lot of us we'd seen pretty much the whole thing and been involved in almost all the major events of the war. Perhaps it was understandable that we had said little to others in the intervening years, yet we hadn't even told each other.

And so, from that evening, the first grain of an idea formed: to write the untold story of the helicopter war in the Falklands.

Back in England after the Falklands War, I'm ready for a mess dinner in the wardroom at Royal Naval Air Station Yeovilton.

Key Characters

Almost 500 helicopter pilots, aircrewmen and observers flew in the Falklands War. The following are some of the key personalities who feature in this book.

845 Squadron (Wessex 5)
Pilots: Roger Warden (commanding officer, Ascension Island), Jack Lomas (A Flight commander), Nick Foster (B Flight commander), Mike Tidd (C Flight commander), Mike Crabtree (E Flight commander), Andy Berryman, Mark Evans, Ric Fox, Ian Georgeson, Richard Harden, Paul Heathcote, Steve Judd, Dave Knight, Richard Morton, Andy Pulford, Kim Slowe

Aircrew: Arthur Balls, Kev Gleeson, Dave Greet, Jan Lomas, Steve MacNaughton, Smiler Smiles, Ian Tyrrell, Tug Wilson

846 Squadron (Sea King 4)
Pilots: Simon Thornewill (commanding officer), Bill

Pollock (senior pilot), Alan Bennett, Martin Eales, Bob Grundy, Ray Harper, Bob Horton, Paul Humphreys, Dick Hutchings, Trevor Jackson, Dave Lord, John Middleton, John Miller, Nigel North, Pete Rainey, Peter Spens-Black

Aircrew: Splash Ashdown, Kevin Casey, Pete Imrie, Michael Love, John Sheldon, Colin Tattersall, Alf Tupper

847 Squadron (Wessex 5)
Pilots: Mike Booth (commanding officer), Rob Flexman (senior pilot), Peter Hails (B flight commander), Neil Anstis, Harry Benson, Ray Colborne, Willie Harrower, Tim Hughes, Dave Kelly, Norman Lees, Paul McIntosh, Adrian Short, Pete Skinner, Jerry Spence, Mike Spencer, George Wallace

Aircrew: Mark Brickell, Jed Clamp, Neil Cummins, Al Doughty, Chris Eke, Steve Larsen, Jock McKie, Sandy Saunders, Reg Sharland, Smudge Smyth, Bill Tuttey

848 Squadron (Wessex 5)
Pilots: David Baston (commanding officer), Chris Blight (A Flight commander), Mark Salter (B Flight commander), Ralph Miles (D Flight commander), Ian Brown, Ian Bryant, Ian Chapman, Pete Manley, Dave Ockleton, Paul Schwarz, Jerry Thomas

Aircrew: Ginge Burns, Martin Moreby

737 Squadron (Wessex 3)
Pilots: Ian Stanley (HMS *Antrim* flight commander), Stewart Cooper

Aircrew: Chris Parry (*Antrim* observer), Fitz Fitzgerald

825 Squadron (Sea King 2)
Pilots: Hugh Clark (commanding officer), John Boughton, Brian Evans, Steve Isacke, Phil Sheldon

Aircrew: Roy Egglestone, David Jackson, Tug Wilson

829 Squadron (Wasp)
Pilots: John Dransfield (HMS *Plymouth*), Tony Ellerbeck (HMS *Endurance* Flight commander), Tim Finding (*Endurance*)

Aircrew: Joe Harper, Bob Nadin (*Endurance*), David Wells (*Endurance* observer)

3 Commando Brigade Air Squadron & 656 Squadron Army Air Corps (Gazelle and Scout)
Pilots: Peter Cameron (3 BAS commanding officer); Gervais Coryton, Andrew Evans, Ken Francis (Gazelle); Sam Drennan, Jeff Niblett, Richard Nunn (Scout)

Aircrew: Eddy Candlish, Pat Giffin (Gazelle), Bill Belcher (Scout)

42 Squadron RAF (Chinook)
Pilots: Nick Grose, Dick Langworthy, Andy Lawless, Colin Miller

Other
Pilots: HRH Prince Andrew (820 Sea King), Keith Dudley (senior pilot, 820 Sea King), Chris Clayton

(HMS *Cardiff* Lynx), Ray Middleton (HMS *Broadsword* Lynx), John Sephton (HMS *Ardent* Lynx)

Aircrew: Peter Hullett (*Cardiff* Lynx)

Helicopters in the Falklands War

Altogether 170 British helicopters were deployed with the task force to the South Atlantic and actively involved during the Falklands War. They were used in four main roles:

Sea King HC4

Wessex HU5

Chinook

1. *Junglies* and other transport helicopters: fourteen Sea King HC4 (Helicopter Commando Mark 4) and forty-six Wessex HU5 (Helicopter Utility Mark 5) of the commando squadrons; ten anti-submarine Sea King HAS2 stripped of their sonar equipment and converted to troop carriers, and four RAF Chinook twin-rotor heavy-lift helicopters. These bigger helicopters did the vast bulk of the lifting and shifting of people and equipment. Wessex could also carry anti-tank missiles or rockets.

Gazelle AH1

Scout AH1

Lynx HAS2

Wasp HAS1

Sea King HAS2

Sea King HAS5

Wessex HAS3

2. *Teeny weenies*: seventeen Gazelle AH1 (Army Helicopter Mark 1) and fifteen Scout AH1. These small Royal Marines and Army helicopters were used on land for front-line reconnaissance and casualty evacuation. Scouts could also carry anti-tank missiles or rockets.

3. *Small ships*: twenty-four Lynx HAS2 and eleven Wasp HAS1. Frigates, destroyers, and survey ships had one or two of these smaller helicopters embarked, capable of firing anti-ship missiles, anti-submarine torpedoes or depth charges.

4. *Pingers*: twenty-seven Sea King HAS2 (Helicopter Anti-Submarine Mark 2) and HAS5 and two Wessex HAS3. The Sea Kings were based on the aircraft carriers HMS *Hermes* and HMS *Invincible*, and other large ships of the task force. They flew around-the-clock sorties to protect against the threat from submarines. The Wessex were based on the County-class destroyers HMS *Antrim* and HMS *Glamorgan*. All were equipped with radar and underwater sonar and could carry anti-submarine torpedoes or depth charges.

Prologue

The Falkland Islands is a small British dependency in the South Atlantic covering an area the size of East Anglia. There are two main islands, East and West Falkland, and hundreds of small islands. Much of the landscape is remote moorland. The abundant wildlife includes king penguins, sealions, upland geese, albatross and petrels.

The islands are just 250 miles from the Argentine mainland. However, the first settler in 1764 on East Falkland was in fact French, followed a year later in 1765 by the first English settler on West Falkland. Both were forced out by Spanish colonists from Buenos Aires, only for the British to reclaim their settlement in 1771. The British and Spanish garrisons eventually withdrew from the islands, distracted by other colonial wars, leaving behind little more than plaques to indicate their respective claims of sovereignty.

In the early nineteenth century, there were several short-lived attempts to establish settlements on the Falklands. The newly independent Argentine government appointed the most committed of these settlers as commandant in 1829. The British protested that Spanish rights had not transferred to the Argentines and, four years later,

1

sent a garrison to establish administration over all of the islands. British colonisation followed in 1845 at the new capital, Port Stanley, on East Falkland.

Argentina continued to dispute British sovereignty, eventually bringing the issue to the attention of the United Nations in 1965. The geographical location of the islands – so close to Argentina and so far from Britain – argued for a transfer of sovereignty. But this was heavily constrained by the wishes of the islanders to remain a British dependency.

The military junta that took control of the Argentine government in 1976 was determined to press the issue. The establishment of an Argentine military base at South Thule, part of the South Sandwich Islands, provoked the British government to send a naval task force to the South Atlantic in 1977. However, reluctance to eject the Argentine occupiers by force resulted in diplomatic stalemate. This merely encouraged the junta that an invasion of the Falklands would not be resisted.

On Friday, 19 March 1982, Argentine soldiers masquerading as scrap merchants landed on the British dependency of South Georgia, another small group of islands under the administration of the Falkland Islands some 800 miles to their north. South Georgia is notable for its severe mountainous scenery, glaciers, wildlife colonies and appalling weather. The soldiers resisted the efforts of the British Antarctic survey ship HMS *Endurance* and her party of Royal Marines to encourage their repatriation.

Two weeks later, on Friday 2 April, a much larger Argentine force invaded the Falkland Islands, quickly overwhelming the resistance of the Royal Marines stationed at Port Stanley. It was the cue for the small force occupying South Georgia to raise their national flag. The Falkland

Islands and South Georgia were now firmly in Argentine hands. The question now was: How would the British government respond?

Chapter 1

An inauspicious start
22 April 1982

One of the first British acts of the Falklands War was the attempt to recover South Georgia using the elite troops of Britain's Special Air Service. Still buoyant from their dramatic success in releasing hostages from the Iranian Embassy siege in London two years earlier, an SAS team planned to take control of South Georgia by the most unlikely and unexpected route. Inserted by two Royal Navy commando Wessex helicopters of 845 Squadron onto the Fortuna Glacier, the largest tidewater glacier on South Georgia, the plan was for them to march across the spine of the huge mountains and take the unknown Argentine force at the whaling station at Leith by surprise.

Despite warnings about the treacherous and unpredictable nature of the sub-Antarctic weather and conditions high up on the glacier, the SAS were inserted. Overnight, on 21/22 April 1982, the weather duly did its worst: a violent storm, the wind gusting to 100 knots and producing squalls of driving snow, stopped the SAS in their tracks after just a few hundred yards progress. With frostbite and exposure a real concern, the SAS troop commander radioed for the helicopters to return and rescue them.

Below the faint disc made by the whirling rotor blades, Lieutenant Mike Tidd had a clear view over the edge of the glacier and down to the sea far below in the distance. The wind was gusting all over the place. Even on the ground with no power applied, his Wessex was still trying to fly itself sideways across the ice. Tidd glanced inside at the cockpit gauges. The air-speed indicator needle flickered between thirty and sixty knots of wind. Flurries of snow whipped over the surface. Conditions on top of South Georgia's Fortuna Glacier were fearsome, far worse than anything Tidd had previously experienced training in the mountains of northern Norway. The helicopter was shaking viciously from side to side. Frankly it was terrifying. The sooner they were safely off the glacier and back on board ship the better.

The six huddled SAS troops skidded and stumbled their way towards the Wessex 5, away from the limited protection of the rocks, heads down into the helicopter downdraft. A smear of orange dye stained the snow, the remains of a smoke grenade used to pinpoint their location. Dressed in their white Arctic clothing, the soldiers were in varying stages of hypothermia after exposure to a night of sub-zero temperatures, gale force winds and driving snow. Seated just below and behind Tidd, Leading Aircrewman Tug Wilson helped them stuff their kit into the cabin of the Wessex. As they clambered wearily aboard, he poured each of them hot soup from a thermos.

'I think we'd better get out of here.'

Tidd's voice on the intercom sounded electronic, distorted by the throat microphone attached around his neck. He looked out to his left, past the M260 missile sight suspended from the cockpit roof that partly blocked his view. He could just make out the two other Wessex helicopters nearby, still loading their troops. A lull in the weather, between the wild and unpredictable snow showers, presented a window of opportunity.

'Thirty seconds, boss,' called Wilson. 'I'm just getting the last ones in now.'

'Four Zero Six, Yankee Fox. I'm loaded and would like permission to depart. It looks clear right now.'

Tidd radioed across to mission leader Lieutenant Commander Ian Stanley in the adjacent Wessex 3. Equipped with radar and flight control systems, the single-engine Wessex 3 was there as pathfinder for the radar-less twin-engine, troop-carrying Wessex 5s. Stanley had led Tidd in Yankee Foxtrot and his colleague Lieutenant Ian Georgeson in Yankee Alpha, the second Wessex 5, in close formation up to the top of the glacier. The plan was for all three helicopters then to fly back down in formation the same way they had come up, the Wessex 3 keeping them clear of the mountains through the snow and poor visibility.

In the cockpit of the Wessex 3, Stanley and his co-pilot Sub-Lieutenant Stewart Cooper looked at each other and nodded. *OK. Let him get out of here while the going is good.* He had done the same yesterday when they dropped the guys off. Ian Stanley was confident that Tidd would know what he was doing. Both Tidd and Georgeson were far more experienced at flying in these Antarctic conditions, having trained with the Royal Marines in the Arctic.

'Roger Yankee Fox, you're clear to go. See you back there.'

Tug Wilson leaned out of the back of the Wessex, restrained by his aircrewman's harness, and checked that all was clear behind. 'OK boss. Let's go.'

With the wind blowing hard up the glacier, Tidd had only to ease the collective lever upwards a little for the seven-ton machine to jump eagerly into the air. Half a mile ahead lay a snow-covered ridgeline before the glacier sloped steeply downwards towards the sea and relative safety. The escape route ahead looked straightforward enough, passing between the giant forbidding mountains that rose high above them on both sides. The very edge of a snow shower appeared just as Yankee Foxtrot lifted. Tidd accelerated to sixty knots, staying low over the glacier in case he needed to land again. Wilson slid the rear door closed to shut out the icy wind and make best use of the cabin heating system for the benefit of the frozen SAS troops.

The speed and ferocity with which the weather changed was astonishing. Without warning, the snow shower encompassed the helicopter like a tidal wave. 'Tug we've got a problem,' shouted Tidd whose world had suddenly turned white. It was like being submerged in a glass of milk. The ridgeline at the end of the glacier, and the sea behind it, had vanished into the snow. As Wilson quickly slid open the rear door to help look for visual cues, Tidd banked left to try to return to the rocks he had seen a few seconds earlier. It was a fifty-fifty decision that ended up saving their lives.

Disoriented by the sudden whiteout and complete lack of visual references, Tidd glanced into the cockpit at his instrument panel. The radio altimeter (radalt) was now unwinding at an alarming rate. Realising that collision with the ground was inevitable, Tidd hauled in power with his left hand and flared the aircraft nose up with his right to cushion the impact. The tail and left wheel of the Wessex hit the snow at about thirty knots, sheering away the undercarriage and causing the aircraft to come crashing down on its left side. The aircraft slid onwards for fifty yards. The left side of the cockpit filled up with debris and snow as the windows imploded. Had a co-pilot been sitting in the left seat, he would undoubtedly have been killed, crushed between the missile sight and the ice below.

As the helicopter ground to a halt, the inertia crash switches in the aircraft's nose automatically shut down both engines. Tidd still had no real idea whether or not they would survive. Lying on his side, he reached down to turn off the fuel cocks and electrics to find the central panel and entire left side of the cockpit submerged under snow and broken glass. The only sounds were the howling wind outside and the cockpit windscreen wiper squeaking vainly up and down. Through the relative silence, Wilson's distant voice shouted up from the back: 'Everyone seems to be in one piece.' Tidd slid open the flimsy cockpit window, now unfamiliarly above him, and clambered up onto the side of the aircraft to help Wilson open the rear cabin door.

From their position on the ice further up the glacier, Ian Stanley and Stewart Cooper had watched helplessly as the Wessex helicopter disappeared into the front edge of the snow storm ahead before banking left and sinking into a dip just before the ridgeline. Stanley's only words were 'Oh shit!' as he saw Yankee Foxtrot's rotor blades plough into the snow and the aircraft then crash and slide along on its side.

The snow shower passed as suddenly as it had appeared. Visibility improved once more. 'Yankee Alpha, I'm going to hover-taxi up to them. Follow me and take care,' radioed Stanley to Ian Georgeson as he lifted gently away from the ice and taxied the few hundred yards down the glacier. There was now no shortage of visual cues. Bits of Wessex tail rotor and other assorted debris lay dotted on the snow.

As the helicopters landed either side of the stricken Wessex, Georgeson's aircrewman Jan Lomas jumped out and headed off to inspect the damage. Wilson and the SAS troops clambered up out of the wreck. Miraculously it appeared that nobody had been killed. The only injury was to one SAS staff sergeant who had been cut above his eye by the cabin machine gun.

Dazed, Tidd wandered over to the Wessex 3. Stanley's crewman Fitz Fitzgerald plugged Tidd's helmet into the cabin intercom. 'God you're a messy bastard,' said Stanley from the cockpit above. 'You've left the windscreen wiper on.' It was the words of an experienced leader easing the pressure from the situation.

'If you can find the fucking switch, you go and turn it off,' replied Tidd with feeling.

Out on the snow, the two crewmen Fitzgerald and Lomas divided the soldiers between the two remaining helicopters. The SAS troops were not at all happy about having to leave their kit behind and keep only their side-arms. But they were given no choice. The helicopters were already at maximum weight and could lift no more. While Georgeson jettisoned fuel directly onto the glacier to reduce weight further, Tidd and two troops squashed into the back of Stanley's Wessex 3. Wilson and the remaining four troops went with Georgeson's Wessex 5. With ten people now crammed into the Wessex 3 and fourteen people in the Wessex 5, Stanley radioed Georgeson to 'follow me'. The depleted formation rose to the hover once again.

The shocking scene on Fortuna Glacier just after Mike Tidd's Wessex 5 crashed on its side. The engine is still smoking. Ian Georgeson's helicopter is in the background. This photo was taken from the cockpit of HMS Antrim's Wessex 3. The SAS men inside this helicopter were split between the two surviving helicopters. Georgeson's Wessex crashed ten minutes later as he crossed the glacier's ridgeline in white-out conditions.

In the back of the Wessex 3, Stanley's observer Lieutenant Chris Parry sat crouched over the radar screen. His job was to keep the formation clear of the cliffs to the side of the glacier. What he couldn't see was the ice ridge in front of him; the forward sweep of the radar was blocked by the helicopter's main gearbox just in front of the radar dome. As Stanley crossed the ridge, Georgeson was following a few rotor lengths behind in Yankee Alpha. Another ferocious snowstorm hit the formation just at the wrong moment, barely ten seconds after launch. As the Wessex 3 dropped rapidly down over the ridgeline, automatically maintaining a low altitude over the steeply descending glacier, Georgeson lost sight of the aircraft in front. 'I'm getting whiteout,' he announced calmly to his crewman Lomas, who reopened the cabin door that he had only just shut. Trying to maintain level flight in order to regain visual contact with the aircraft in front, Georgeson was completely unaware that he was in a dip in the ice and on the wrong side of the ridgeline. Just as with Tidd minutes earlier, he saw the radalt unwinding rapidly and pulled in power. There was a fateful inevitability as the Wessex touched down on the snow.

They almost got away with it. However, the forty-knot wind slewed them around so that they were drifting slowly sideways. The starboard wheel caught in a small ice crevasse and the aircraft toppled over onto its side.

In the lead aircraft, Cooper had been peering behind him through the left cockpit window giving his crew a running commentary on the position of the second Wessex. 'OK, OK. Fine. He's still with us. Fifty yards. Steady. Oh God. He's gone in.' The huge spray of snow and the complete disappearance of the Wessex suggested a huge crash into the cliffs. 'It looks like they have really totalled themselves.'

With no radio contact, an overloaded helicopter and appalling weather conditions, there was nothing for it but to return to HMS *Antrim*, the County-class destroyer from which they had launched two hours earlier. The journey back was subdued. They cleared the mountains and crossed the coast. Parry radioed disconsolately ahead to the ship: 'Four Zero Six departing coast now. ETA fifteen minutes. Regret we have lost our two chicks.'

There was a long pause.

'Roger.'

After the horrific conditions high up on Fortuna Glacier, the normally taxing task of landing on a bucking ship in a mere gale now seemed curiously routine. The scrum of soldiers and crew tumbled out of the back of the Wessex 3 onto the flight deck. Tidd approached the hangar surprised to see Stanley's senior maintainer, Chief Fritz Heritier, and his team laying out a load of drips and stretchers. 'Guys, you don't need that, our only injury is a gashed cheek.' It was painfully obvious that Tidd, who had been disconnected from the intercom in the crush of the returning aircraft, didn't know about the second crash.

When he heard, it was like a kick to the stomach. Ian Georgeson, Tug Wilson and Jan Lomas were good friends as well as colleagues. Tidd went up to the bridge to talk to *Antrim*'s captain, Brian Young, task group commander. A former aviator himself, he knew what it was like to lose friends.

Up on the glacier, Yankee Alpha had toppled over on its right side with a sickening thud. After spraying its rotor blades to the four corners, it had juddered a few yards onwards down the glacier. The cabin of the aircraft was a tangle of bodies, backpacks and ammunition. Lomas lay at the bottom of the pile, pinned down by Wilson, in turn pinned down by one of the SAS soldiers. Looking sideways, Lomas could see Georgeson's feet kicking to his right. 'Are you alright, boss?' shouted Lomas.

'Yes, I'm just stuck,' came the reply.

Freeing themselves from their own tangle, neither crewman was able to reach the emergency exit above them. This time movement was almost comically restrained by their goon suits, the tight waterproof immersion suits they wore to keep them dry in the event of a ditching in the sea. One of the taller SAS troopers finally reached up to the yellow and red handle and jettisoned the bubble windows above them. The gaggle of thirteen men scrambled out one by one. There was some concern that the aircraft might either disappear down into a crevasse or burst into flames at any minute. So it was with considerable bravery that Lomas and Wilson managed to clamber up onto the fuselage, past the steaming exhaust, and reach down to free a smiling and grateful Georgeson. As luck would have it, the only minor injury was to the very same SAS staff sergeant who had been injured in the first crash. He now had a matching pair of identical injuries from two crashes within ten minutes.

Sheltering downwind in the protection given by the crashed aircraft, the team crouched and discussed what to do next. The surface of the glacier was like nothing they had seen. In parts it was flat and snowy. Elsewhere it was cruelly serrated with waves of ice interspersed with blue crevasses disappearing into the depths. Walking off the glacier was not a sensible option. And it seemed highly unlikely that their only source of rescue, the Wessex 3, would return to rescue them that afternoon. The SAS troops had already survived one tumultuous night out in the open. All the aircrew had been on survival training courses where the mantra was: protection, location, water, food. Protect yourself against the elements and work out how you are going to get out before you worry about water and food. The team set about preparing themselves for another night on the glacier.

One group of SAS soldiers roped themselves together. They set off the few hundred yards back up the glacier to retrieve some of the equipment left behind in the crashed Yankee Foxtrot. The aircrew and remaining troops inflated Yankee Alpha's nine-man liferaft for protection and ran out the HF radio antenna to tell *Antrim* they were still alive. Ian Georgeson, as the tallest person present, was elected aerial holder. The aircrew all carried search-and-rescue SARBE short-range UHF radios in their lifejackets. But these would only be useful for talking to the rescue aircraft when it was more or less within earshot. If it came at all.

Out at sea on *Antrim*, a wave of relief swept over Tidd as he was given the good news that his team were all well. To him, it was as if the dead had been raised. Meanwhile Stanley and his crew were already on their way back to the glacier armed with blankets and medical supplies. The weather was worsening with thicker cloud and violent squalls. Stanley managed to hover-taxi up the side of the glacier all the way to the top. Despite making contact with Georgeson on his SARBE via the emergency frequency 243 megahertz, there was no sign of the crashed Yankee Alpha. A depressed Stanley reluctantly returned to *Antrim* to consider his options. It was late afternoon.

After a thorough check of the Wessex 3 by the engineers, Stanley decided to have one last crack at rescuing the survivors. It seemed like tempting fate to fly a sixth mission to the top of the glacier with just one engine to support them. Stanley had twice experienced engine failures during his career, once on land, once into the sea. Fortuna Glacier would be a bad place to experience a third.

With low cloud scudding over the ship, Stanley lifted off for the final attempt of the day armed with a new strategy. He would punch through the cloud and try to approach the glacier from above. To a *junglie* pilot, this strategy would be utterly incomprehensible. Flying into cloud is a recipe for disaster. Without radar control, coming back down is likely to end in tears. But to a radar equipped anti-submarine pilot, this was bread-and-butter stuff.

Although the clouds were fairly thin over the sea, the mountain tops ahead were now shrouded in a thick layer of cloud. Flying clear at 3,000 feet, the prospect of getting down onto the glacier, let alone spotting the wreck, seemed remote. Yet as the Wessex flew above where the glacier should be, a hole appeared magically in the cloud beneath them. There in the middle of the hole lay a single orange dinghy perched on top of the glacier. It was an unbelievable stroke of luck. Stanley spiralled rapidly down through the hole and landed on the ice just as the cloud closed in above them.

The SAS team were yet again extremely reluctant to leave behind their kit and equipment on the glacier with the wreck of Yankee Alpha. But faced with the choice of another night of hypothermia and frostbite, there was really little option. The problem still remained of how on earth to fit fourteen large passengers into the tiny cabin of the Wessex 3. For Stanley's first rescue hours earlier, the rear cabin had been cramped with two crew and six passengers. Even if they could cram in a further eight people, the Wessex would be dangerously overloaded way beyond the design limits of the rotor gearbox and the capacity of the single engine.

One by one, the team squeezed into the back. Bodies were everywhere. Observer Parry worked his radar screen whilst sitting on top of one trooper lain across the seat. Arms and legs hung out of the door and windows. Eventually everybody somehow crammed in. Any kind of emergency, such as a crash or ditching into the sea, would be utterly disastrous. With the strong wind assisting their take-off, the helicopter slid off the side of the glacier and headed back to the ship. There was little scope for conversation because of the cold and wind blowing through the open doors and windows. Although smoking was supposedly not permitted on board, Stanley and Cooper both lit up cigarettes and looked at each other in astonishment: 'Wow. That was fun!'

Behind them and out of sight of the pilots, most of the crew and passengers did likewise.

There was still the small matter of landing their overweight helicopter on the heaving deck of *Antrim*. Their only hope was lots of wind over the deck, which would reduce the power needed to maintain a hover. They would only have one attempt at landing. Should they misjudge their approach, the helicopter would have absolutely no chance of recovering for a second attempt. Ditching into the icy black sea would mean certain disaster for most or all of them in the back.

Stanley radioed ahead for the ship to get onto a heading that gave maximum wind over the deck. His final approach was judged to perfection. The helicopter descended straight towards the deck avoiding the usual careful hover. In amongst the crush of bodies in the back, Jan Lomas could make out the air speed indicator on the observer's panel. It wavered around sixty knots at the moment they touched down on the deck. A controlled crash would have been good enough. Instead it felt like a smooth landing. Lomas was gobsmacked.

The near disaster on Fortuna Glacier was a worrying start to Britain's campaign to reclaim South Georgia and the Falkland Islands. One failed mission by the SAS; two crashed helicopters. But for the astonishing skill of the Wessex 3 crew, it could have been so much worse.

Chapter 2

Junglies
1979–82

When I left school, I didn't bother with university because I'd always wanted to fly. I tried for British Airways and failed the interview. The military was the obvious next step. The RAF didn't appeal for the not terribly convincing reason that I didn't fancy being stuck on some German airfield for years. My stepfather introduced me to a friend of his, a Royal Navy captain, who opened up the possibility of flying with the Navy. It also didn't hurt to see the Fleet Air Arm adverts of the day showing Sea Harrier jets and helicopters. Underneath was the line 'Last week I was learning to park my dad's Morris Marina . . .'. I followed the recruitment trail and applied to the Admiralty Interview Board.

And so on a wet October day in 1979, I found myself squashed into a minibus heading for Britannia Royal Naval College in Dartmouth, Devon, one of forty apprehensive young men hoping to become Royal Navy pilots and observers. I was now Midshipman Benson, aged nineteen years and one week.

*   *   *

For many years, pilots and aircrew of the naval air commando squadrons have been proud to call themselves *junglies*. The original *junglies* were the crews of 848 Naval Air Squadron who operated their Whirlwind helicopters in the jungles of Malaya from 1952. Operating in support of the Gurkhas and other regiments, the commando squadrons became known for their flexibility and 'can-do' attitude, an approach that has continued to the present day in Iraq and Afghanistan.

The very first commando assault took place during the Suez crisis of 1956 when twenty-two Whirlwind and Sycamore helicopters of 845 Naval Air Squadron landed 650 commandos and their equipment in a mere one and a half hours. Given the limited capability of these underpowered helicopters, it was an astonishing feat. In 1958, naval air commando squadrons were involved with support operations in Cyprus and Aden. From 1959, 848 Naval Air Squadron operated with Royal Marines from the first commando carrier HMS *Bulwark*, and later from HMS *Albion*, mainly in the Far and Middle East. It was at Nanga Gaat, the forward operating base deep in the jungles of Borneo during the Indonesian confrontation of 1963, using Whirlwind 7 and Wessex 1 helicopters, that the nickname *junglies* was born. The new twin-engined Wessex HU (Helicopter Utility) Mark 5 entered service in 1965 in Aden, Brunei and Borneo, bringing with it a substantial improvement in lifting capability. The Sea King Mark 4 increased capability further, entering service with 846 Naval Air Squadron in 1979.

By early 1982, Britain's political and military priorities had altered dramatically. In place of the Far East adventures, the typical *junglie* could expect to spend a substantial part of their winter training in Arctic warfare in northern

Norway and the rest of the year on a couple of six-week rotations in Northern Ireland.

It was into this environment that I emerged as a baby *junglie* on Monday 1 March 1982. Officially we were Royal Navy officers first and Royal Navy pilots second. Unofficially we all knew exactly who we were. *Junglies* first, Navy second.

My training was fairly typical. After convincing the Admiralty Interview Board that I had sufficient leadership potential as a young officer and sufficient coordination as a trainee pilot, I joined Britannia Royal Naval College Dartmouth in the autumn of 1979. For many of my new friends and colleagues, this was the first time they had been away from home. For me, with ten years of boarding school under my belt, the routine and discipline of Dartmouth was a piece of cake.

My naval and flying training took nearly two and a half years from start to finish. Along every step of the way lurked the ever-present threat of being 'chopped'. Most of us survived our first thirteen hours of flight experience in the antiquated tail-dragging Chipmunk aeroplane at Roborough airport near Plymouth. The similarly antiquated instructors at Roborough were all experienced assessors of young aviators. Those of us with sufficient aptitude passed. Those who didn't got chopped.

After passing out of Dartmouth, I spent the summer of 1980 on 'holdover' at RNAS Yeovilton in Somerset. Holdover was the Navy's attempt to slow down the flow of pilots to the front line. Defence cuts meant that there were simply too many aircrew in the system. Yeovilton was home to the *junglies*, flying Wessex 5 and the new Sea King 4, and *stovies*, flying the Navy's shiny new Sea Harrier vertical take-off and landing jets. My few months at Yeovilton were brilliant fun. I knew that either *junglie* or *stovie* would be an attractive option once I finished flying training.

Towards the end of 1980, I resumed my place in the training pipeline and completed a range of ground courses. My fellow trainees and I spent a gruesome week being schooled in aviation medicine and advanced first aid at Seafield Park in Hampshire. Here we learnt how easy it was to become extremely disoriented whilst airborne. Each of us was strapped in turn into a rotating chair that was spun around. Starting with our heads down and eyes closed, we were then asked to lift our heads up and open our eyes. Watching others become completely unbalanced and fling themselves involuntarily out of the chair was a lot more entertaining than when we had to experience it for ourselves. The most shocking demonstration was to sit in the chair with eyes closed while the chair was spun up very slowly indeed. I was not aware of any movement at all. Opening my eyes to discover the world rushing past at a rate of knots was extremely disconcerting, though highly entertaining for onlookers.

In an adapted decompression chamber we all experienced a few minutes of hypoxia, the state of drowsiness that ensues at high altitude, and which can lead to death if insufficient oxygen reaches the brain. The staff set up a realistically simulated helicopter crash scene for us to use our first-aid skills. All Royal Navy aircrew have a special memory of the horribly realistic sucking chest wound that blows little bubbles of blood and the supposedly wounded leg that turns out to be completely severed.

We also spent eight days in the New Forest on survival training. This involved being dropped in the middle of nowhere with only the clothes we were wearing and a tiny survival tin full of glucose sweets. The first twenty-four hours were not fun. Ten of us were invited to swim across a freezing lake to clamber into a nine-man liferaft that simulated a ditching at sea. Discomfort, sudden attacks of cramp, and one of our colleagues with the runs, made the time pass very slowly indeed. It was a relief to be able to swim back to the shoreline and start an eighty-mile trek over the next three days. The last five days were spent building a shelter called a 'basher' and practising our survival skills – setting traps, carving spoons out of bits of wood, and skinning and cooking a rabbit that had been temporarily liberated from the local pet shop. I lost a stone in weight during these eight days.

Our final noteworthy course was one well loved by all Navy aircrew. Colloquially known as 'the dunker', the underwater escape trainer is a diving tower filled with water. The purpose of the dunker is to teach aircrew how to survive a ditching at sea. Perched on the end of a hydraulic ram above the water is a replica of a helicopter cockpit and cabin. The aircrew, dressed in normal flying gear and helmets, strap into the cockpit at the front or the cabin at the back. The module then lurches downwards into the water rolling neatly upside down some twelve feet underwater. Our mission is to escape before we all drown.

The staff took us through the ditching procedure. As soon as you know you're heading for a swim, the first thing is to pull the quick release lever that jettisons the door. In the dunker, we simply had to simulate this. As the helicopter hits the water, with one hand you grab onto a fixed handle in the cockpit, with the other you prepare to release your straps. As the helicopter disappears under water, you grab one last gasp of air. When all movement stops, you release your straps, haul yourself out using the handle as a reference point, and allow buoyancy to take you up to the surface.

My first experience of the dunker was unnerving and

disorienting, which is of course the point. But after a couple of goes, we became confident and even cocky. With six of us plonked in the rear cabin, a sign language game of 'After you', 'No really, after you', 'No please, I insist' then ensued, to the growing irritation of the excellent Navy divers who were there to watch that we didn't get into trouble. The module only stayed under for less than a minute. The really cool customers were the divers who watched us vacate the module safely before strapping themselves in to ride it back upright and out of the water. We also practised the same escape in darkness with the tower windows blacked out. The dunker saved lives: those aircrew who survived crashes or ditchings at sea which killed their passengers, undoubtedly did so because of their sessions in the dunker.

Learning to fly helicopters is an expensive business. The Navy wants to make sure its pilots can learn as quickly and efficiently as possible. It's far cheaper to get used to the unfamiliar environment of being airborne in a fixed-wing aircraft than a rotary one. So the first seventy-five hours of our flying training involved a few months based at RAF Topcliffe in Yorkshire learning to fly the Bulldog, a small single-engine propeller-driven aeroplane that was a vast improvement on the Chipmunk. After just eight hours flying, the instructor stepped out and left me to fly my first solo. Aerobatics, navigation training, night-flying and formation flying were all progressively introduced to us. The Bulldog was easy to fly and our time passed all too quickly.

We moved down to Cornwall and our first real taste of proper Navy life at RNAS Culdrose for Basic Flying Training on the Gazelle helicopter. All helicopters are inherently unstable. Left to their own devices, they would much prefer to roll over and crash than remain in stable controlled flight. Having arrived with a confident belief that our ability to fly Bulldogs made us masters of the universe, we were put firmly in our place by our feeble slapstick attempts to hover a helicopter.

In any helicopter there are three sets of controls. The collective lever sits in the left hand. Raising it up adjusts the pitch on all of the blades at the same time. Increasing the angle of attack to the wind through the blades causes the helicopter to rise up. The cyclic stick in the right hand alters the angle of attack of the blades at only one point in the rotor disc, causing the entire disc to tilt forwards, backwards, left or right. The pedals increase or reduce the angle of attack in the tail rotor, whose purpose is to counter the torque or twisting motion of the aircraft. Newton's laws tell us that every action has an equal and opposite reaction. If the main rotor blades are spinning one way, the aircraft fuselage will try to spin the other. The tail rotor prevents this from happening.

Learning to use any one control at one time is easy enough. The problem is in learning to use all three at the same time. Pulling in power on the collective requires simultaneous use of the pedals to correct the tendency to yaw. But the additional downdraft on the aircraft fuselage means that an adjustment is also needed with the cyclic stick. For the Gazelle, a vertical take-off means lifting the collective, pushing smoothly on the right pedal, and easing the cyclic back and to the right. Now comes the hard part. A movement on the cyclic to tilt the disc also means that the thrust from the disc is no longer vertical. A compensating increase in power is required. Raise the collective lever and all the other controls need further adjustment. And so on. Hence the comedy value of trying and failing to maintain a hover for the first time within an area the size of a football field. Concentrating on adjusting our height above the ground, we would neglect to stop the helicopter from racing sideways across the ground. All of us very quickly became hopelessly out of control.

Fortunately our instructors were tolerant of our early incompetence, up to a point, and we either learnt fast as expected or faced being chopped. Six months and eighty hours flying time later and most of us were completing our captaincy checks before being awarded our wings. My own captaincy check was fantastic fun. I had to recce and land on top of Longships Lighthouse, just off the coast of Land's End. Wings are the motif that Navy pilots wear on their left sleeve. Being awarded my wings was an extremely proud moment.

Little did I know that I would be on my way to war exactly a year after my first solo flight in a helicopter. Altogether I spent eighty hours learning to fly these sporty Gazelles, based at RNAS Culdrose in Cornwall, before progressing onto the bigger Wessex at RNAS Yeovilton in Somerset.

At this point, our training course of nineteen pilots went their separate ways. Twelve pilots were appointed to stay at Culdrose and do their Advanced and Operational

Flying Training on anti-submarine Sea King Mark 2 helicopters. They would become *pingers,* named after the pinging sonar that Sea Kings dip into the sea in order to hunt submarines. I and six others were appointed to head up to Yeovilton to become *junglies,* the Navy's commando squadron aircrew tasked to support the Royal Marines.

And so we learnt to fly the Wessex HU Mark 5. By the time I flew my first Wessex in 1981, the old bird had already been around for sixteen years. The Wessex was a whole different animal compared to the Gazelle. Whereas the Gazelle was light, fast, and handled like a sports car, the Wessex seemed heavy, slow, and handled more like a tractor. But once we got to know her, we quickly fell in love. The controls may have seemed sluggish at first. But we learnt to see them as forgiving. For a large helicopter of seven tons at maximum all-up weight, the Wessex was extraordinarily manoeuvrable. My personal record was of throwing a Wessex into a 110-degree wingover turn. That's as near to upside down as I could get without the rotor blades flapping vertically upwards and applauding my impending crash. Having both frightened and impressed myself in equal measure, I resolved to be a little less ambitious in my aircraft handling. It never lasted. The Wessex was simply too much fun to fly.

Once started, the Wessex was incredibly reliable; the problem was getting it started. The electric cables didn't seem to like damp weather. I only ever had three emergencies in 700 hours flying a Wessex before, during and after the Falklands War. And they all happened on consecutive days. An engine failure was the first. I lost the primary hydraulic system on the very next flight and the secondary system the day afterwards. Had these latter two happened at the same time, I would now be dead. Without hydraulics, seven tons of air through the rotors would have caused the cyclic stick in the cockpit to thrash around wildly out of control.

Our Advanced Flying Training on the Wessex was spent mainly at Merryfield, south-west of the busy main airfield at Yeovilton. Our Gazelle training mostly took place in the same way at Culdrose's satellite airfield Predannack. The ten-minute transit to and from Merryfield became a familiar routine that was usually an enjoyable journey free from practice emergencies thrown at us by our instructors. After just seven hours flying time of circuits and basic emergency drills it was an exhilarating feeling when my instructor Lieutenant Mike Crabtree jumped out and let me loose on my own for the first time.

Over the next few months, we practised basic circuits, instrument flying in cloud, navigation, night-flying and formation flying. On almost every sortie, we would practise autorotation, the emergency procedure needed when everything turns to a can of worms. If either the engines or transmission or tail rotor fail on a helicopter, the pilot's only weapon to avoid making a big hole in the ground is the momentum in the rotor blades. In the same way that winged sycamore seeds spin around of their own accord as they descend from a tree, helicopters can descend without power under some semblance of control. Of course for a seven-ton helicopter (about the same weight as an old red London double-decker bus) the rate of descent is more akin to a flying brick than a graceful sycamore seed. But the principle holds. By dumping all power immediately you sense a problem; the blades continue to rotate on their own – hence 'auto-rotation' – driven by the wind now passing up through them as you descend.

So when disaster strikes, the pilot's first job is to dump the collective lever immediately. You have about one second to do this before the rotor blades slow down irreversibly. Dumping power reduces the drag on the blades. But it also reduces the lift that keeps you in the sky. As you descend rapidly, you are looking out for some suitable field or other landing point just in front of the helicopter's nose. The choices are fairly limited once your helicopter has become little more than a rotary glider. At a critical moment, some 100 to 150 feet above the ground, you ease back on the cyclic to raise the nose, reduce forward speed, slow your rate of descent, and give the blades a bit of extra momentum as the wind through them increases. At about ten to twenty feet above the ground, you are aiming to wind up the flare so that the helicopter almost reaches a stationary hover. But with no power to keep the blades rotating, you are only going one way. Down. The final task is to haul on the collective lever and use all the remaining momentum in the blades to cushion the landing. We practised endless 'autos' from a variety of positions in the sky: from 1,000 feet, 200 feet, upwind, downwind, from high and low hovers. To our instructors' considerable credit, and despite the huge size of the Wessex, none of us ever pranged.

Now that we could handle the basics, we moved on to Operational Flying Training where we learned to use the Wessex in its operating role. This involved winching, day and night load-lifting, troop-carrying, low-level flying, confined area landings, tactical formation, mountain flying (in Wales), search-and-rescue procedures, day and night deck-landings and 2-inch rocket firing.

Rocket firing at the range in Castlemartin, South Wales, was especially good fun. The seven students and two helicopter warfare instructors, Lieutenants Pete Manley and Paul Schwarz, took three aircraft away for a couple of days. Each of the Wessex was fitted with rocket pods.

We could carry a maximum of twenty-eight rockets, seven in the top half and seven in the bottom half on each side. The firing range was an area of moorland and scrub leading to a cliff edge by the sea. Perched at the end was an old Second World War tank. The technique for firing was to approach the range at low level, about ninety degrees off target, pull up to about 1,000 feet and roll into a steep dive towards the target. The sighting system involved little more than lining up the cross hairs on a glass sight with a point on the windscreen behind it, marked with a chinagraph pen. It was hardly high-tech stuff and our accuracy reflected this. Although I did manage one hit out of the many rockets I fired, the proof of the pudding was that the tank was still there after years of Wessex firings and misses. Still, rockets might keep people's heads down if ever used in anger.

Castlemartin was also fun for the evening entertainment. Those of us who hit the tank more by luck than judgment were required to buy champagne for the boys from the officers' mess bar. Any excuse will do. But *junglies* are also known for their high jinks. Being a firing range, there was a plentiful supply of thunderflashes, very loud bangers that are used to simulate explosions or mortar fire. My very own personal introduction to the thunderflash came whilst minding my own business seated on the loo early in the evening. I heard the match strike. I saw the brown tube roll under the door. I saw the fizzing fuse. I leapt frantically out of the way into the corner of the cubicle and covered my head. Stupidly I failed to cover my ears. The rest of the evening in the bar passed with little need for conversation as I could hear nothing above the ringing in my ears.

The final training exercise, effectively completing my two and a half years of naval officer and pilot training, involved four days of military exercise ('milex') out on Dartmoor. We based four Wessex helicopters in the hills south of Okehampton. Aircrew and maintainers spent the next few days operating out in the field, working with a Royal Marine troop who alternated between the role of enemy troops attacking our base at 3 a.m. and friendly troops that we were tasked to support. It is extraordinarily demanding to fly a helicopter around Dartmoor at ninety knots at a height of fifty feet or less in loose tactical formation, whilst trying not to bump in to either the ground or the other aircraft, keep up with our fast-moving location on featureless terrain using a fifty thou' ordnance survey map, and avoid wallpapering the cockpit with said map. As if this was not enough, our instructors added a few extra degrees of difficulty by occasionally switching off some valuable piece of avionics and telling us one of our radios or hydraulic systems or engines had failed. Or they would tell us to take over the lead and bring the formation into the planned drop zone. This meant actually knowing where we were rather than just following the leader and pretending. It meant thinking very quickly how best to approach the landing site and transmitting the new plan to the other aircraft. And it always meant taking in to account wind direction and tactical considerations. The expression 'one-armed paper hanger' was very familiar in *junglie* pilot circles.

Two friends on my course were chopped in the final weeks before going front line, one just before milex, one just after. The official explanation was that they weren't good enough. Nevertheless both went on to become highly experienced commercial pilots. The unofficial explanation was defence cuts.

The remaining five of us completed our training and, on 1 March 1982, we joined 845 Naval Air Squadron as newly qualified Royal Navy pilots. More importantly, we had become *junglies*.

Friday 11 June 1982, Port San Carlos, Falkland Islands. Neil Cummins and I headed out across the muddy grass in the darkness. It was cold and windless. The first signs of dawn stretched across the horizon. A junior engineer followed just behind us to help with getting the Wessex started.

The huge green bird that was ours for the day sat with its rotor blades drooping heavily, restrained by red 'tip socks' that tied them to the fuselage like a bonnet. I could just make out the letters XL, X-Ray Lima, on the side. Between the three of us, we removed the tip socks and gathered together the other covers that protected the engine intake and exhausts from rain and water.

Remembering all of the vitally important checks around the aircraft ought to have been unnecessary as the maintainers had already thoroughly checked and serviced the aircraft earlier. But pilots are sticklers for procedure. I did a thorough walk around the helicopter as a final check. Human error is an easy way to kill yourself.

As I clambered over the aircraft, using brief flashes of my torch to check whether oil levels were sufficient and hatches were closed, I could see little flashes around me from the dozen other Wessex pilots getting ready for launch. I wondered what little idiosyncrasies I would find on this particular helicopter. I smiled as I opened the platform that allowed me to check the gearbox oil level. At least I knew there was some oil in this one.

A minute or so later I was putting on my helmet and Mae West lifejacket and climbing up into the cockpit. This aircraft had no heavy window armour, so I slid the door shut, adjusted the height of my seat, fiddled with the pedals, and strapped myself in. A hundred switches, knobs, levers and dials stared at me, challenging my next move. I flicked on the battery switch, plugged in my helmet lead, and adjusted my microphone. Neil Cummins was wearing his throat mike which, picking up vibrations in the vocal chords, gave a curiously metallic sound to his voice. I deciphered the inevitable 'How do you read, boss?' with practised ease.

'Loud and clear.'

'Loud and clear also.'

'Ground power in please.' He plugged the lead from the spare batteries into the side of the aircraft just below the exhaust pipe. It would give us an extra electrical boost when starting the first of our engines.

My hands and eyes ran quickly over the switches on the centre console between the pilots seats, switching some on, leaving others off, testing warning lights and generally preparing the electrics for start-up. I then raised my left hand to the radio panel in the roof and selected all the different frequencies I would require from my four radio sets, checking the numbers against what I had written on my knee pad during the pre-flight brief. Looking down onto the instrument panels I had a good look at every dial, running my eyes over them from left to right. Co-pilot's dials, engine gauges, fuel flow meters, torque, and across to the pilot's flight instruments in front of me that would tell me height, speed, rate of climb and aircraft attitude, amongst other things. With a full waggle of the two sticks, cyclic in my right and collective in my left, and a good kick on both pedals, I was ready to start in less than a minute.

'Starting port,' I said.

'Roger,' came the reply as I pressed the starter button down and held it. The engine beneath the co-pilot's feet wound up slowly while it waited for ignition. The ignition unit crackers below me did their stuff. With a roar from the port exhaust outside the window to my left, the engine lit. I moved my hand to the fuel cut-off in case the temperature went too high. But after its speedy upward rise, the temperature needle dropped back as the increased airflow through the engine cooled things down. With a slight increase on the speed select lever or throttle, the generators came on line and I called for ground power to be unplugged. After checking that all the generator-powered electrics had also come on, I repeated the start procedure with the starboard engine. The engine roared into life with a loud blast outside below my window. I remembered to switch on the anti-icing system that prevents ice from building up in the intakes and damaging the engines.

As first light was breaking, I circled my finger in the air to the maintainer now standing on the ground just beyond the tip of the rotor blades. He had a last look around and replied with the same hand signal. 'Engaging rotors,' I said as I eased the rotor brake off and checked that it was locked off. I then moved the starboard speed select lever slowly forward to accelerate the engine that was now driving the four huge blades. As the blades sped up, the aircraft started to rock slowly from side to side.

As the blades reached flying speed the rocking slowed. With speed select fully forward, the fuel computer would make sure the engine maintained that speed, neither too fast nor too slow. I put the port engine into drive and advanced the lever to the gate. As it reached the gate, it started to help drive the rotors and I saw the starboard fuel flow reduce as the port increased. With a little tweak of both speed select levers, the fuel flows were balanced, showing that the two Rolls-Royce Gnome engines were now taking equal strain.

With the rotors going, I checked that both hydraulic systems were running and the autopilot functioning properly. Neil Cummins checked the winch and load hook. We were ready to roll. I called out my final pre-take-off checks, called for the wheel chocks to be lifted off the grass and put in the back, and prepared for launch with a final adjustment of the friction on my collective lever.

A nearby Wessex announced on the squadron frequency that he was departing from the east side of the hillside. I called him to check my radio was working. The powerful downdraft from his aircraft then buffeted me as he rose up into the dawn air to my right. I called a quick warning that I was departing. 'X-Ray Lima now lifting from the western side.' I eased gently up on the collective lever, simultaneously pushing my left foot slowly forward and moving the cyclic stick slightly back and to the left. The faint outline of the disc made by the rotor blades moved upwards and I felt the undercarriage oleos extending as the blades took the strain. With the controls, I felt for the balance needed to keep the aircraft pointing straight and to lift the aircraft vertically. The starboard wheel left the ground followed by the port wheel and finally the tail wheel. A little extra power on the collective and we rose cleanly above the ground.

Normally I would ease off the power and hover at fifteen feet to check the systems were working well. Today, I needed to get clear of the other helicopters that were also starting up. We rose smoothly up into the air and, as I ran my eyes quickly through the cockpit instruments, I eased the cyclic stick forward and increased power a touch more to drop the nose, build up speed and clear the area. A bit of pressure on the left foot corrected the urge to yaw.

As we increased speed, I felt the slight judder of the aerodynamic forces on the blades. I was aware of the other

Wessex half a mile in front of me as we passed above the farm buildings of Port San Carlos settlement. I accelerated smoothly up to ninety knots, about a hundred miles per hour, and headed out into San Carlos Bay, flying at fifty feet above the sea. It was hugely exhilarating. I headed into the anti-clockwise pattern around the bay, partly set up to avoid collisions, mostly to identify any intruders.

We had been told to get to HMS *Fearless* where we would get our first instructions for the day. In front of the dark shadow of the hills on the far side of the bay lay the dozen or so ships. The huge amphibious assault ship *Fearless* had a *junglie* Sea King from my sister squadron burning and turning on one of its two helicopter spots. The other assault ship *Intrepid*, various frigates, a BP fuel tanker and several landing ships were also dotted around the bay. We flew past the frigate HMS *Plymouth* that had survived a Mirage attack two days earlier. A large black hole in her funnel revealed the target of the bomb that had passed right through it without exploding.

The first breaths of wind were starting to break up the calm water surface. There was patchy cloud at high level above. In the early morning light, the Falklands scenery was stunning. I lowered the collective lever and flared the aircraft to reduce our forward speed, smoothly bringing X-Ray Lima into a hover alongside the flight deck of *Fearless*.

The flight-deck officer waved me across to the spare landing spot clear of the Sea King. My landing was confident and firm, just as it was supposed to be. 'Good stuff boss, I'm just disconnecting to get our tasking.'

Cummins then walked out to get our instructions from the flight-deck officer now in front of me.

It was a beautiful day to be at war.

Chapter 3

April Fools
2 April 1982

Throughout late March, Argentina ignored Britain's protests about the landings in South Georgia. On the morning of Friday 2 April, a large force of Argentine marines landed on the Falkland Islands near the capital Port Stanley. The British force of sixty-eight Royal Marines of Naval Party 8901 engaged the invaders in a brief fire-fight, killing one Argentine marine and wounding several others. Overwhelmed by sheer numbers, there was no real choice but to surrender. Falkland Island Governor Rex Hunt and the party of Royal Marines were flown out to Argentina and repatriated to the UK. Many of them would be back within weeks.

The following day, a smaller force of eighty Argentines attempted to secure the British Antarctic Survey base at King Edward Point, near Grytviken on South Georgia, little knowing that the position was occupied by twenty-two Royal Marines dropped there days earlier from HMS Endurance. The Royal Marine detachment put up a spirited surprise defence, crippling an Argentine Puma helicopter *and the navy frigate ARA* Guerrico, *killing several Argentines and wounding many more, at a cost of one Royal Marine wounded. Realising that further action would lead to a pointless bloodbath, Lieutenant Keith Mills RM raised the white flag and negotiated a peaceful surrender. As prisoners, their excellent treatment and repatriation by the Argentines helped set the tone for subsequent prisoner handling on both sides.*

We could have let the Falklands go. But the invasion offended British national pride. Most importantly, it offended Prime Minister Margaret Thatcher. Within just a few frantic days, a naval task force was assembled to sail the 8,000 miles and retake the islands. Despite the activity, nobody thought we were serious.

Thursday 1 April 1982. Sub-Lieutenant Paul 'Hector' Heathcote sat in his flying overalls in the aircrew room of the RAF station at Aldergrove, near Belfast. Heathcote was one of six pilots, three aircrew and twenty maintainers making up 845 Squadron's Northern Ireland detachment. The role of the unit was to support Army operations throughout the province. Co-located alongside the resident RAF squadron, each unit provided two Wessex helicopters on permanent call. It was a considerable source of pride that the Royal Navy *junglies* managed this with just four Wessex helicopters whereas the 'crabs', as the RAF are known by the other services, needed twelve. The resulting banter between the two services was usually friendly, but occasionally bubbled over into something more fractious.

The lead story in the newspapers that morning was all about the illegal landing of Argentine scrap merchants on the British protectorate of South Georgia. Heathcote thought it would be amusing to play an April Fools' joke on his fiancée Linda back in England. What if 845 were deployed down there to deal with them? Later that afternoon he rang her up from the officers' mess payphone. 'Sorry darling, we're all off to the Falklands for three months. We've got to go and do something.'

He had no idea that this was exactly what was to happen for real.

'Where are the Falklands? Off Scotland?' she replied, echoing the same question that would resound around the country just a few hours later.

At RNAS Yeovilton the following day, the phones were ringing red hot. Squadron commanding officers had been instructed to recall their aircrew, many of whom had just left for Easter leave, in response to news of the early morning invasion of the Falkland Islands by Argentine special forces. In 845 Squadron staff office, commanding officer Lieutenant Commander Roger Warden, senior pilot Lieutenant Commander Mike Booth and air engineering officer Lieutenant Commander Peter Vowles discussed their plans. The initial requirement was to assign crews and aircraft and send them off as detachments as soon as possible. For a commando squadron, this was bread-and-butter stuff. As well as frequently rotating aircraft and crews to and from Northern Ireland, there were regular detachments of either two or four aircraft to land bases in Norway or Germany and to various Royal Navy and Royal Fleet Auxiliary ships.

As air engineer officer, Vowles was primarily concerned with the usable hours available on each airframe, gearbox and engine. All helicopter parts have a limited lifespan before needing replacement or overhaul. His expertise lay in assigning the right aircraft and components based on their remaining life and likely use. The maintainers in each detachment would take with them a 'flyaway pack' of plastic boxes filled with basic parts and a spare engine.

While Vowles sorted out aircraft availability, Mike Booth's first conversation was with Lieutenant Nick Foster. Foster and his flight had returned a few weeks earlier from Northern Ireland and were about to go on leave. Instead they were told to get themselves and two aircraft ready to embark in a Belfast transport aeroplane and head on down to Ascension Island on the equator. His second conversation was a phonecall to Lieutenant Commander Jack Lomas at home. 'Jack, I want you back asap to take a pair of gunships up to *Resource* in Rosyth. You're going with Oily.'

Lieutenant Dave 'Oily' Knight had recently returned from Norway and was also at home, mixing concrete out in the sunshine for a new patio. 'Drop everything, Oily. Get your arse back to Yeovilton. You're off to Scotland tonight,' Booth told him. The patio would have to wait.

Along the corridor at Yeovilton, 846 Squadron commanding officer Lieutenant Commander Simon Thornewill was also pulling his team together at short notice. He had been telephoned at home at two in the morning and told to get his squadron of Sea Kings onto the aircraft carrier HMS *Hermes* the same day. The Sea King crews had also just returned from detachments, this time to the north of England and the North Sea. With his senior pilot Lieutenant Commander Bill Pollock and air engineer Lieutenant Commander Richard Harden, they had assembled the squadron aircrew for a brief. Even with crews readily available, departure of the whole squadron in one day was a tough call. The more realistic plan was to embark the following day.

During the day, Simon Thornewill took a phone call from fellow test pilot, Lieutenant Commander Mike Spencer, at the Royal Aircraft Establishment Farnborough.

Spencer had been testing out the latest generation of night vision goggles and invited Thornewill to come up to Farnborough and try them out.

By late afternoon, the first Wessex was ready to leave Yeovilton for Rosyth, the Royal Navy base in Edinburgh. At the controls of callsign Yankee Tango, Oily Knight taxied out to 'point west', the standard take-off point for helicopters at Yeovilton. Within an hour of lifting off, he was followed by Jack Lomas in Yankee Hotel. Darkness fell as Lomas passed Newcastle on the flight north. An air traffic controller wondered why they were flying so late on a Friday night. 'Can't say,' replied Lomas, whereupon the well-wishing controller burst into song: 'Don't cry for me Argentina . . .'. Both aircraft embarked safely on the flight deck of the Royal Fleet Auxiliary supply ship *Resource* late that night. The aircraft weapon platforms and other equipment were on their way up by truck.

The next morning, a bemused Lomas was summoned to fly all the way back down from Scotland to Plymouth on a Heron aircraft for an embarkation meeting with representatives from 3 Commando Brigade Royal Marines and Commodore Amphibious Warfare (COMAW). There Lomas was relieved to see the familiar faces of fellow *junglies* Simon Thornewill and Lieutenant Commander Tim Stanning, his former Wessex boss, who was now in charge of helicopter tasking for COMAW.

To Lomas, the meeting seemed a shambles. 'In essence, we haven't a clue how we're going to do this,' he thought; 'but let's get everything onto the ships, do our planning and exercising on the way down there, and sort out all the kit onto the right ships when we get to Ascension.'

It may have been shambolic. But it was all that was needed.

* * *

On Saturday 3 April, Simon Thornewill led the first nine Sea Kings out from Yeovilton heading towards Portsmouth, staggering their departure so as not to arrive all at once on the already-frantic flight deck of the carrier *Hermes*. The following evening, three of his most experienced pilots were sent off to join Mike Spencer and Lieutenant Pete Rainey at Farnborough to test out the night vision goggles. Each pilot spent forty-five minutes flying around the darkness of Salisbury Plain in the left-hand seat of a specially adapted Puma helicopter under Spencer's instruction. The Sea King pilots couldn't believe how good the goggles were. They were all able to make a few landings in complete darkness. The pilots returned to *Hermes* at three in the morning along with seven sets of goggles and Pete Rainey to teach them how to use them.

Days later, Pollock and his three Sea Kings embarked for the South Atlantic on the assault ship HMS *Fearless* at Portland.

Back at Yeovilton, Mike Booth and Peter Vowles were busy assigning the next three Wessex flights. They were now sleeping on camp beds in the office as calls were coming in throughout day and night, amending embarkation requirements, particularly the armament pack – what guns, missiles or rockets were needed. Six more Wessex were being stripped down ready to be moved to Ascension in the back of the Belfast transport aircraft now parked on the dispersal in front of the squadron offices. In a flurry of activity, the first two Wessex – Yankee Delta and Yankee Sierra – departed Yeovilton on Sunday 4 April. Nick Foster and his team flew in an accompanying RAF Hercules. The next few days saw Mike Tidd and his team, along with the ill-fated Yankee Foxtrot and Yankee Alpha, set off in another Belfast and Hercules, while Roger Warden and his team set off with Yankee Juliett and Yankee Kilo.

Within a week, thirteen Sea Kings and eight Wessex had been successfully despatched from Yeovilton for the South Atlantic, each of them folded up and squeezed into the back of transport aircraft.

From the sea, Ascension Island looks a bit like Treasure Island. A huge mountain grows out from its centre. It really ought to be a tropical paradise. Unfortunately, setting foot on the island immediately dispels the illusion. The landscape is mostly dusty and brown. The ground is unforgiving, made of volcanic rock that would happily skin the soles off your feet. Ascension is little more than a giant lump of volcanic rock parked in the middle of the Atlantic Ocean just south of the equator. It was first garrisoned by the British in 1815 as a precaution after Napoleon was imprisoned on St Helena.

In 1982 Ascension Island was an ideal halfway staging post along the 8,000-mile journey from the UK to the Falklands and therefore the initial target for all ships and aircraft. As a British protectorate, Wideawake airfield and its giant runway was loaned out to the US military and NASA. On 5 April, Nick Foster and his flight were the first Brits to arrive in Ascension. Although made welcome by the American base staff, they had no spare bedding or accommodation and so spent the first couple of nights sleeping under pool tables.

Wideawake very quickly became a hub of activity. The first Royal Navy warships and their auxiliary supply ships arrived off the island on Tuesday 6 April, diverted from Exercise Spring Train in the Mediterranean. Stores began to arrive on RAF transport aircraft, load-lifted out by the ships' own helicopters. The sudden build-up of stores and aircraft threatened to descend into chaos. The Wessex crew watched in horror and amazement as a Royal Marine Scout helicopter lifted its load off the ground before the groundcrewman attaching the load had time to clear. With his arm stuck through the net, the poor crewman dangled helplessly underneath the Scout as it transitioned away. Somehow air traffic control managed to communicate the situation with sufficient calm for the pilot to return safely to dispersal, whereupon the load and passenger were dropped unceremoniously.

The Wessex engineers did a remarkable job of preparing the first two helicopters. Within thirty-six hours of arrival the two aircraft had been unfolded, assembled, ground-tested and made ready to fly. They embarked on the giant 23,000-ton stores ship RFA *Fort Austin* on 7 April, joining the three Lynx helicopters already embarked. *Fort Austin*'s first task was to get down to the South Atlantic as quickly as possible to resupply the 'red plum', HMS *Endurance*, the much smaller Antarctic survey ship, which was fast running out of fuel and stores.

Non-aviators have told me that watching a helicopter hovering steadily adjacent to a ship that is ploughing through the waves seems mystifyingly impressive. How on earth does the helicopter keep moving ahead at exactly the same speed as the ship? They have less to say about the actual landing on a pitching and rolling flight deck. Perhaps having achieved the miraculous by synchronising aircraft and ship movement, the landing looks just like more of the same.

The reality for the pilot inside the cockpit is pretty much the reverse. Hovering alongside the ship is the easy part. It's the landing that can get quite exciting. To an experienced Navy pilot, deck landings vary in difficulty depending on wind and sea conditions. However, they are merely part of the remarkable routine of flying at sea.

Learning the technique that turns this potentially dangerous task into the safely routine is an unnerving experience. I first learnt from Lieutenant Graham Jackson towards the end of my training on 707 Squadron. 'Jacko' was great fun to fly with, everybody's friend and an excellent instructor. He gave the appearance of being slightly wild but, like most Navy pilots, was in fact superb at his job. It was a mystery how he remained so amiable in spite of our best efforts to crash with him.

He took me out for my first ever deck landing on a sunny but hazy winter's day off the coast of Portland. I flew the Wessex out across the Dorset coast and on towards the RFA *Green Rover*, a small fuel tanker with a single gantry at the front and large flight deck on the back. I tried to kid myself that I would be cool and professional as I first sighted the ship and began my descent; my waterproof immersion suit held in all the heat and sweat that revealed my true state of mind. Jacko was relaxed and casual as he talked me down. 'OK, Harry, line yourself up off the port quarter. Start your descent now. When you get to about half a mile, bring your speed off so that you end up alongside the deck.' He must have been as nervous as I was but never showed it.

'No probs, sir,' I lied.

It's easier to gauge distance to the ship by approaching from a slight angle rather than directly from the stern. The idea is then to follow an imaginary glide path that ends about twenty feet above and twenty feet to the left of the flight deck. Our aircrewman Steve Larsen in the cabin behind us had gone quiet as I set up the approach. As I got nearer the ship, I gradually increased power to compensate for the slower speed, eventually bringing the big helicopter to an unsteady hover alongside the flight deck. 'Fuck,' I said. 'Do you really want me to do this?'

Graham Jackson laughed. Ignoring my question, he continued talking me through the approach in a matter-of-fact way.

Hovering next to a moving ship is not terribly different to hovering next to a stationary building or a tree. In each case the wind is always relative to the helicopter. The difference is that the sea around the ship is moving whereas the land around the building or tree is not.

It was really hard to keep my eyes on the ship and not be distracted by the rush of water swooshing past. Although the sea was fairly calm, *Green Rover* was also rolling gently from left to right and pitching up and down on the mild swell. I was very aware that my landing site was moving around.

The rushing water and rolling ship made me want to compensate for every little movement. I started to swing around in the hover just like my first slapstick attempts in the Gazelle nine months earlier.

'Try not to move the controls so much. You're overcontrolling.'

I let the cyclic stick in my right hand return to its spring-loaded upright position and my hover immediately stabilised. I could keep steadier if I focused on an imaginary horizon way out in the distance and ignored all of the movement around me. I also had to shut out the thought that this would be my first deck landing.

'Keep your eyes on the base of the hangar and watch the flight-deck officer with your peripheral vision.'

In fact there wasn't a hangar on the *Green Rover* but I knew what he meant. The base of the superstructure at the front of the flight deck was the place nearest to the centre of the ship that therefore moves around the least.

I could see the flight-deck officer waving his bats to clear me across to land on his deck. My next temptation was to hold back so that I didn't drive my blades into the ship's superstructure.

'You need to come forward a bit so that you can then move across directly above the bum line.'

A thick white line painted across the deck showed me where my rear end needed to be. So long as I stayed above the line, I wouldn't drift forward into the superstructure or backward and miss the deck altogether. The superstructure ahead of me looked mighty close to the helicopter's whirling blades.

Although requiring accurate flying, it turned out to be the easiest part of the whole deck-landing process. All I had to do was edge the helicopter sideways and drift along the line. As I moved across the deck, I also descended to five feet. There was an uncomfortable shudder through the flying controls as the Wessex moved into the turbulent air behind the ship. With another small movement on the cyclic, I stopped my sideways drift.

The flight-deck officer now had his arms and bats held outwards to tell me to hold my position. In rougher seas, I came to realise how important it was that the flight-deck officer knew his ship. Even in the roughest seas, all ships stop rolling eventually and stabilise for a short while. At that moment, the flight-deck officer waves the pilot down. As he waved me down, my hover started to wobble again. I needed to land vertically and had to stop the sideways drift. I held the cyclic stick steady for a second or two so that my hover stabilised. I then lowered the collective lever in my left hand.

'Firm and decisive,' said Jackson.

We collapsed onto the deck with a wobble from one wheel to the other.

'Keep lowering the lever.'

The helicopter sunk down heavily on its oleos and the bouncing stopped. We were down.

The flight-deck officer lowered his bats. A quick thumbs-up sign from me and four groundcrew ran in with nylon strops to lash the helicopter to the deck.

Jackson turned to look across at me. 'Well done, Harry. Your first deck landing.'

It hadn't been a thing of beauty. But I'd get better at it, much better.

After a few circuits and landings, Jackson unstrapped and climbed out of the cockpit onto the flight deck, leaving me and Steve Larsen to it. We then did a few circuits and landings on our own before he jumped back in and we flew back to shore.

The following night we repeated the process, this time in the dark. Night deck landings are far more unnerving. On the approach to the ship, I had to keep flicking my eyes from the flight instruments to the lights on the ship. It's much harder to judge distance and speed just from a couple of vertical lights on top of the ship and a row of horizontal lights behind the flight-deck officer's head. But at least there's no swooshing water to distract you. Instead of watching the ship roll around, I learnt to keep a steady hover whilst watching the row of flight-deck lights rolling around.

For my first day deck landing I had somehow managed to avoid a nasty effect known as 'ground resonance'. Wessex were especially prone to this problem. Just because of the slightly lopsided way helicopters hang suspended in the hover, landing almost always involved bouncing from one wheel to the other. Left unchecked this bouncing can degenerate rapidly into ground resonance, an unstable condition that can eventually cause the helicopter to topple over. If the bouncing isn't too bad, lowering the full weight of the helicopter onto the deck usually solves the problem. On my subsequent deck landings, I went into ground resonance a few times and we had to lift quickly back up into the air to calm things down. Experienced pilots almost never get into ground resonance. Unfortunately both aircrew and groundcrew knew this. So it was embarrassing when it happened.

Compared to landing, taking off from the little *Green Rover*, or indeed from any ship's flight deck, was a piece of cake. It was much the same procedure in reverse. First I gave a thumbs-up sign to the flight-deck officer. The four groundcrew ran in and removed the strops, moved clear of the disk, then turned and held them up clearly for me to confirm. The flight-deck officer signalled I was clear to launch by holding his bats out again. I didn't want to hang around on a pitching and rolling deck for long after that, pulling in power cleanly and decisively to lift off. As the Wessex continued rising, I cleared to the left and accelerated away from the ship.

After sleeping on the floor of Ascension for two nights, Nick Foster and his team were hugely impressed with the comfort and splendour of the RFA *Fort Austin*. It was as big as a medium-sized cruise chip, with cranes and gantries where cabins might otherwise have been, and it had some of the comforts of a cruise ship. As flight commander, Foster had a cabin to himself, complete with double bed, sea view, ensuite bathroom and even shared use of a steward. The maintainers also thought it was great because they were each assigned two-man cabins. The low point of the trip was undoubtedly when the chief steward was forced to apologise. The normal seven-course sit down dinner would be reduced to a mere five courses, since they didn't know how long they would be away. 'If you're going to go to war,' thought Foster, 'go to war on an RFA.' It was luxurious compared to the cramped conditions of a Royal Navy warship.

On 9 April, after embarking a 120-strong combined group of SAS and SBS special forces, *Fort Austin* became the first British ship to set off south from Ascension. At first there was a vague notion that *Fort Austin*, *Endurance* and its two AS12 air-to-surface missile-equipped Wasp helicopters might comprise a sufficient task group to retake South Georgia. Fortunately, in the absence of a Navy warship to act as escort, this unwise idea was vetoed.

Three days out from Ascension, *Fort Austin* met up with *Endurance* in the rough South Atlantic waters. Lieutenant Kim Slowe took off in Yankee Delta to begin the 'vertrep', vertical replenishment, of eagerly awaited fresh food and stores across to *Endurance*. Unfortunately, part way through the vertrep, a fuel computer malfunction on the Wessex caused one of the engines to run down to idle. Slowe felt the aircraft begin to sink because of the lack of power. To the horror of the hungry *Endurance* onlookers, he was forced to jettison the load into the sea just to stay airborne, and then coolly flew the Wessex on one engine back to *Fort Austin*.

The following night, Nick Foster took off in Yankee Delta to test the repaired aircraft. All seemed as well as it ever does on a night flight over the sea when you can see little or nothing outside and only the dimly lit instruments inside your cockpit. Soon after take-off the computer on the same engine ran down to idle yet again. In the dark night of the South Atlantic, Foster felt the tail of the aircraft start to shake badly. 'Oh God, I think we've got a tail rotor problem,' he told his crewman. His mind immediately switched to the prospect of ditching into the sea. It only lasted a few seconds before he realised that in fact the adrenalin of the situation was making his knees shake. The movement on the pedals was in turn making the tail shake. Rather less coolly, Foster recovered safely on one engine to *Fort Austin*, which was now heading back north to Ascension.

Meanwhile, in the North Atlantic, Jack Lomas and Oily Knight were heading south with their Wessex gunships on RFA *Resource*. Having been the first to embark up in Scotland, it soon became apparent that they had departed in haste: for the AS12 missiles to be effective, the M260 missile sight in the left seat of each aircraft needed to be recalibrated. Fortunately, a few days later, *Resource* was sailing past the Dorset coast: Lomas and Knight returned back to Yeovilton for the necessary adjustments and rejoined the ship on the same day. The two gunships carried out a successful test-firing of four missiles just before arrival in Ascension.

Like Nick Foster in *Fort Austin*, Jack Lomas was going to war in style. *Resource* was essentially an ammunition ship. In other words, a giant bomb. Soon after heading off, the ship's captain told Lomas about his approach to action stations. 'There's two ways we can play this, Jack,' he said. 'We can be totally pucker, strip down the ward-room, close the bar, and take it all terribly seriously like *Hermes*. Or we can be sensible. We are sitting on 27,000 tons of high explosive. If an Exocet missile gets us, the next bang you hear will be your arse going through your head. You won't need a lifejacket. You'll need a parachute.'

The bar stayed open. Throughout the journey south, the Wessex team lived and dined like kings. This provided an irresistible opportunity for one-upmanship to Oily Knight. It was already a depressingly murky day when

Knight flew across to the aircraft carrier *Hermes* in search of spares. After shutting down on the huge deck behind a row of Sea Harriers, he headed towards the little door at the foot of the superstructure and went below decks.

He was appalled by the cramped conditions he met on board the aircraft carrier. There were bodies asleep on camp beds along the corridors. Lunch on board appeared little short of dumplings and some sort of gruel. Returning to *Resource*, he typed up a 'typical' dinner menu, embellished ever so slightly with lobster, foie gras, steak and salmon, cheese, biscuits and liqueurs, washed down with port. The menu was then despatched to a 'friend' on the *junglie* Sea King squadron on *Hermes*. Knight knew that morale was already low. He was delighted to hear that on receipt of his menu it had now plummeted below the floor. Taking the piss was all part of the game, according to Knight. Thankfully for the rest of us, his moment of comeuppance lay ahead.

A typical Wessex 'flight' comprised a couple of helicopters, aircrew and engineers, stuck on the back end of an auxiliary ship. Communication with the outside world was limited or difficult. Keeping up to date with events in South Georgia and the Falklands meant an almost total reliance on the BBC World Service news, transmitted over HF radio. Keeping in touch with the squadron hierarchy back at Yeovilton, let alone other flights dotted around the growing British fleet now heading south, was nigh on impossible apart from the odd few words on a signal. Flight commanders held a considerable degree of autonomy and responsibility as a result, relying on the ingenuity and experience of the entire flight to resolve unforeseen issues.

One such issue for Lomas and his team involved the flotation canisters that were normally plugged into the hub of each main wheel on the Wessex. These canisters contained a giant balloon that fired off, just like an airbag, in the event of a ditching at sea. The priority was not so much to save the aircraft but to keep the aircraft afloat long enough to improve the odds of escape for aircrew and passengers. The previous summer off the coast of the USA, a Wessex flown by Lieutenant Phil Doyne-Ditmas had suffered a tail rotor failure and ditched into the sea. Although only one 'flot can' fired, causing the aircraft to flip upside down under water, all of the crew and passengers managed to escape. The problem for Lomas was that it was impossible to fit the flot cans as well as the 2-inch rocket platform. Without a commanding officer or senior pilot to talk to, Lomas flew across to *Fearless* to talk to former boss Tim Stanning. 'What the hell am I supposed to do, Tim? Our rocketry kit has been aligned. But it doesn't seem a terribly sensible idea to be flying around the Bay of Biscay over water without flot cans.'

Stanning's reply was straightforward. 'You're a gunship. Keep it that way.' Sometimes it was good to have another experienced *junglie* around.

Even though the Royal Navy had been flying Wessex helicopters at sea for seventeen years, there were always situations that tested the initiative and creativity of the crew. Some procedures were made up on the hoof. One of the key threats the Wessex was thought likely to face, should the task force see action, came from fixed-wing aircraft. With his background as a Helicopter Warfare Instructor (HWI), Lomas and his team decided to turn the attack capabilities of the Wessex into defence. Instead of firing the rockets downwards onto a ground target, what would happen if they were pointed upwards at an incoming jet?

Lomas, Knight and their two other pilots, Sub-Lieutenants Richard 'Noddy' Morton and Steve 'Wannafight' Judd, had a fantastic time experimenting with flying past the ship at low level, raising the aircraft nose slightly, and firing off pairs of rockets. The rockets were designed to explode either on impact or after a period of time. Making notes after each firing, the crews soon worked out that they could get the rockets to explode fairly reliably a couple of miles away at about 500 feet. Although the likelihood of actually hitting an attacking jet was zero – it was bad enough trying to hit a stationary tank – it might make the pilot's eyes water. And it was good for morale.

Chapter 4

Not a 'first tourist' day
21 April 1982

The SAS never do things the easy way. Inserting a troop onto the top of the remote and inhospitable Fortuna Glacier in appalling weather was always going to push the survival skills of Britain's finest to the limit. And that was assuming the 845 Squadron Wessex pilots could get them up there in the first place.

The most challenging element of an ambitious mission plan was to send the helicopters up there in close formation at night. As if the plan wasn't tough enough already, a practice formation session confirmed that night-time was not the time to do it. The SAS plan launched in daylight marked the beginning of Operation Paraquat to take back South Georgia.

Two weeks after the initial Argentine occupation of South Georgia and the Falklands, the whole venture remained in the realm of a good April Fools' joke. Many people still thought it would turn out to be just a bit of fun. Before long the politicians would get their act together and everyone could come home again. It was about to become very clear indeed that this was not to be the case.

Like Hector Heathcote, Mike Tidd was also in Northern Ireland when it all kicked off on Friday 2 April. He was surprised and disappointed not to get a phone call from Yeovilton asking him to get back fast. Eager not to miss out on the fun, he phoned in to Yeovilton. 'Wait a few days and see how things pan out,' said Booth.

A few days later, Tidd was taxiing his Wessex in to dispersal at Aldergrove after a long day flying in South Armagh. In front of him stood the grinning face of Lieutenant Ray Colborne (known to all as 'Uncle Ray'), who was holding up a brown travel bag. After the rotors stopped turning, Colborne wandered over and handed Tidd the bag, telling him, 'You're off, my son! See that British Airways Tristar on the other side of the airfield? Best you get changed. You're in the jump seat.' The rest of Tidd's team were already on their way, having been replaced by Colborne, two other experienced Wessex pilots, and three of the new baby *junglies*, including me.

Now dressed in civilian clothes and perched between the Tristar's two British Airways pilots, Tidd looked down at the Irish Sea 30,000 feet below. Suddenly a cold sweat came over him. He realised he could feel his loaded 9mm pistol still hanging in its holster inside his bomber jacket. Heathrow security were unlikely to take kindly to a loaded weapon passing through their airport with no paperwork, especially coming from Belfast. On arrival he collected his flying kit bag and, thinking fast, grabbed a policeman. 'Excuse me, old chap, I'm on my way to the Falklands and I've got a lot of kit. Any chance of some help?' The unwitting policeman then led the armed Tidd all the way through customs and safely out the other side.

On the morning of Tuesday 6 April, Tiddles and his

newly formed Wessex flight of Ian Georgeson, Sub-Lieutenant Andy 'Boy' Berryman, and RAF exchange pilot Flight Lieutenant Andy 'Pullthrough' Pulford, were the second team to arrive on Ascension. Two days later, they were assisting Nick Foster's flight, lifting stores and troops out to *Fort Austin*. On 11 April, the flight embarked on RFA *Tidespring*, a large oiler, destined to head off with the warships *Antrim* and *Plymouth* for South Georgia. After collecting a few more stores from the returning *Fort Austin* en route, the group continued south to rendezvous with HMS *Endurance*.

It was at this stage that the SAS hatched their bold plan to launch from one of the ships by helicopter, land a team of sixteen men on Fortuna Glacier, march down the central spine through the mountains, and take the Argentine troops by surprise from the rear. As if this plan wasn't sufficiently daring and risky, the initial plan was to do it all *at night*.

It meant the Wessex helicopters would have to get to and from the glacier in the dark in close formation. And so on the evening of Thursday 15 April, Tidd and Berryman took off in one aircraft, with Pulford and Georgeson in the other aircraft, to practise night formation without lights. Bearing in mind the drama to come just one week later, the thought today still sends shivers down Mike Tidd's spine. Having flown a night-formation sortie in a Wessex myself, I can vouch for the only word that begins to describe the experience. Terrifying. White knuckles and tight sphincter muscles are unavoidable.

Night formation is simple in theory. On the tips of the rotor blades and along the spine of the Wessex are about a dozen beta lights. These give off a faint green glow in the dark. The effect is to produce a disk of light from the spinning rotors. The pilot flying in echelon judges his position using the shape of the disk and the angle of the lights on the spine of the lead aircraft. He judges his distance by the extent to which he can see the red lights of the lead aircraft cockpit. If he can barely see the cockpit lights, he's too far away. If he can actually read the instruments, he's about to collide. It's quite an adventure.

The first problem is that flying smoothly enough to stay in stable close formation is hard enough during daylight, let alone in the pitch black. Fear and uncertainty lead to inevitable overcontrolling and wild swings in aircraft positioning. The second problem is how on earth to join up after launching from a ship where a formation take-off is impossible. As the more experienced pilot, Tidd put Berryman in the pilot's right-hand seat. This meant that Tidd's head was squashed in behind the M260 missile sight in the aimer's left seat. After 'frightening themselves fartless' trying to join up with the other Wessex, the idea of a tactical night insert was quietly and sensibly binned.

Although Tidd, Pulford and Georgeson all had experience of Arctic mountain flying in northern Norway, any notion that South Georgia would be a similar environment was quickly disabused following an extensive briefing from Lieutenant Commander Tony Ellerbeck, Wasp flight commander from *Endurance*. His description of the Antarctic weather sounded pretty unpleasant. None of them fully realised quite how unpredictable and violent it would turn out to be. As for the SAS plan, Ellerbeck was not impressed. 'They are out of their tiny trees,' he told *Antrim*'s Ian Stanley.

Nevertheless, against the advice of all those with local experience of the severe conditions, the SAS mission went ahead. On the morning of Wednesday 21 April, with *Antrim* positioned some fifteen miles off the coast of South Georgia, Ian Stanley and his crew took off in their anti-submarine Wessex 3 from *Antrim* to attempt a recce of Fortuna Glacier.

For the first time, Stanley began to grasp the sheer scale of the task. The scenery was awe-inspiring, breathtaking. Gigantic black granite cliffs rose 2,000 feet vertically out of the sea. Fragmented shoulders of ice spilled off the edge of glaciers. The wind whipping around the bays produced considerable turbulence even before they got into the mountains. An engine failure in these freezing waters would be bad enough. The thought of climbing up into the mountains in these hostile conditions, even with a working engine, was not remotely appealing.

Stanley returned to *Antrim* to load the few troops he could take into his cramped cabin. He cleared the deck to make way for Yankee Foxtrot, flown by Mike Tidd, and Yankee Alpha, flown by Andy Pulford, to load up their aircraft one at a time with the bulk of the troops. The three aircraft formation then set off across Cape Constance and into Antarctic Bay towards the foot of Fortuna Glacier. However, a heavy snowstorm made further progress impossible and the formation returned to *Antrim*.

With the weather changing rapidly and violently, Stanley returned for a further recce with the SAS mission commander Cedric Delves and team leader John Hamilton. This time conditions had cleared sufficiently for them to hover-taxi at low level up the face of the glacier. As they climbed, co-pilot Stewart Cooper was mesmerised as the radio altimeter flickered from 30 feet to 200 feet and back almost immediately. The aircraft was crossing deep blue crevasses that cracked the white icy surface of the glacier. At the top of Fortuna, it was clear that Hamilton was less than thrilled at the prospect of legging it over the top of the mountains. Ian Stanley chuckled wryly as he heard Delves tell him: 'You've got to get on John.'

Back one more time to *Antrim*, the formation loaded up, delayed yet again by a heavy snow shower. This time all three Wessex managed to work their way back up the glacier, buffeted violently in the heavy turbulence and snow squalls. One moment an aircraft would be in full autorotation with no power applied and yet still climbing. Another, they would have full power applied and still be going down. On each occasion, the pilots had to trust that the updraft or downdraft would reverse direction before too long.

This is one of the two ill-fated Wessex 5s on their way to drop SAS troops on the top of Fortuna Glacier in South Georgia. The massive cliffs give a hint of the awesome scale and power that lay ahead of them up in the mountains.

Stanley's first attempt to put his wheels down on the glacier was nearly disastrous. Only a warning from the crewman, Fitzgerald, and quick reactions from Stanley prevented the Wessex 3 from slipping into a crevasse. Behind him, Tidd was unable to bring his aircraft to a hover at all and was forced to circle round again. Pulford managed to land using the lead aircraft as a reference point. His crewman, Jan Lomas, voiced what all the other aircrew were thinking: 'What a bloody stupid idea this is.'

Visibility shifted from clear to zero to clear with alarming speed. Still flying their aircraft on the icy surface with the wind gusting sixty knots, the pilots watched the SAS troops unload their equipment. All three aircraft were now profoundly unstable as the Wessex airframes shook from side to side.

Tidd was first to clear out his passengers, commenting to Tug Wilson in the back: 'What on earth are these prats coming up here for. They'll be lucky not to fall into one these crevasses.' Eager to get off the treacherous mountain, Tidd decided to lift off early in order to take advantage of a clear gap in the weather that had suddenly opened up in front of him. It was a precursor to his fateful decision the following day. After receiving a thumbs-up from the SAS troop commander Hamilton, the two other Wessex gladly lifted off and headed down the glacier to join Tidd for the trip back to *Antrim* and *Tidespring* out at sea. 'Thank God we'll never have to do that again,' announced a relieved Tidd on arrival back on board, prematurely as it turned out.

That night was a shocker. The weather worsened dramatically. The barometer dropped thirty millibars within an hour; the wind gusted to over 100 knots, and the seas became huge and burst over the bow of the rolling ships. On the flight decks of both *Antrim* and *Tidespring*, a Wessex remained open to the appalling weather, partly because of the danger of moving the aircraft into their respective hangars, partly to keep aircraft available on alert. On *Tidespring*, the Wessex maintenance crew were forced to lash heavy manila ropes to stop the blades thrashing themselves to death. The normal tipsocks were simply inadequate for the task. On *Antrim*, wardroom film night was abandoned as the projector became too hard to hold down. On Fortuna Glacier, the SAS troops had only moved a few hundred yards and were vainly digging themselves into the ice to gain even a few inches of shelter from the driving wind and snow.

It was no surprise the following morning, Thursday 22 April, when the signal came through from Hamilton requesting emergency evacuation. His team were suffering from frostbite and exposure. Tidd's roster put Ian Georgeson and Andy Berryman in the frame to fly the two Wessex 5s. But whereas he was happy for Arctic-trained Georgeson to fly in these appalling conditions, he was less willing to let the less experienced Berryman go, despite the fact that Berryman was an extremely competent young pilot. 'It's not a "first tourist" day,' said Tidd.

The three Wessex set off again with conditions improved from the overnight storm to a mere gale. Stanley led in the Wessex 3 with Georgeson and Tidd following, having decided that he couldn't put Andy Pulford through a second dose of Fortuna Glacier. As the formation approached the foot of the glacier, Stanley told the two other aircraft to land on a flat promontory and wait while he recced the mountain. Violent changes in wind direction made it hard for Stanley to control his tail rotor as he climbed the glacier. He decided to abort the recce and recalled the other aircraft back to the ships for a refuel. An hour later, at lunchtime, the trio set off for a further attempt. This time the weather was clearer and calmer as the rescue team landed next to the orange smokes set off by the SAS teams on top of the glacier. Under normal circumstances conditions would have been considered appalling. The wind was gusting to sixty knots. The aircraft were still sliding around on the ice.

In the back of Yankee Foxtrot, Tug Wilson had closed

the door and was pouring hot soup out for the frozen SAS troops. Mike Tidd made his fateful call for permission to go while the going was good.

Aside from the loss of the two troop-carrying Wessex 5s, *junglie* involvement in the taking of South Georgia was otherwise minimal. For the next few days, Tidd and Georgeson made themselves useful on board *Antrim*. However, an important and unusual role lay ahead.

Having discovered that the route over the top of Fortuna Glacier was impassable, the SAS now attempted to insert their patrols covertly in rubber inflatable Gemini boats. This method resulted in no greater success. Ian Stanley and his crew spent a day searching for and rescuing broken down Geminis that were now floating around the freezing Antarctic waters.

To the Royal Navy aircrew, the SAS were a peculiar bunch and a law unto themselves. Having refused to speak to anyone or take advice beforehand, suddenly they were now everybody's best friends. Maybe it was the relief at surviving near disasters. Maybe it was the camaraderie of having been into battle together, at least against the weather. The Wessex aircrew were even invited onto the subsequent assault, causing Jan Lomas to comment afterwards that 'the SAS were lovely!'

Three days after the crash on Fortuna Glacier came news that an Argentine Guppy-class submarine was in the area. The ARA *Santa Fe* had already landed a party of marines at South Georgia and now posed a serious threat to the British surface fleet. On the morning of Sunday 25 April, the Wessex 3 crew spotted the *Santa Fe* on the surface leaving Grytviken in gloomy weather conditions. Ian Stanley immediately ran in from behind the submarine at low level, lobbing two depth charges into the water just ahead of it. As the Wessex banked hard to clear away from the area, the crew strained their heads behind them to watch the outcome of the attack.

The effect was dramatic. Huge explosions in the water blew the rear half of the submarine completely out of the water, its tail hanging suspended in the air before crashing back down into the sea. Amazingly the submarine remained afloat, although it had turned, zigzagging its way back towards land. From the Wessex 3 cabin, Fitz Fitzgerald fired his entire supply of machine-gun ammunition into the conning tower of the submarine. Shortly afterwards, HMS *Brilliant*'s Lynx arrived on the scene, dropping a Mark 46 torpedo into the water alongside the surfaced submarine without effect. They followed up with their own burst of machine-gun fire, steering away when fire was returned at them from the tower of the submarine.

Next on the scene was Tony Ellerbeck in HMS *Endurance*'s Wasp helicopter. Sighting the submarine's fin from two miles away, the Wasp launched one of its AS12 anti-ship missiles. From the left seat, aimer David Wells directed the wire-guided missile directly into the fin. The missile passed straight through the thin skin exploding in the sea on the other side. The impact was enough to blow the Argentine machine gunner off his firing position and down into the control room below. The second missile was not as successful.

In the air, the attack threatened to degenerate into chaos. The two *Endurance* Wasps couldn't talk to anyone else because they had a different radio fit. Their first missile attack had therefore taken the Lynx crew completely by surprise. *Brilliant*'s second Lynx now appeared, circling overhead whilst firing her machine gun into the submarine hull. Meanwhile Tony Ellerbeck's Wasp returned to *Endurance* and rearmed with two more missiles, launching both in quick succession. This time the first missile flew into the sea whilst the second went through the submarine fin.

A second Wasp, flown by John Dransfield from HMS *Plymouth*, now had a crack with its single AS12 missile. Aimer Joe Harper guided his missile right onto the submarine itself, exploding so close that it caused further damage to the hull.

By now the submarine was approaching the jetty at Grytviken. Machine-gun tracer fire was streaking in all directions, coming up from the Argentine ground forces and down from the helicopters. A third Wasp, also from *Endurance* and flown by Tim Finding, now lined up for the attack. His aimer, Bob Nadin, achieved a miss with his first missile and a hit with his second on *Santa Fe*'s fin.

Six helicopters were now competing exuberantly for the prize of sinking the Argentine submarine. As it became obvious that the sub was limping back to the pier at King Edward Point, the helicopters began to withdraw away from the ground fire. *Santa Fe* and her sixty-man crew were going nowhere. However, Tony Ellerbeck wasn't finished, having rearmed and returned for his third attack. The first missile failed to fire, but the second hit the fin, this time exploding noisily. Eight missiles, one torpedo and a whole load of machine-gun bullets had now been fired at the *Santa Fe*. But it was the original two depth charges that did the damage.

In order to sustain the momentum of this attack, it was decided to begin the land assault straight away. The main body of troops had been held off in RFA *Tidespring* to avoid the submarine threat. So a hastily assembled landing force combining SAS, SBS and Royal Marines was flown in by the *Antrim* Wessex and both of *Brilliant*'s Lynx. Mike Tidd and Ian Georgeson organised the flow of troops to the flight deck in order to free up extra Royal Marines.

The Royal Navy warships sailed towards Grytviken firing their guns and with their huge battle ensigns flying. It was a stirring sight, even if *Antrim*'s ensign did wrap itself around the radar mast.

The destroyer HMS *Antrim* sails towards Mount Paget in South Georgia. In this bay, *Antrim*'s Wessex 3 blew the Argentine submarine *Santa Fe* out of the water with two depth charges. Various Wasp helicopters then followed up with an enthusiastic, but largely futile, volley of AS12 missiles.

Demoralised by the intensity of the naval gunfire barrage and the reappearance of their damaged submarine, the Argentine garrison surrendered as the landing force approached. Shortly afterwards, the British Prime Minister Margaret Thatcher was able to stand on the steps of 10 Downing Street and read out the emotive signal sent by HMS *Antrim*'s Captain Brian Young. 'Be pleased to inform Her Majesty that the White Ensign flies alongside the Union Flag in Grytviken South Georgia. God save the Queen.'

*   *   *

Having run out of helicopters, Mike Tidd realised that his team were the obvious choice to look after the Argentine prisoners from the garrison and *Santa Fe*. Young was grateful for the offer. The *junglies* could make themselves useful again.

Some very rapid planning was now called for. Back on RFA *Tidespring*, with help from Ian Georgeson, Andy Pulford and Andy Berryman, Mike Tidd set about organising a system of prisoner management and accommodation. Within just eighteen hours, the ship's team banged together shelves and cushions as sleeping accommodation, and makeshift toilets using forty-gallon drums cut in half with wooden seats fitted.

With help from a detachment of nine Royal Marines from *Antrim*, a total of 260 prisoners were processed through *Tidespring*'s flight deck and down into allocated compartments below. Argentine special forces troops were assigned one magazine, the crew of the *Santa Fe* the other; the scrap merchants from the original invasion were sent to the now-empty aircraft hangar, and the remaining force of Argentine marines were housed in the hold.

By Saturday 1 May, the force was sailing north toward warmer waters, ultimately to offload the prisoners using the two Wessex that were based at Ascension Island for onward repatriation to Argentina. Altogether the prisoners were on board for two weeks, testing the initiative and patience of Tidd and his team throughout. Problems included how to keep the huge holds warm in the freezing Antarctic waters; how to make sure young naval engineers didn't shoot one another or themselves with their unfamiliar SMG sub-machine guns; how to apply the more obscure aspects of the Geneva Convention, which had been written for the confines of land and not sea; and how to dissuade the friskier prisoners from causing trouble.

One of those prisoners included the especially trouble-some Lieutenant Alfredo Astiz, an army officer known internationally as *El Ángel Rubio de la Muerte* ('The Blond Angel of Death') who was wanted for the forced disappearances, torture and murder of thousands of political prisoners in Argentina in the 1970s. He was eventually segregated from his compatriots and taken north on board *Antrim*. Although questioned by British police, he was repatriated to Argentina a few weeks later. French and Swedish governments continue to seek his extradition and legal action was renewed against him in Argentina.

Argentine officers in general treated their conscripts like dirt. After observing officers pushing their men out of the way when food was served in the ship's hold, Tidd caused dismay when he informed the Argentines that, whilst in his care, they would follow the British tradition of feeding the men first and officers second. The prisoners included many Argentines with British connections. One Argentine marine officer commented on the irony that his father was decorated as an RAF Spitfire pilot during the Second World War and now he, the son, was a prisoner of the British. Another was greatly saddened that he was unlikely to be able to take up his place at Oxford University that summer. Several of the submariners had been part of a naval contingent that collected two Type-42 destroyers from shipyards on the Tyne for service in the Argentine navy. Some of the 845 Squadron engineers had joked with the Argentines that they were being taken to a prisoner of war camp in England. 'Excellent. Could we go to Newcastle? We like Newcastle,' they asked.

As the prisoners were offloaded from *Tidespring* at Ascension, Mike Tidd and his team were touched that several Argentine officers came over to shake hands and thank them for the way they had been looked after. In different circumstances, they might have been friends.

Chapter 5

Kicking off
1–6 May 1982

The task force had sailed from Britain in indecent haste. A huge volume of stores had been piled into ships and needed reorganising, while helicopters and crews were dotted around the fleet unable to contact one another.

Yet an excellent plan was beginning to emerge. The fleet would assemble at Ascension Island, halfway to the Falklands, and use the helicopters to 'cross-deck' stores between ships and bring new stores from the air base. The carrier group was to set off and win the naval battle around the Falklands before the amphibious group left the safety of Ascension Island to land the troops on the islands. Throughout the journey south, soldiers, sailors and airmen trained for an assault on the Falklands. Still nobody really thought it would come to all-out war.

Within hours of the carrier group's arrival off the coast of the Falklands, Britain's dispute with Argentina was about to get very serious indeed.

* * *

With the demise of Britain's empire abroad and a tightening of the political purse strings at home, the savage defence cuts announced by Secretary of State John Nott in 1981 called an end to the need for expensive naval aircraft carriers and outdated amphibious landing ships. Britain's interests would now be focused on her contribution to NATO and the defence of Northern Europe from an expanding Soviet Union. Thus when Argentina invaded the Falklands, Britain's ageing helicopter carrier, HMS *Hermes*, was heading for the scrapyard; the first of three new through-deck cruisers, HMS *Invincible*, had already been sold to the Australians; the commando assault ship HMS *Intrepid* was in mothballs, and several Royal Fleet Auxiliary supply ships were en route to other navies around the world. Had the Argentines timed their invasion a matter of weeks later, there would not have been enough ships to make up a task force, let alone retake the Falklands.

The task force that sailed from Portsmouth on Monday 5 April amidst much fanfare and razzamatazz had been thrown together with great speed, enthusiasm and ingenuity. National pride was at stake. The two big carriers *Hermes* and *Invincible* were earmarked for Sea Harrier operations. With just twenty Sea Harriers initially, the task force was utterly reliant for air defence on this tiny group of vertical and short take-off and landing jets and their two mobile airfields out at sea. Any kind of amphibious landing would be led by the venerable assault ship *Fearless*, backed by a handful of landing ships logistic. On Friday 9 April, 3 Commando Brigade's force of Royal Marines (known to all as either 'royal' or 'bootnecks') and 2 and 3 Para, followed on the requisitioned cruise ship SS *Canberra* from Southampton. *Fearless*'s sister ship HMS *Intrepid* was rapidly extracted from mothballs and sailed for the South Atlantic on 26 April after a work-up at Portland.

From *Fearless*, helicopter tasking commander Tim Stanning wondered what kit had made it on board in the mad rush to depart from Portsmouth. Prior to arriving at Ascension, his job would be to put together the immense list of tasks that enabled the helicopter crews to cross-deck stores, troops and equipment from the wrong ships to the right ships. Furthermore, he was also to construct the Helicopter Assault Landing Task sheet, the 'HEALT'. The plan was to conduct a full-scale rehearsal of an amphibious assault on the Falklands whilst the fleet was at Ascension waiting for events to unfold.

Although Oily Knight and Jack Lomas in their Wessex claimed the prize for being the first *junglies* to leave Yeovilton, the *junglie* Sea Kings were the first squadron to leave en masse soon afterwards. Nine aircraft had embarked with *Hermes*, while three more sailed with *Fearless*. One other had followed by air with the fourteenth and final Sea King following later on HMS *Intrepid* along with Mike Crabtree's Wessex flight.

Even if they were slightly more ungainly and less manoeuvrable, the new Sea Kings were far more powerful than the Wessex they had replaced. Because of their extra size and power, they would be expected to do much of the cross-decking in Ascension and also much of the subsequent offload of ammunition and stores when the time came for an amphibious landing in the Falklands. They had one other remarkable advantage, as yet untested, in the shape of the seven sets of night vision goggles that would allow them to fly at extremely low levels in the dark. All this lay in the future.

Eleven days after setting off from Portsmouth, the first

few British ships arrived off the coast of Ascension Island. Having tasked his flight to get on with their contribution to the cross-decking operation, Jack Lomas went ashore to try to track down spare batteries for his Wessex. Landing at Wideawake airfield, he was delighted to see 845 Squadron's Mobile Air Ops Team (MAOT), led by Lieutenant Brad Reynoldson, marching up and down the huge dispersal area amongst a mass of loads with large green A43 radios strapped to their backs and hooking-up loads. Inbound helicopter crews called up 'helicom', on the radio frequency 258.8 megahertz, whereupon Reynoldson and his team would tell them which load needing taking to which ship. 'MAOT's running the place. Everything's going to be fine!' thought Lomas.

For Sea King and Wessex helicopter crews alike, the biggest problem during cross-decking was finding the destination ship amongst the widely scattered fleet. Armed with a list of ships' names and the daily changing alphanumeric codes, the pilot would see, for example, that 'Hotel Three Alpha One' was the landing ship RFA *Sir Galahad*. With six identical-looking ships of this type to choose from, and all ships' names painted over for security, crews resorted to the use of blackboards in the back of the helicopter. Coming to a hover alongside the flight deck, the crewman would hold up the board, 'Are you *Sir Galahad*?' – a question which invariably prompted a burst of laughter between pilot and crewman. The more serious reply from the flight deck would either be a thumbs-up or a frantic pointing at another nearby ship. Aircrew recognition of RN and RFA ships was already generally excellent. After two hours of load-lifting, crews had worked out where pretty well all the ships were parked.

As well as reorganising stores, the stop at Ascension was an opportunity to reorganise the helicopters. Five of the original *junglie* Sea Kings remained on *Hermes*, freeing up more space for Sea Harrier operations. This group included four night-flying Sea Kings.

During the journey south, the cockpits of these four aircraft had to be specially adapted by the squadron engineers so they could be flown with the night vision goggles. The dim red lighting that normally lit the Sea King's cockpit instruments at night-time would look like dazzling bright sunshine when viewed through the ultra-sensitive goggles. The other four Sea Kings from *Hermes* were spread between the roll-on, roll-off ferry MV *Elk* and the P&O cruise liner *Canberra*. The new arrival from Ascension replaced Mike Crabtree's two Wessex on HMS *Intrepid*, which then made their way to the fuel ship RFA *Tidepool*. Bill Pollock and Simon Thornewill swapped ships so that Pollock could take charge of the special forces night-flying programme from *Hermes*, and Thornewill, as squadron commanding officer, could liaise with the landing force commanders on *Fearless*.

Just two days after arriving at Ascension, the carrier group led by HMS *Hermes* departed south, leaving behind the amphibious group to continue cross-decking and preparing for the eventual landings. The amphibious ships and landing forces weren't to set off until the naval battle was won.

On board RFA *Resource*, news of the two Wessex crashes on South Georgia was beginning to filter through via the BBC World Service. 'Fuck me,' said Jack Lomas. 'Thank God Tiddles and his boys didn't get themselves killed. But two Wessex lost. What a start!'

The following day the atmosphere became decidedly sombre with news that one of the Sea Kings on *Hermes* had flown into the sea at dusk, killing Petty Officer

Aircrewman Kevin 'Ben' Casey, the first British fatality of war. As if it were needed after the fiasco on Fortuna, the tragic accident was an unpleasant reminder that conditions in the South Atlantic would pose every bit as much of a threat to aircrew as direct action by the Argentine enemy.

As the fleet sailed further south, they left behind the balmy tropical weather of Ascension and entered the wildly changing conditions of the South Atlantic. On some days the sea would be completely flat calm and the surface almost oily. On others, the wind would whip up heavy seas making conditions for take-off and landing terrible. Often visibility was appalling. Finding ships out in the fleet in such weather, and getting back safely, required skill, ingenuity, and a healthy dose of self-preservation.

Without radar to guide, Wessex 5 crews mostly relied on a method of navigation called 'dead reckoning'. It didn't matter exactly where the aircraft was over the sea. What mattered was where the aircraft was in relation to each ship. Dead reckoning meant applying a mental combination of wind and ship direction. The big assumption of course was that the ship's heading didn't change. Hence there was always a need to add a large margin for error. All naval aircrew have experienced the unnerving situation of returning to where 'mother' should be only to find a vast expanse of sea and no sign of a ship.

The only navigation aid for the Wessex crew was a direction-finding needle on the cockpit panel that swung left or right in response to a radio signal, should the ship be generous enough to use its radio. But with radio silence the norm in the fleet, relying on wits and caution was usually the best strategy for avoiding a cold swim. In especially poor visibility, pilots would deliberately offset the return journey in order to cross a mile or two behind the ship and find the wake. It was then a simple matter of flying up the wake and hoping you then arrived at the right ship.

Along the way, the floating bomb that was RFA *Resource* regularly transferred ammunition to other ships. Some of this was done by 'replenishment at sea', an impressive manoeuvre whereby both ships would sail close alongside one another. Lines would be shot from one ship to the other, followed by heavier lines. Stores could then be hauled across by lines of sailors while the ship transferred fuel by hose suspended from a separate line. The two Wessex helicopters were used extensively to assist in the ammunition transfer by underslung load. However, the containers used to hold the 4.5-inch shells for ships' guns were in limited supply. Under threat of attack during action stations, some of these boxes were simply despatched off the back of the flight deck, making the shortage even worse.

On board *Hermes*, the 846 Squadron Sea King detachment now had seven sets of second- and third-generation night vision goggles. To work properly, the goggles needed a minimum level of light from the moon or stars, so they couldn't be used in the pitch-blackness of heavy cloud cover. In most weather conditions, the goggles enabled the pilots to fly their aircraft visually, almost as if it were daylight, albeit in monochromatic green. However, it wasn't quite as easy as flying in daylight. The image presented was two-dimensional, not allowing any perception of depth, and making distance and closing speeds very difficult to assess. Bill Pollock compared it to peering through a tube of bog roll underwater.

Using the night vision goggles and the Sea King's automatic height hold, linked to the radio altimeter, pilots could keep their aircraft just twenty feet above the land and fifty feet above the sea. The stop at Ascension had given 846 Squadron a chance to show off their new skills to some very interested observers from special forces. A night flight around the island followed by a landing in total darkness told them all they needed to know: flying at night and at extreme low level was the ideal way to get the troops in and out of the Falklands covertly.

Getting the troops to the right place was another matter. The Sea Kings were equipped with a Tactical Air Navigation System that could be aligned with the ship's own navigation system just before take-off. Without a satellite or beacon to provide constant updates, the system relied on what the instruments within the aircraft were telling it. Over time, tiny errors would creep in and the system would drift, becoming less and less accurate. But by cross-checking several aircraft systems against each other at periodic intervals of flight, it was hoped that the errors would average out. Flying in from the sea as a formation, the plan was to aim to hit land, offset to one side of a known point. That way they knew which direction to look for it, updating their systems as they coasted in. The formation would then split up and each Sea King would complete its individual mission. Concordia Rock was chosen as the known point, because of its distinctiveness and remoteness.

Pollock realised that he was going to have to work hard to keep his pilots and aircrew alive. The training on the way south had shown that crews could cope with long periods of flying at extremely low level over the sea using the night vision goggles. But the extra hour, and often much longer, of flying and navigating over the featureless terrain of the Falklands was going to increase the workload in the cockpit dramatically. Keeping crews rested and aircraft serviced meant his four night-flying Sea Kings would not be available for flying during the day. Dealing with the many frustrations this posed meant keeping good relations with Admiral Sandy Woodward's staff who were running the campaign, the captain's staff who were running the ship, and the aviation staff who were running aircraft operations.

Planning was also complicated, split between the 3 Brigade command on board *Fearless*, still parked off the coast of Ascension Island, and the planning team on board *Hermes*, some 4,000 miles south. Wardroom Two on *Hermes* was closed off for special forces planning. None of the aircrew or troops actually involved in the missions was allowed inside so as not to compromise other missions if they were captured and interrogated. But coordination was needed to make sure each individual mission was achievable and that aircraft wouldn't suddenly run into one another in the dark.

Somebody also needed to make sure the returning helicopters weren't going to get shot down by their own side. Low-flying aircraft unexpectedly approaching the fleet at night from the direction of the Falklands were likely to have a brief and unpleasant encounter with a Sea Harrier or a Sea Dart missile. The fleet needed to know when the Sea Kings were going out and when they were coming in. Somebody had to negotiate this complex chain of command and make sure everybody knew what they needed to know. Only Lieutenant Commander Bill Pollock knew all the details. It meant he wasn't going to get much flying done himself.

On the evening of Friday 30 April, the British carrier group entered the 200-mile Total Exclusion Zone (TEZ) now declared around the islands. Any non-British ship or aircraft entering this zone could expect to be fired upon without warning. The Falklands War kicked off for real approaching midnight as Lieutenant Nigel North's flight of three *junglie* Sea Kings lifted off from the deck of *Hermes*.

North had started his preparation four hours before launch time with a briefing of all the crews, followed by the individual brief for his particular mission. It was a pleasant night as he walked out across the flight deck of the carrier. The dark shapes of the three Sea Kings with their drooping blades awaited their occupants. As mission leader, his first job was to lead the formation of Sea Kings across the eighty miles of South Atlantic now separating *Hermes* from Concordia Rock.

As the crews prepared each of the Sea Kings for start-up, heavily laden SAS and SBS troops boarded the aircraft with their huge bergens. With rotors turning and a final fix of their position from the ship, the formation lifted off and disappeared into the blackness. The Sea Kings flew low across the sea. Without goggles, the world outside was black and unmoving. With them, a green sea scrolled beneath the aircraft as the pilots headed towards a green horizon. After a couple of position checks from the other aircraft, North was satisfied that he was to coast in on track at the right place.

The sea transit in formation went well. Even so, North felt mighty relieved to hit landfall within a mile of Concordia Rock. The navigation system was working. The formation then split to go their separate ways and North now concentrated on his own individual mission. Apart from flights around Salisbury Plain and Ascension Island, this was the first time any of the crews had flown at low level over land at night. Throughout the journey south, all of the crews had spent hours poring over maps of the Falklands to try to memorise the main features and get a mental picture of what was to come. What North and his co-pilot Lieutenant Alan 'Wiggy' Bennett had not expected was that the ground seemed to be covered in snow. Cursing the 'met' man on *Hermes* for failing to forecast accurately, they continued on.

The drop-off point for the SAS team was just north-west of Estancia House, a collection of farm buildings some twelve miles from the capital Port Stanley. Depositing their troops on the ground with surprising ease, the crew were convinced the roar of the helicopter would be heard throughout the entire Falklands. But shielded from the capital by a line of hills, it was doubtful whether anyone would have heard them. After lifting off, aircrewman Colin Tattersall leant forward to say he had cut a piece of Falklands heather for the pilots to take back to the ship, but he had seen no sign of snow. It was just how the grassland looked through the goggles. The met man was reprieved.

Still feeling nervous about the noise they were making the pilots focused on getting back to the sea and relative safety as quickly as possible. In the back, Tattersall was pointing a radar-warning receiver in all directions. There were no emissions. The Argentines didn't even know they were there.

Having set off in formation, the three aircraft dropped their teams and returned to *Hermes* individually. Bob Horton and Paul Humphreys in one of the other Sea Kings had seen another aircraft, most likely Argentine, but evaded successfully. The first covert mission of the war had been a remarkable success.

Later on board *Hermes*, Bill Pollock went to debrief Captain Lyn Middleton, and presented him with some heather: 'A piece of the Falkland Islands for you, sir.'

'Bloody hell,' replied Middleton. 'If we're going to take the Falklands bit by bit, it's going to take a long time.'

* * *

Just before dawn on 1 May, an RAF Vulcan bomber from Ascension Island, 4,000 miles to the north, conducted an extreme long-range bombing raid on Port Stanley airfield. This mission was the first of seven codenamed 'Black Buck'. As an exercise in logistics it was genuinely impressive and remarkable. Eleven Victor tankers and two Vulcans took off from Wideawake airfield at midnight in order that one Vulcan could drop its load of twenty-one 1,000-pound bombs diagonally across the runway.

The effectiveness of the mission itself was rather more questionable. Only one of the bombs hit the runway, with negligible effect on Argentine operations. Subsequent bombing missions missed the runway altogether. Even if they had hit, the crew forgot to arm the bombs on their second mission, according to the commanding officer of 801 Sea Harrier squadron. It was an unbelievable error after all the effort to get them there. Later missions launched Shrike missile strikes against radar installations. For this, the radars had to be switched on in order to allow the missile to home in. Realising the threat, the Argentine operators simply switched their radars off. The missions achieved little.

The RAF publicity machine subsequently tried to talk up how the Black Buck raids demonstrated their ability to bomb the Argentine mainland. However, a single unescorted Vulcan bomber would have been easy meat for an Argentine Mirage fighter. It was an empty threat. The credit claimed for the Vulcan raids demeaned the actual RAF contribution of pilots, engineers and aircraft, which, even if relatively small, was both important and significant. This was neither. The entire Black Buck mission turned out to be an expensive and ineffective exercise in inter-service politics.

What Black Buck One undoubtedly achieved was to

wake up the Argentine defences in time for the surprise dawn raid on Port Stanley airfield by the Sea Harriers of 800 Squadron. Launched from *Hermes* a hundred miles north-east of Stanley, nine Sea Harriers attacked the airfield at low level. Two toss bombs hit the runway scarring it; others bombs left the airfield facilities in smoke and flames. The other three jets attacked the grass airstrip at Goose Green, to where all of the twelve Argentine Pucara twin turboprop attack aircraft had been moved. One Pucara was destroyed in the attack by a direct hit and two others were damaged.

Meanwhile, out at sea, Jack Lomas was at the controls of his Wessex, Yankee Hotel, oblivious to the drama unfolding ashore. In the rear cabin was his crewman Petty Officer Steve MacNaughton. After dropping off passengers and stores on the deck of *Hermes*, he now received curt orders over the radio from *Hermes*' 'flyco'. 'Yankee Hotel, clear the deck immediately and hold as close as you can on the starboard quarter. Expedite.'

Lomas lifted off straight away and circled round to bring the Wessex to a hover just to the rear and to the side of the carrier. After a wait of ten minutes or so, Lomas called flyco for an explanation.

'You're planeguard. Confirm you are equipped.' They were to act as search-and-rescue cover in case any of the returning Sea Harriers ditched into the sea.

'I have one winch and one crewman. I'm also short of fuel. Request a quick suck.'

'Negative, hold.'

Almost immediately Lomas heard the first of the Sea Harriers call up on the radio as the ship began a turn into wind to assist their recovery. Lomas was more concerned about his fuel state to think much about the sailor wandering a few yards in front of him towards the triple chaff launchers just behind the *Hermes* bridge super-structure. Chaff comprises thousands of tiny strips of aluminium foil that form a bloom. This then creates a big false target on radar to an attacking missile or jet.

With a giant *whoosh*, one of the chaff launchers suddenly fired its rocket up through Yankee Hotel's rotor blades before bursting high above the helicopter. Lomas's heart leapt in his mouth at the shock. 'Fuck me. What the fuck was that?' he shouted to MacNaughton before transmitting to *Hermes*: 'You've just fired chaff through my rotor blades.' His message was ignored.

He was also almost too shocked to notice the Sea Harriers landing on the deck, one by one, just a few yards to his left. The historic event was reported later on the BBC news by correspondent Brian Hanrahan: 'I counted them all out and I counted them all back.'

'OK you can leave now,' a seemingly unconcerned *Hermes* told a still stunned Lomas.

Of course *Hermes* was correct to prioritise the Sea Harriers. Without them, there would be no task force. A single Wessex was well down the pecking order. But the brusque way that the situation was handled seemed unnecessary. Barely coaxing Yankee Hotel back to land on *Resource* with well below minimum fuel left in the tanks, Lomas told Steve MacNaughton, 'My God, that was frightening.'

The other half of Jack Lomas's flight, Oily Knight, Noddy Morton, Petty Officer Aircrewman Arthur Balls, and Royal Marine Colour Sergeant Tommy Sands, had deployed the previous afternoon to the County-class destroyer HMS *Glamorgan*, sister ship of *Antrim* which was operating in South Georgia. Tommy Sands had been embarked with the flight as military trainer. But for reasons of practical operational efficiency, he had been trained up by Arthur

Balls and Steve MacNaughton to act as an additional aircrewman.

It was a tight squeeze landing Yankee Tango on the flight deck of *Glamorgan* with the ship's own Wessex folded and stowed in the hangar. To Oily Knight, operating two Wessex from one deck looked like an accident waiting to happen, should one aircraft be stuck on deck with the other needing an urgent suck of fuel. Still, he thought, close cooperation between crews should minimise the risk.

Two helicopters parked on a single spot flight deck. These ones are actually on HMS *Antrim*, sister ship of *Glamorgan*. Ian Stanley's Wessex 3 is on the left next to Mike Crabtree's Wessex 5 on the right.

It wasn't entirely clear to any of the crew what their task was as they arrived on board. Their confidence did not improve when they woke up the following morning within sight of land. *Glamorgan* and two sleek Type-21 frigates, *Arrow* and *Alacrity*, had been tasked to provide naval gunfire support for the raids on Stanley with their 4.5-inch guns.

Their first mission, requested by *Glamorgan*'s captain

Mike Barrow, was to fly up to 3,000 feet and drop a few blooms of chaff at decent intervals so that they looked like ships to any attacking aircraft's radar. Armed with AS12 missiles on either side of the aircraft, Arthur Balls sat in the left seat behind the M260 missile sight as Oily Knight drove from the right seat. Noddy Morton and Tommy Sands sat in the back as stand-in crewmen. Next to them was a supply of brown paper parcels containing chaff.

Oily Knight was not at all impressed with the idea. First, all *junglies* hate heights. Staying at low level avoids the perceived problem of high-altitude nosebleeds, a common *junglie* concern, and the rather more real danger of having to descend blind through cloud. Second, it seemed obvious to Knight that chaff might fool an incoming missile, but it wouldn't fool an attacking aircraft. The pilot would see the sudden magical appearance of several big echoes behind a small slow-moving echo on their radar and draw the obvious conclusion: they're not ships. Third, opening the parcels through the open door of a windy helicopter inevitably meant that half of the thousands of tiny bits of foil would fill the cabin rather than the sky below. Nonetheless, having restrained himself from the temptation to express these concerns, Knight set off to complete the task professionally, as ordered, before returning to *Glamorgan* to refuel.

The second mission of the day was to conduct a surface search along the coastline. There had been talk of a possible submarine sighting near Port Stanley. This would be where the AS12 missiles might come in handy. Flying south of the capital, the crew of Yankee Tango had a good view of the bleak Falkland Islands coastline. The plan was to fly close enough to keep land in sight but not too close to come within range of any shore-based Argentine positions.

The low-lying land brought them closer in to the coast than they had intended. Through the long-range setting of his missile sight, Arthur Balls could see a column of smoke way out to the west, most likely a result of the earlier Sea Harrier raid on the airstrip at Goose Green. But if he could see so far inland, others much closer on land could also see them. Knight and Morton both spotted the missile launch out to the right side of the aircraft at the same time. A very bright white light source left the coastline and gradually climbed towards the Wessex at what seemed like a slow pace. Inside the aircraft there was a short pause as the situation sunk in. *'Fuck, we're being shot at.'* Knight's immediate reaction was to apply fighter-evasion techniques. He pushed the nose of the Wessex forward dropping low and fast towards the surface of the sea, trying to stay at right angles to the incoming missile.

When practising fighter evasion, the trick that always seemed to fool fighter pilots expecting an easy win was for the helicopter to achieve a maximum crossing rate. As the fighter closes with the helicopter at high speed, the attacking jet has to tighten its turn progressively. This would affect the targeting system enough for the jet to overshoot. I've seen how effective this can be at first hand, having sat next to a frustrated and surprised fighter pilot in the cockpit of a Hunter jet as we overshot a formation of low-level Wessex helicopters beneath us. At least this was the theory as Knight pushed the Wessex down to sea level. He hoped the same principle would apply against an attacking missile.

With Yankee Tango now powering across the line of the missile, the crew realised the missile was wire-guided. The flame from the missile produced a white light that was now bobbling about as it sped towards them. After a few further jiggles, the missile splashed harmlessly into the sea well short of its target. But there was no time to relax.

Almost immediately a second missile launched. This time, the white light angled straight upwards until it disappeared into the cloud base at 1,000 feet. This was far worse for the crew who were now becoming distinctly unnerved. 'Shit, I can't see it any more but I know it's still heading our way,' exclaimed Knight trying to extract as much speed from the Wessex as possible. A few seconds later, the missile emerged from the cloud much closer. From the back, Morton called out distance even though there was no real way of being sure how far away it was. 'Two miles. One and a half miles and closing. One mile. *Shit.*'

From the front, Knight prepared his crew for the worst: 'Right boys, you'd better hang on. There might be a bit of a bang.' There then followed a moment of pure absurdity as Sands was seen trying to put his fingers in his ears, despite wearing a helmet.

In fact, once the missile was right on them, Knight's plan was to pull up hard and head for the sky. A trained missile-aimer himself, he knew that the aimer on land would never be able to keep up with the rapid vertical movement. The missile response would also be delayed because of the length of the wire now stretched out over the sea. Provided he timed his pull-up right, the missile would pass safely underneath before splashing harmlessly.

Knight never found out whether his plan would have worked. Mercifully for the crew, the missile exploded in an orange fireball just out of range. Afterwards, the crew speculated that the missiles were most likely Tigercats, the land-based version of the Seacat missile found on many Royal Navy ships. 'Tigercat is obviously as useless as

Seacat,' joked a remarkably relaxed Knight. Asked years later whether he had been scared during the attack, Knight replied, 'No. I think I lacked imagination! Anyway, it was never going to get me. I was twenty-six and immortal.'

Now back up at a safer height above the sea and judiciously further out from the coastline, Yankee Tango returned towards *Glamorgan*, perhaps not now totally confident in the presumed immortality of its pilot. There was still the known threat from Argentine Mirage jets and Canberra bombers to contend with. As they headed back, HMS *Arrow*'s Lynx called up over the radio: 'All callsigns, air raid warning red, look out for inbound intruders coming around the coast.' The Lynx's first reaction to the threat was to climb up to hide in the cloud; Yankee Tango meanwhile disappeared down low to hide amongst the waves. No sooner was the Wessex down at low level than the Lynx called up again: 'Yankee Tango, you might want to come up a bit. I can see your wake on my screen.' A grateful Knight raised the nose and climbed, but only a bit.

This particular group of three Mirage jets was in fact heading for a low-level attack on *Glamorgan*, *Arrow* and *Alacrity* engaged in naval gunfire support against the airfield at Port Stanley. From three miles away, Morton watched cannon shells strafe one of the Type-21s followed by bombs that produced huge plumes of water. Two of the bombs exploded either side of *Glamorgan*, blowing her stern clear out of the water. Amazingly, there was no serious damage.

Although the attackers escaped from this particular raid, other Mirage jets were not so lucky. Sea Harriers from 800 and 801 Squadrons both made successful interceptions with other raids before and after the attack on the ships. It was two RAF pilots flying the Navy jets who claimed the first air-to-air successes of the war by shooting down a Mirage jet using their AIM9L Sidewinder missiles. A third Mirage, damaged by a Sidewinder, was subsequently shot down by their own defences over Port Stanley. Later that afternoon, a Canberra was shot down by a Sea Harrier from 801 Squadron based on *Invincible*.

Returning to *Glamorgan* with precious little fuel remaining, Yankee Tango was forced to wait in the hover alongside while the Wessex 3 was cleared from the deck. Safely back on board, this incident prompted Knight and his crew to investigate whether in-flight refuelling was an option. The idea was to plug the fuel hose and connector into the side of the Wessex whilst in the hover alongside the flight deck. Should the flight deck ever be completely out of action, airborne refuelling would give the Wessex enough time to divert elsewhere. Although routine for Sea Kings, helicopter in-flight refuelling (HIFR) had never been done in a Wessex because the crewman would need to push in the connector at an impossible angle. The crew worked out that they could achieve HIFR using a crewman standing on the edge of the deck to connect up. It was an innovative solution but one that was never tried for real.

By the early hours of 2 May, the naval gunfire support group of ships led by *Glamorgan* withdrew from the coastline and Yankee Tango returned to *Resource* the following day.

Sunday 2 May was a momentous day. During the night a reconnaissance flight by a Sea Harrier had detected a group of surface targets that included the Argentine aircraft carrier ARA *Veinticinco de Mayo*, named after Argentina's National Day, possibly as close as 150 miles to the west of the British fleet. All ships of the British carrier group went to action stations anticipating an attack from the carrier-borne A-4 Skyhawk jets. The attack failed to materialise because a radar problem with the Argentine carrier's Tracker aircraft meant the exact location of the British fleet was not known.

The second Argentine naval task group did not fare so well. Later that day the British nuclear-powered submarine HMS *Conqueror* attacked and sank the cruiser ARA *General Belgrano* using two Mark 8 torpedoes. *Belgrano*, formerly the USS *Phoenix*, was an old US Navy light cruiser that had been sold to the Argentine navy in 1951. As the *Phoenix*, the ship had survived the attack on Pearl Harbor by the Japanese in 1941. She now became the only ship to have been sunk by a nuclear submarine, and only the second to have been sunk at all since the Second World War.

The immediate consequences were the death in the icy South Atlantic waters of 323 Argentine seaman and the permanent withdrawal of the Argentine navy, including the *Veinticinco de Mayo*. The action was considered politically controversial because the *Belgrano* was outside the 200-mile Total Exclusion Zone and heading away from the Falklands. Militarily, it was a devastating blow. At a stroke the naval threat to the British fleet was removed. While the politicians argued over the rights and wrongs, the way was now clear for the British amphibious group to set sail from Ascension a few days later.

With the Argentine navy out of the way, the main threat to the British fleet was from the air. Two days later, on Tuesday 4 May, two Argentine Super Etendard jets headed inbound from the mainland towards the British fleet at low level. The raid was detected by one of the ships as a fast-moving pop-up target. The 801 Squadron Sea Harrier on Combat Air Patrol (CAP) was immediately directed towards the target. The Sea Harrier's Blue Fox radar had already proved its worth, detecting the Argentine fleet at night a few days earlier. Its deterrence effect alone was also powerful. Several Mirage raids had been seen to turn away when faced with an encounter with the 'black death'. Those that had not turned away had not fared well. Inexplicably the Sea Harrier was ordered off-station and given another job. Whether through bad luck or bad judgment, it left a hole in the air defences. The Argentine jets continued their run unopposed and released their load of two Exocet sea-skimming missiles with deadly effect.

It was mid-morning. The Type-42 destroyer HMS *Sheffield* was out to the south-west of the fleet on 'picket duty': the awful responsibility of being second line of defence after the Sea Harriers but the first target for the enemy. There was a mild swell and good visibility. One missile flew harmlessly past the frigates *Yarmouth* and *Alacrity* and dropped into the sea. The other slammed into the side of HMS *Sheffield* with what its captain Sam Salt described as a 'short, sharp, unimpressive bang'.

As the day's search-and-rescue helicopter, Jack Lomas and Steve MacNaughton scrambled Yankee Hotel from *Resource* as soon as news of the strike came through. By the time Lomas brought the Wessex to the hover just short of *Sheffield*, other ships and aircraft had already reached the scene. It was one that was hard to digest. Lomas and MacNaughton just couldn't believe what they were seeing; they couldn't take it in.

Sheffield had begun to smoke behind her forward circular radome (radar dome) but the smoke hadn't yet started billowing. The dark entry hole made by the Exocet missile was visible on her starboard side just above the water line. Men in blue number eight uniforms and anti-flash gear – the white cotton balaclavas and gloves that protect head and hands against flash burns – were standing on the foc'sle. A body lay on the deck. The Type-21 frigate HMS *Arrow* was already alongside transferring survivors and spraying water across *Sheffield* in an attempt to cool the fire. *Arrow*'s Lynx and an anti-submarine Sea King were flying burned and bedraggled survivors across to the carrier *Hermes*. Amazingly, *Sheffield*'s Lynx survived the attack and recovered to *Hermes* later that day. The frigate *Yarmouth* was firing off mortars, spooked by the possibility of a submarine threat; there had been claimed sightings of torpedo tracks in the water. Everybody was shocked and nervous, but calm.

As the Wessex hovered over *Arrow*'s foc'sle, MacNaughton winched several walking wounded with blackened faces on board and the Wessex headed off for *Hermes*. Altogether twenty-one men died from the missile strike. Many of those burned had injuries made worse by the polyester uniforms which melted into their skin. It was a bad day for the Royal Navy.

To compound the day's tragedy, two hours after the Exocet strike on *Sheffield* news came that a Sea Harrier flown by Lieutenant Nick Taylor had been shot down during a second bombing raid on the airstrip at Goose Green. His death was a terrible blow to the Yeovilton-based aircrew who knew him.

The day after the attack, Lomas flew Yankee Hotel back to the stricken *Sheffield* several times to take firefighters on board to investigate the extent of the damage, to remove recoverable parts, and to see if the hull could be salvaged. The paint on the ship's hull had blistered more or less everywhere and the deck was still steaming. It was with a curious fascination that the crew circled the ship to look at the gaping entrance hole. It should have been macabre but it wasn't. Subsequently the burning hulk of *Sheffield* was left to drift eerily for several days. During an attempt to tow the ship to South Georgia, the sea came up and the *Sheffield* sank.

RFA *Fort Austin* and her Wessex flight arrived on the scene from Ascension. Nick Foster's first task in Yankee Delta was to collect *Sheffield* survivors from the frigate *Arrow* and take them over to *Resource*. The Wessex was too big to land on *Arrow*'s deck so he maintained a low hover. The crewman chucked a net onto the deck with instructions for the survivors to put in any spare kit before being winched on board.

Each *Sheffield* survivor had been issued with a blue number eight shirt and trousers, lifejacket, a pair of voluminous Y-fronts, white plimsolls and, of all things, a string vest. To Foster, in a strange preview of things to come, the survivors looked incongruous in their white daps. The string vests soon became carrier bags for whatever extra they managed to beg, borrow or steal. For whatever reason, the men had not been issued with decent clothing and Foster thought how demeaning it was for them. The helicopter's net remained unfilled as the dishevelled survivors pathetically clung on to all that they owned. With their glassy stares and sullen looks they appeared to have lost the fire in their bellies. 'So that's what happens when you've been sunk,' thought Foster with a surge of sympathy.

Around half of the survivors from *Sheffield* were temporarily housed in *Resource* while waiting to be repatriated via Ascension. The ship's master, Captain Seymour, wisely told the aircrew: 'Take them into the bar, give them a few drinks and get them to talk about it. It's the best thing you can do.' The four pilots did exactly that. It proved an extremely emotional time. One young medic told of how he felt he had let the ship's crew down because too many people had died. He was distraught. Two of the pilots took him back to his cabin to put him to bed, sat down and stroked his head like a child to try to get him to sleep. It was the only way to cope with such trauma.

For many and perhaps most of those in the British task force, whether in the carrier group in the South Atlantic, in the amphibious group about to depart from Ascension, or still in the UK as I was, *Sheffield* was the turning point. For the Argentines, much the same could be said about *Belgrano*. These were deeply shocking events. There was a general hardening of resolve on both sides. It was the time when we realised that this was for real. We were actually going to go into battle. The land war would be fought.

As the world looked on horrified at the escalation of conflict between two former friends over a scrap of land in the middle of nowhere, it was clear that too much blood had now been spilt to step back. Our two nations were at war.

Chapter 6

Preparing to land
7–19 May 1982

The gloves were off and there would be no pulling back. With the Argentine navy no longer a threat, the British amphibious group and its embarked troops could now set off into the South Atlantic. The problem was that most of the troop-carrying helicopters needed to support them were in the North Atlantic or back in the UK.

All remaining Wessex and Sea King aircrew were now formed into new squadrons and promptly despatched to the Falklands. At last I would be on my way. By mid-May, some forty-six Wessex, twenty-four troop-carrying Sea Kings, and four heavy-lift RAF Chinooks were making their way to the South Atlantic.

By mid-April, commando helicopter support available to the commanders planning the amphibious assault was pretty modest by any standards. The main lift capability rested with the dozen *jungle* Sea Kings from 846 Squadron, which were en route to Ascension Island on board *Hermes* and *Fearless*. A further six Wessex 5s from 845 Squadron were on board the RFAs *Resource, Fort Austin* and *Tidespring*. Already at Ascension were two more Wessex 5s, one *jungle* Sea King and one RAF search-and-rescue Sea King, making a grand total of just twenty-four troop-carrying helicopters.

On board *Fearless*, Tim Stanning and his fellow taskers were more concerned at the lack of available deck space for the forthcoming amphibious landings. Even at this early stage of planning, it was the relatively small number of ships involved in the landing that would determine the tasking rather than any shortage of helicopters. The early assumption was that most troops would disembark by landing craft while most ammunition, equipment and supplies would be load-lifted ashore in Sea King-sized loads. Once the troops were ashore, however, a great deal more helicopter lift would be needed in support of the subsequent land campaign.

Meanwhile, the last of the 845 Squadron personnel not in Northern Ireland were despatched by Lieutenant Commander Mike Booth to embark on the reprieved HMS *Intrepid* off Portland. On Tuesday 20 April, Lieutenant Mike 'Crabbers' Crabtree and Hector Heathcote flew the first of the two Wessex out to the ageing assault ship. Heathcote had come back from Aldergrove on the same flight as Mike Tidd. Like Tidd, he had also managed to conceal from Heathrow security the fact that he had a loaded 9mm Browning pistol inside his jacket.

Intrepid was an old friend to many Wessex aircrew, whether through squadron detachments over the years, or in its role as Dartmouth Training Ship for young officers. Hector Heathcote and I had joined the Navy together on the same day in October 1979. Our first experience of life at sea came a few months later on board *Intrepid*, sailing from Taormina in Sicily up to Trieste in the north-east corner of Italy, and then back around to Livorno on the west coast. On a day trip to Florence our group of twenty aspiring helicopter pilots pretended to be terribly cultured. Of course we were really only interested in drinking lots of Italian beer.

The young officer's training programme was meant to build character by giving us a taste of life at the bottom. The staff laughed at our expense as we were sent off to find the ship's billiard-room keys. (Think about it.) The ship's company enjoyed seeing the young midshipmen given shitty little jobs, such as cleaning out boxes of rotten courgettes in the ship's galley. It was the Navy's idea of a joke. But because we knew it only lasted a few weeks, we loved it. We especially loved scrubbing down the flight deck because we could gaze longingly at the ship's detachment of Wessex 5s and dream of flying them ourselves one day.

Flickering thoughts of his time on *Intrepid* two years earlier barely interrupted Heathcote's concentration as he brought the Wessex into a hover alongside the huge flight deck, as they joined the assault ship for what was called a 'work-up'. The point of these sea trials was to iron out some of the inevitable teething problems that arise when a ship tries to operate aircraft after a long break. Procedures get forgotten. Skills become rusty. A typical example might involve a ship-controlled approach where the helicopter is given instructions on how to approach the ship in poor weather conditions by using the ship's radar. Telling the pilot that he has still one quarter of a mile to run as the helicopter speeds past the flight deck is not good. Either the radar picture is not set up properly or the helicopter controller is not on the ball.

The two Wessex re-embarked for the journey to

Ascension on Monday 26 April. Yankee Charlie was flown by Crabtree and Heathcote, and Yankee Whiskey by Lieutenant Mark Evans RM and Sub-Lieutenant Sparky Harden. Evans was known to all as 'Jayfer' (Joke Flight Royal), from his time as the only Royal Marine on Nick Foster's flight, which was affectionately nicknamed 'Joke Flight' by the squadron senior pilot. Behind his disarmingly gentle and joking manner was an exceptionally capable and professional pilot. One of Sparky's claims to fame was an enduring popularity that allowed him to get away with a casual disregard for the status of his course mate, HRH Prince Andrew, now flying an anti-submarine Sea King from the carrier HMS *Invincible*. Harden coined the nickname 'H' for the Prince, treating him in exactly the same offhand manner that he treated the rest of us. We loved it. His other claim to fame was a reputation for enthusiastic low flying, a habit that led two years later to a subsequent crash, court martial and dismissal from the Navy.

Ten days and 4,000 miles later, *Intrepid* arrived at Ascension on Wednesday 5 May to join the armada of ships that formed the amphibious group. The sight of so many ships was both shocking and impressive. Later that day, Crabtree and his flight transferred from *Intrepid* to the fuel tanker RFA *Tidepool*, sister ship of *Tidespring*, for the next stage of their journey to the South Atlantic. On 7 May, the two Ascension-based Wessex, Yankee Juliett and Yankee Kilo, were flown onto *Intrepid* and then, with blades folded, winched down into the cavernous hold of the assault ship for use as reserve replacement aircraft. With the Argentine navy now out of the way, the amphibious fleet led by *Fearless* and *Intrepid* set off from Ascension on Saturday 8 May. Meanwhile, four more Wessex were flown out from Yeovilton in the back of a

Belfast to replace the Ascension aircraft that were now in the hold of *Intrepid*, and to provide a fresh set of aircraft for Mike Tidd's ill-fated flight.

By mid-April all of the *junglie* Sea Kings had left the UK. But there were plenty more Wessex. For a while there was talk of expanding 845 Squadron into one giant monster squadron, incorporating the training squadron and anyone else available. Instead, on Monday 19 April, the training squadron instructors and their aircraft were recommissioned with front-line status at Yeovilton.

The first new squadron, 848, was formed mostly from the aircraft and crews of the Wessex training squadron from which I had emerged just a couple of months earlier. It was a proud moment for commanding officer Lieutenant Commander David Baston to reclaim the name of the original *junglies* with the motto '*Accipe Hoc*' – 'Take that!'

Most of the pilots and aircrew were either highly skilled instructors or pilots taken from the course following my own – that is, still technically in training – to make up numbers. The first two Wessex of the newly formed squadron, led by Lieutenant Commander Chris Blight, had already been despatched to the supply ship RFA *Regent* which was embarking in Plymouth Sound the same day. Another two were to be despatched to the fuel tanker RFA *Olna*. But most of the aircraft and crews were to sail south on the giant roll-on roll-off container ship the SS *Atlantic Conveyor*, one of six similar ships owned by Cunard, two of which, *Conveyor* and *Atlantic Causeway*, had been requisitioned by the MOD.

David Baston and several of the aircrew took an aircraft down to Plymouth dockyard to have a look at their new ship. Looming over them at the dockside, *Atlantic Conveyor* was simply massive. A giant bridge superstructure towered over a vast forward deck that stretched out several football-field lengths in front. Behind the high bridge was a smaller deck, still comfortably big enough to take at least one helicopter. The forward decking appeared to be awash with men brandishing angle grinders. Containers were being lifted into place by a giant crane and were being stacked one on top of each other to line the sides of the deck as protection from the South Atlantic weather. Men were moving around levelling the new deck structure in preparation for the Harriers and helicopters that were to operate from it. Trailing behind them was a man carrying the biggest paint roller any of them had ever seen. The colour of the paint was the ubiquitous 'pussers' grey.

There were several false starts before the squadron was able to embark for the first time. Two of the Wessex became unserviceable while waiting at the Royal Marine base in Plymouth and needed replacement from Yeovilton. Last-minute modifications to the ship meant more delays. On Sunday 25 April, the six Wessex helicopters finally embarked on *Atlantic Conveyor*, underway in Plymouth Sound. Lieutenant Pete Manley conducted a first-of-class load-lifting trial.

The safe arrival of *Atlantic Conveyor* in the Falklands was crucial. In the giant holds underneath the flight deck was a huge volume of stores. This included an entire tent city for 10,000 people, sufficient to house both 3 Brigade, already en route on *Canberra* and *Norland*, and 5 Brigade due to head off shortly on the *Queen Elizabeth II*. There was also a portable runway, JCB diggers to build it, and all the ancillary equipment needed to operate Harriers ashore, including giant plastic fuel pillows. There was even a squadron of black raiding craft, presumably belonging to special forces. *Conveyor*'s holds were so vast that even this huge volume of kit and equipment failed to fill them.

The container ship arrived at Ascension on Wednesday 5 May. As well as the six Wessex, *Conveyor* also carried other valuable aircraft including replacement Chinook and Lynx helicopters. They were joined at Ascension by six RAF Harriers and eight Royal Navy Sea Harriers, each landing vertically on the huge forward flight-deck area of the ship. Helicopters and jets were then parked in rows between the walls of containers and wrapped in plastic for further protection. In the rush to get aircrew south, a further flight of four Wessex pilots and three crewmen also embarked on the troop carrier MV *Norland* at Ascension, with the intent of being allocated aircraft later.

Behind *Conveyor*'s bridge was the smaller deck jutting out to the stern of the ship. A ramp, used for access to the huge spaces underneath, folded up behind the deck. During a brief stop at Ascension Island, Pete Manley had paid an unofficial visit to the local golf club to acquire important stores. In calm weather, Manley figured that the ramp would be the obvious place for a South Atlantic cocktail party on a balmy evening. With a plentiful supply of hundreds of beer barrels on board *Conveyor*, obtained by clambering over the reserve supply of cluster bombs, all that was needed was a handle, some gas and a suitable umbrella. The golf club generously obliged with the beer equipment but no umbrella.

With all of the Wessex and Sea Kings either despatched to the Falklands or on detachment to Northern Ireland, 845 Squadron senior pilot Mike Booth was now virtually the only *junglie* left at Yeovilton. To meet the demand for more troop-carrying helicopters, he was asked to form a new squadron out of the detachment in Northern Ireland plus various extra aircraft and aircrew engaged with search-and-rescue duties, plus the odd test pilot and those 'flying desks'. It was a huge relief to all of us stuck out in Northern Ireland. We were increasingly worried that we had been forgotten.

848 Squadron show how to squeeze several Wessex onto the stern deck of *Atlantic Conveyor*. The pilot of this Wessex will have felt very uneasy watching his blades whirling so close to the other helicopters. This is where you really have to trust the white lines.

This second new squadron, 847, was assigned to embark in *Atlantic Causeway*, twin of *Atlantic Conveyor*, and in RFA *Engadine*, a flat-bottomed training and support ship. Because of problems trying to find sleeping space for everybody, the new squadron had to be split disproportionately. It was not an ideal solution. Four of the aircraft and fifteen pilots embarked on *Engadine*. The remaining twenty aircraft embarked on *Atlantic Causeway* with just four pilots.

On Sunday 9 May, Major Adrian Short and I flew X-Ray Mike down to Plymouth and landed on *Engadine* which lay alongside the dock. I was assigned a cabin with one of the *Engadine* junior officers and my fellow Sub-Lieutenant Dave Kelly. As we dumped our kit bags on our bunks, Kelly peered out through the scuttle. 'Oh look,' he said smiling, 'our cabin is about nine feet above the waterline. What flies at nine feet, Harry?' He then smiled again as he informed me that *Engadine*'s sister ship had reportedly rolled over and sunk in the Irish Sea. Not surprisingly, *Engadine* and its flat bottom had never been south of the equator.

Having contemplated this happy news, the fear of missing out once again became our number one concern when we learned that *Engadine*'s maximum speed was twelve knots. It would take forever to reach the Falklands. We quickly calculated that the earliest we could get there would be by Saturday 5 June, twenty-six days hence. It could all be over by then. We could swim faster.

Three days after *Engadine* sailed, the four pilots of 847 'B' flight led by Lieutenant Commander Peter Hails shuttled their twenty aircraft the short journey across from where they had been dropped off in Plymouth by 'A' flight onto *Atlantic Causeway*. *Causeway* also embarked 825 Squadron, whose Sea Kings had their anti-submarine pinging kit stripped out in order to convert them to troop carriers. The very much faster *Causeway* set off on Friday 14 May and quickly overtook the plodding *Engadine*. There were further frustrations as we were forced to divert to Gibraltar overnight for engine repairs.

Now that the task force's additional aircraft had set off, the *QE2* sailed from Southampton on 12 May with the task force's additional soldiers of 5 Brigade, comprising Scots Guards, Welsh Guards and Gurkhas.

For all squadrons and flights heading south, the long journey was an opportunity to practise deck landings, load-lifting, winching, cabin gunning, formation flying, instrument approaches, and navigation over the sea.

847 was the newly formed Wessex squadron with which I went to war. This badge was sewn onto the sleeve of my flying suit. The squadron motto *Ex alto concutimus* translates roughly as 'We zap them from on high'!

Our new senior pilot, Lieutenant Commander Rob Flexman, was pleased to be going; he had only just returned from an exchange tour with the French navy flying Super Frelon helicopters. However, with such a top-heavy squadron, he was concerned that there might be friction with some of his more experienced colleagues who might feel they should have been appointed number two in his place. He also wondered how he would perform individually in action. His first task back in the Wessex saddle was to get up to speed with deck landings.

Some of my colleagues found it hard to conceal their

glee after watching the senior pilot bouncing wildly across the flight deck in ground resonance a couple of times. For me, it simply diluted the embarrassment when, on my own first sortie at sea, six out of eight attempts at deck landing resulted in the same ground resonance and the need to take off again in a hurry. Coached and generously encouraged by my experienced senior colleagues, Lieutenant Commanders Neil Anstis, Mike Spencer and Mike Booth, I learnt how to do it properly. On most days and a handful of nights, I got airborne for short sessions of deck-landing practice. These flights felt fantastic. My confidence grew as my landings on the moving flight deck got better and better. I began to feel more like a Royal Navy pilot. Over the next two years as a front-line Wessex pilot, I would complete over 400 deck landings at sea, both at day and night.

The highlight of my trip south was the 847 Squadron flying competition. The challenge was to spill the least amount of water whilst dangling a bucket from the winch, navigate the most accurate triangle pattern to end up exactly overhead the ship, and land most precisely on the required spot on the flight deck. The squadron was divided into teams of two, one pilot, one aircrewman. Petty Officer Aircrewman Chris Eke and I were pitched against the formidably experienced opposition. We won. I accepted congratulations with all the modesty and reserve that I didn't feel. I couldn't have been more thrilled.

Our progress south remained painfully slow. Different kinds of training helped to fill the long hours. I worked on my physical fitness. All of us did. I wanted to go into battle at the peak of health in case I got shot down. We did sit-ups and push-ups and squat thrusts and star jumps and ran laps round the ship until we felt physically sick. Wearing incredibly short shorts – very much the fashion of the 1980s

– we played a relentless amount of deck hockey. We did military training, firing machine guns, rifles, pistols and light rockets – usually at the few seagulls trailing behind the ship. The lowlight of my trip south was my embarrassing failure to wake up one morning in time for a training session on the handheld 30mm Light Anti-tank Weapon. My well-deserved punishment was to be handed the manual and told I was to brief all of the pilots after lunch on the use of the LAW weapon. I didn't miss any training after that.

Skimpy shorts were very much the fashion in the 1980s. When we weren't flying, my colleagues on 847 Squadron and I played endless games of deck hockey on the flight deck of RFA *Engadine*.

The air and sea temperature rose noticeably as we approached the equator. It was a delight and a distraction to lean over the guard rail and watch the flying fish darting out from the side of the ship. Every now and then we would spot a shark or giant stingray from the air. Passing through the equator inevitably meant paying our traditional dues to King Neptune for first-timers like me. This involved a thoroughly unpleasant and humiliating 'crossing the line' ceremony on the flight deck. Our duty was to bow down before Neptune, the bearded Neil Anstis wearing blue paint, long dangly hair and a thoroughly unattractive dress-like garment. We were then made to drink a foul brown concoction that included alcohol, chocolate and pepper, and were then sprayed with a disgusting fluid of origin unknown.

Heavy drinking on this day, and throughout the entire journey south, was almost inevitable. The party stopped only when Mike Booth decided to close the bar a few days before we reached the Total Exclusion Zone (TEZ) around the Falklands.

During the second week of May, Sea Harrier operations in the TEZ were constrained by persistent poor visibility, low cloud, rain and fog. In the early hours of Thursday 6 May, two Sea Harriers on night patrol from *Invincible* were vectored to investigate a fast-moving low-level contact. Having descended toward sea level, nothing was heard or seen of them again. It was presumed that they had collided. Following the death of Nick Taylor and the Exocet attack on *Sheffield*, the loss of two more Sea Harrier pilots, John Eyton-Jones and Al Curtis, was a terrible blow.

On 9 May, Sea Harriers crippled an Argentine fishing trawler, the *Narwhal*, suspected of intelligence gathering. Cannon fire from both jets ripped great holes in the trawler above and below the waterline. Two bombs were dropped but failed to arm. Had they done so, the trawler would have blown apart. Two *junglie* Sea Kings were launched from *Hermes* along with a radar-fitted anti-submarine Sea King as guide. They stopped by *Invincible* to pick up a boarding party of SBS troops along the way.

After a 150-mile transit directly towards the Falklands, Bill Pollock and his co-pilot Lieutenant Dick Hutchings RM in the lead Sea King arrived to a scene of desolation. The trawler was stopped in the water; there was nobody on deck. The ship looked lifeless. After a quick circuit, Pollock hovered over the apparently empty craft, despatching their SBS troops onto the deck by rope. It soon became clear that there would be no resistance from the ship's crew. They were hiding below decks, clearly in fear for their lives. One crew member had been killed.

With the ship slowly sinking, the Sea Kings began to winch the surviving crew, body bag and SBS troops on board. The first two Sea Kings set off straight away while Pollock, Hutchings and aircrewman Doc Love were still winching their mix of British and Argentine passengers on board. After such a long time getting there and then hanging around, fuel in Pollock's Sea King was becoming very tight indeed. Worse, an anxious radio discussion with *Invincible* revealed that the carrier was fifty miles further away than expected. The aircraft was simply not going to make it back. In all there were twenty people on board. One way or another, they were going to need rescuing.

The Type-42 destroyer, HMS *Glasgow*, sister ship of the *Sheffield*, was instructed to head at high speed towards the Sea King. Pollock ran through his calculations again, realising that it was still unlikely to be enough. They would be swimming. There was one radical solution that might help. Pollock remembered an incident from a few years back when he was flying a Wessex. He had been caught out a long way from his ship with a diminishing supply of fuel. The aircraft manual claimed that, in an emergency, shutting down one engine would use up less fuel. The working engine would compensate by taking up the strain, but it wouldn't be double. There was no real problem flying on one engine. But if you have two engines, you should use them. This was very definitely an emergency. It had worked in the Wessex. Now it was time to see if it would work in the Sea King.

Holding their collective breath, Pollock and Hutchings went through the procedure for shutting down an engine in flight. Miles from anywhere and with so many lives at stake, it was a nerve-racking experience. The crew watched in awe as the working engine took up the slack. Overall fuel consumption dropped by a quarter, exactly as promised. It just might give them the extra miles they needed.

As the needles on the fuel gauges edged their way remorselessly towards zero, HMS *Glasgow* came into sight, steaming straight at them. Pollock turned the helicopter onto final approach while the other engine was restarted to give them the extra power they needed for landing. The flight deck of a Type-42 destroyer is designed for the much smaller Lynx. Sea Kings are not cleared for landing for several reasons: there's not enough room on the deck; there's no margin for error to prevent the helicopter blades from smashing into the ship's hangar; and the deck is not stressed for the extra weight of a Sea King. But far out in the South Atlantic with just seconds of fuel remaining, the options were to attempt an unorthodox landing on *Glasgow* or ditch in the sea and hope to survive.

The ship was pitching around in the swell. With guidance from the flight-deck crew, Pollock lowered the Sea King onto the deck, holding power on in a 'wheels-light hover' so as not to put its full weight on the deck. From the cockpit it looked awfully tight. And it was. The wheels just held on the outer edges. The blades were just feet from the hangar.

The flight-deck crew now rushed in with the fuel hose and plugged into the side of the Sea King. Pollock lifted back off the deck into a hover to continue the refuel. With huge relief, the two pilots watched the fuel needle creep slowly upwards. The passengers never even knew how close it had been.

On board *Fearless* there had been considerable debate as to whether to make an amphibious assault on East Falkland or establish a beachhead and airfield on West Falkland. San Carlos was chosen mainly because the surrounding hills provided protection for the landing ships against air attack. However, several threats and obstacles needed to be overcome before the landings could take place. The Sea Harrier attacks on Goose Green had the unintended consequence that the surviving Argentine Pucara aircraft had been moved across to the grass airstrip at Pebble Island on the north side of West Falkland. Just minutes flying time from San Carlos, these aircraft from Pebble Island had the capacity to seriously disrupt a successful landing.

On the night of Tuesday 11 May, Nigel North and his crew took off from *Hermes* in a solo Sea King. It was pitch black and overcast. In the cabin of the aircraft was an eight-man SAS observation team and their canoes. Using instruments and night vision goggles, the Sea King flew low over the sea towards Pebble Island on West Falkland. Without modern satellites or beacons, the on-board equipment inevitably drifted off a little during flight. This time the pilots used the promontory of Cape Dolphin on East Falkland as their reference point to update their navigation equipment. The Sea King flew onward across Falkland Sound dropping to wave-top height in the darkness.

In order to avoid alerting the Argentine troops at Pebble Island with the sound of the helicopter, the SAS team were to be dropped off ten miles away. The team had brought two canoes with them in order to cross a narrow strait onto the island itself. But once on the ground, it became obvious that the size of the crashing waves at the planned crossing point would make launching the canoes impossible. The Sea King lifted them quickly on to their alternate drop-off point before covertly flying back to *Hermes* in the blackness. Bad weather caused further delays and it was only forty-eight hours later that the SAS managed to report back to *Hermes* the presence of eleven enemy aircraft on Pebble Island.

On board *Hermes*, it was a nervous time for the Sea King crews waiting for their first active encounter with the enemy. All of the previous night-time missions onto the Falkland Islands had been for reconnaissance. The next mission would be to fly into battle.

On Friday 14 May, after a false start the previous night, *Hermes* and her two escorts, *Broadsword* and *Glamorgan*, closed to just forty miles from Pebble Island in order to give the heavily loaded Sea Kings as much flying time as possible in the strong winds and heavy seas. The huge amount of day-flying done at Ascension and night-flying on the islands ought to have taken its toll on the Sea Kings. Frankly it was amazing that all four night-flying aircraft were able to fly at all.

To save space on the flight deck of *Hermes*, already crammed with Sea Harriers, the Sea Kings remained beneath in the hangar with their rotor blades folded back. Spreading the blades back out again would have to be done carefully to avoid damaging them. High winds lashing the carrier's flight deck now made this impossible. Yet the mission had to go ahead somehow. Three of the four Sea Kings started their engines and spread their blades unconventionally inside the hangar before being taken up on the flight-deck lift one by one.

Timings for the SAS attack on Pebble Island were non-negotiable. *Hermes* and its priceless load of Sea Harriers needed time to withdraw well away to the east of the islands before dawn. Getting caught in daylight close to the islands by the Argentine air force was simply not an option. The agonising forty-minute delay before the Sea Kings could finally launch now put huge pressure on the SAS to get in and out as quickly as possible. The new timings would give them just ten minutes on the airstrip.

Three of the four aircraft, again led by Nigel North, launched into the darkness and out towards Pebble Island. Strong headwinds made progress slow. But the actual insertion went well. Up until then, the Sea Kings had done plenty of night-flying in formation using night vision goggles. This was the first time the aircrews had done a night landing in formation.

They were just a few miles short of the Pebble Island airstrip. The assault group of fifty-eight SAS troops were out of the three helicopters within a minute. The only hitch was that they were supposed to bring back the original recce party's canoes, which were nowhere in sight. As the other two helicopters lifted off behind him, North stayed on a little longer for a brief but fruitless search. For all of the helicopters, the return journey to *Hermes* was over quickly, sped up by the wind now coming from behind them.

By the time the SAS had covered the three-mile march to the airstrip, through the darkness, they were already running late. They elected to open fire from the edge of the grassy airstrip to disable the enemy aircraft. Seeing no response from Argentine troops, the SAS attackers then ran onto the strip and, climbing directly up onto each aircraft, used grenades and explosive charges to sabotage them.

Meanwhile the original three Sea Kings launched once again from *Hermes* into a strong headwind. First to launch were Pete Rainey and Dick Hutchings. They had to complete a complicated resupply mission of food and equipment to SAS troops hidden in the hills to the west of Mount Kent on East Falkland. Only then could they turn and head north-west towards Pebble Island.

Two hours later, the next two aircraft launched with Nigel North and Wiggy Bennett in the lead and Bob Horton and Paul Humphreys behind them. A fourth aircraft followed another ten minutes later. The extra aircraft was needed to take out the original eight-man observation team dropped three days earlier.

In a remarkable piece of well-timed coordination in the darkness, Rainey's Sea King joined up with North's formation at Cape Dolphin on their final low-level run-in to the pick-up point. It was a team effort, the result of superb navigation by North's co-pilot Wiggy Bennett and the usual rigorous preparation from Bill Pollock. Tonight was another rare chance for Pollock to get airborne. With the night vision goggles in short supply, he and his co-pilot John 'Stumpy' Middleton had just one set between them in the fourth back-up Sea King, ten minutes behind the main formation. While Pollock flew the aircraft on instruments as if for a normal night flight, Middleton wore the goggles and gave him instructions.

As the formation of three Sea Kings approached the pick-up point, all the crews could see through the green light were the flares of explosions at the airstrip beyond the landing point. They had no idea how many men would return from the attack.

The SAS team were already arriving back at the pick-up point as the first Sea Kings landed. Only two men had been injured, the result of a land mine set off by the

Argentines. The first two Sea Kings filled with men and lifted away into the night. North found himself with five troops more than he expected, forcing him to ditch fuel directly onto the ground to reduce weight. He then lifted the heavy aircraft and flew across to the original drop-off point to locate the missing canoes and backpacks for the fourth Sea King. Pollock and Middleton made their approach to the spot where North was now flashing his navigation lights.

The entire demolition and reconnaissance teams were extracted successfully and returned to *Hermes*. The raid had led to the destruction or immobilisation of all bar one of the Argentine Pucara, Mentor and Skyvan aircraft. The mission was a resounding success without the loss of a single man.

Death, where is thy sting? Our biggest fear was bumping into one of these Argentine Pucara aircraft in mid-air. At least we didn't have to worry about these five, crippled by the SAS in their daring night raid on the airstrip at Pebble Island. A sixth Pucara was totally destroyed.

* * *

The night-flying crews had only just returned from their successful Pebble Island adventure when they were ushered in to a meeting with senior pilot, Bill Pollock. He told them that the task force commanders in London had approved an even more audacious plan.

Encouraged by the SAS raid against the local threat, they now hoped to remove the long-range air threat with a raid on the mainland air bases in Argentina. Of particular interest were the Exocet-fitted Super Etendards that had launched from Rio Grande air base, responsible for the sinking of HMS *Sheffield*, and the Mirage jets based at Rio Gallegos. The plan was to insert a small group of SAS soldiers onto the mainland. The only problem, Pollock explained, was that this would be a one-way mission. The Sea King would not be able to carry enough fuel to get there and back. It would also mean missing out on the eventual amphibious landing on the Falklands. Getting an SAS team covertly into Argentina was apparently a more important mission than the loss of a valuable Sea King and crew to the landing forces. Bill Pollock asked for volunteers to come forward by the following evening.

Two days later, Lieutenant Nick Foster watched as a Hercules from Ascension flew past the supply ship *Fort Austin* and despatched a series of parachutes from its cargo door at the rear. Soon afterwards, he was hovering his Wessex over the sea, winching the special forces soldiers and their equipment up into the aircraft and depositing them dripping wet onto the flight deck. They were extremely unimpressed to find one of their pallets had sprung a leak. With the Wessex cleared away into the ship's hangar, Lieutenant Bob Horton landed a Sea King on board to collect them. Nick Foster ran in and connected up his helmet to the intercom. 'So these are your *Latino* boys?' he asked mischievously.

'I don't know what you're talking about,' replied Horton straight-faced.

The volunteer crew for the one-way mission was led by Dick Hutchings, the only Royal Marine pilot amongst the night-flying crews. As the squadron combat survival instructor he was the obvious candidate. He had also completed the SAS-run course at Hereford. Alongside him were co-pilot Wiggy Bennett, one of the best navigators on the squadron, and the highly competent Leading Aircrewman Pete Imrie. The crew were to be accompanied by a nine-man assault team of eight SAS soldiers and one SBS Royal Marine.

Soon after midnight on 18 May, Sea King Victor Charlie launched from *Invincible*, now positioned 300 miles from the Argentine coast. The helicopter had been stripped of all surplus weight and equipment in order to carry the biggest possible load of passengers and fuel. With so many long-range night-flying missions into the Falklands already under their belt, the two pilots were confident that their navigational equipment and skills would get them to the right place even after such a long transit.

As soon as Victor Charlie had lifted from the deck, *Invincible* turned to head back east. The heavily laden Sea King flew westwards at low level in the darkness, slowed by the headwind. The crew were using two of the seven pairs of valuable night vision goggles. Their progress was delayed further by the need for a sudden detour north around an unexpected gas exploration field. Headwind and detour ate up valuable fuel. But worse was to come. Visibility was already reducing as the Sea King hit landfall and the aircraft turned south for the transit towards Rio Grande. The weather deteriorated with every mile. Dick Hutchings was now forced to fly lower and slower until the Sea King was almost hover-taxiing just above the beach in ever-thickening fog. The one positive was that Wiggy Bennett had updated the navigation system as they passed their originally intended landfall point.

With the fog now reducing visibility to dangerously low levels, Hutchings had no choice but to land the Sea King seven miles short of his planned drop-off point. But the SAS troop commander was uncomfortable about their location, even as the first of his troops started to unload from the aircraft. The pilots were unable to convince him that the exact grid reference they had given from their recently updated navigation system was accurate. The troop commander decided to abort the mission and ordered his men back on board.

The only option now was to get out of the area fast. They were just twenty miles from the airbase at Rio Grande. Flying west towards Chile was the only option. Unable to fly below the fog, the aircraft climbed to clear the mountain range ahead of them. A buzz every few seconds in their helmets showed that their movement had been picked up by Argentine radar. Within minutes they had crossed the border into Chile, descending to drop off the special forces team at a remote site on the other side of the mountain range. All that remained was for the Sea King to make for an uninhabited stretch of coastline near Punta Arenas.

The crew's attempt to put down nearly ended in disaster. Hutchings was blinded by the flashing low-fuel warning lights in the cockpit which saturated his night vision goggles. Eventually he grounded the Sea King on the beach and set fire to the aircraft with fuel and flares. The crew smashed the valuable goggles to pieces and buried them in the sand.

After seven days of avoiding capture and sleeping rough, Hutchings, Bennett and Imrie wandered into the town of Punta Arenas where they were picked up by the local police. Two days later, they were repatriated to the UK.

The night insertions and extractions to the Falklands continued with replacement pilots Sub-Lieutenant Trevor Jackson, Martin Eales and Lieutenant Peter Spens-Black joining the night-flying specialists. The loss of two sets of night vision goggles in Chile meant the night flyers had to share five sets. A second batch of fifteen goggles was eventually parachuted into the sea by long-range Hercules from Ascension Island.

Jackson teamed up with Flight Lieutenant Bob Grundy. For their first sortie together, however, Jackson's goggles failed to switch on. He was forced to endure the entire mission in complete darkness apart from what he could see under the suppressed lighting of the instrument panel. For over three hours it was the only indication he had that the Sea King was flying at thirty feet above the ground at 100 knots. It was terrifying: the worst flight of his life.

For the second sortie, the newly tested goggles duly lit up: 'That's fantastic. I can actually see where I'm going.'

What he didn't say was that the quality still seemed poor. After the flight, he asked Grundy: 'How do you fly with these things? It seems so blurred.'

'You *can* adjust the focus!'

Trevor Jackson's third and subsequent sorties were perfect.

As the giant container ship *Atlantic Conveyor* ploughed its way through the South Atlantic waters, the Wessex aircrew high up on the ship's superstructure were treated to a noisy spectacle. Throughout Tuesday 18 May and the following day, the eight spare Royal Navy Sea Harriers and six RAF ground-attack Harriers lifted away from the huge forward deck one by one.

A Sea Harrier launch is a quite extraordinary sight. It doesn't seem right that a fighter jet should be able to defy gravity with such apparent ease. And yet it does, somehow rising vertically up into the air, raising its nose slightly, retracting its undercarriage, and accelerating upwards and away into the distance. Just seconds later, the pilot has taken the jet around in a tight circuit and is now blitzing past at low level at 600 knots – almost 700 miles per hour.

The Harrier sound is distinct and unforgettable. The high-pitch whistle of the powerful Pegasus engine warns you to put your hands over your ears or lose your hearing. As the pilot pushes the throttle to full power, the pitch of the whistle starts to increase, replaced almost immediately by an ear-splitting roar. With the exhaust nozzles pointing downwards, all of the engine thrust will be used to lift the aircraft off the ground. The enormous noise betrays the vast amount of power and energy needed to lift thir- teen tons of fully armed strike fighter off the ground. Once clear, the pilot slowly rotates the exhaust nozzles until they point backwards like a conventional jet.

The biggest advantage of getting all the jets onto the two aircraft carriers is the ski jump. A vertical take-off in a Sea Harrier is undoubtedly impressive. But it also needs a lot of power and uses up a hell of a lot of fuel very quickly. The Sea Harriers could accelerate down the deck of the aircraft carrier gaining airspeed. The ski jump would then bounce them into the air. This simple but clever invention allowed the jets to get off the deck more effi- ciently and thus carry a heavier load of fuel and weapons.

The decks on the carriers were already crowded before the new Sea Harriers and RAF Harriers arrived. Making space meant a further complicated shuffling of helicopters beforehand. Sea King and Lynx helicopters were told to move to the supply ship *Fort Austin*. This then meant moving some of the Wessex helicopters elsewhere. Nick Foster and Sub-Lieutenant Ian Brown, one of my fellow trainees, made the mistake of landing on *Hermes* during an air raid and were told to 'shut down'. Now the lowest priority aircraft on the ship, the Wessex was packed away in the hangar. Humble pleas for release fell on deaf ears. After three days of waiting patiently with only their increasingly foul-smelling goon suits for company, Foster and Brown were eventually allowed to transfer to *Atlantic Conveyor* and join the other Wessex.

Just days to go before the San Carlos landings, three more vital events had to take place before the operation could get underway. Falkland Sound needed to be checked for mines. On the morning of Wednesday 19 May, HMS *Alacrity* was given the job of expendable guinea pig, bravely sailing between West and East Falklands. An Argentine observation point overlooking Falkland Sound and the entrance to San Carlos also had to be neutralised, while an SBS patrol had also warned of an Argentine commando base recently set up at Port San Carlos. These infantry units needed to be dealt with before the arrival of the British amphibious group. Finally the concentration of 3 Brigade troops on *Canberra* needed to be dispersed. In calm seas out in the South Atlantic, 40 Commando Royal Marines transferred by ropes and landing craft across to the already crowded *Fearless*. Three Para did the same to the similarly crowded *Intrepid*, while 2 Para remained on board *Canberra*.

In preparation for the landings, the eleven Sea Kings repositioned themselves so that the four night-flyers were

On my way to the Falklands as a newly qualified Wessex pilot. Twenty-one-year-old 'Acting' Sub Lieutenant Harry Benson RN of the newly formed 847 Naval Air Squadron.

Half of my squadron sailed to the Falklands on the flat bottomed helicopter support ship
RFA *Engadine*. The sea wasn't always as calm as this, just south of Ascension Island. At a
painfully slow twelve knots, it took us four weeks to get from Plymouth to San Carlos.
We could have swum faster.

Bill Pollock's 'night flyers' were one of the keys to the British success in the Falklands. A last
minute acquisition of seven sets of night vision goggles allowed four specially-adapted Sea Kings of
846 Squadron to fly SAS and SBS patrols in and out of the islands at night completely undetected.

Until early May, few of us thought the Falklands war would actually take place. What changed was the sinking of two ships. For the Argentines, it was the torpedoing of the *Belgrano*. For the British, it was the Exocet strike on HMS *Sheffield*, seen here with HMS *Arrow* bravely alongside.

(*Above*) My colleagues in Yankee Charlie were the only Wessex crew to take
part in the D-Day landings. Their first task was to collect a paratrooper who
had damaged his back. But within hours, they had attended to two shot-down
helicopters, watched most of the air attacks by the Argentine air force, been
strafed by a Mirage and finished their day with a dramatic rescue of two sailors
from the icy sea next to the burning HMS *Ardent*.

(*Right*) On the day of the San Carlos landings, Simon Thornewill
and his seven 'day' Sea Kings of 846 Squadron disembarked over 900,000 pounds
of stores and equipment and over 500 men. These two Sea Kings are operating
from the rear of the two specially built flight decks on the liner SS *Canberra*.

(*Main picture*) Weather was always going to be a crucial factor in the D-Day landings at San Carlos. The morning started really well with overcast skies. But the clouds quickly burnt off, giving the Argentine jets a clear run at the British ships. Amazingly, throughout the war, not one British ship was successfully attacked within San Carlos water.

Even with the arrival of *Atlantic Causeway* and thirty more helicopters, helicopter lift was in short supply. Here a newly arrived Sea King of 825 Squadron lifts an underslung load while the troops of 5 Brigade have to walk.

The two amphibious assault ships HMS *Fearless* and *Intrepid* were the focus of both the San Carlos landings by 3 Brigade and the move forward to Fitzroy by 5 Brigade. This shows the stern being flooded to allow landing craft in and out. A Sea King of 825 Squadron is refuelling on the rear of the two landing spots.

now on *Intrepid* and seven day-flyers were spread amongst *Fearless*, *Canberra* and *Norland*.

It was at dusk, during a final transfer of troops from *Hermes* to *Intrepid* that Lieutenant Bob Horton's twelfth Sea King crashed into the sea, rolled over and sank. The official explanation was that the aircraft had suffered a catastrophic system failure after hitting an albatross. The two pilots escaped. Most of the passengers weren't so lucky. The appalling loss of life was amongst the worst of the war: twenty young men died in the cabin of the aircraft, including eighteen SAS soldiers, the only RAF fatality of the war and the 846 aircrewman, Corporal Doc Love.

The two Wessex crashes on Fortuna Glacier had preceded what was ultimately a successful land campaign on South Georgia. The question was whether this considerably more disastrous Sea King accident would precede a similarly successful land campaign on the Falkland Islands.

Chapter 7

D-Day
20–21 May 1982

Incredibly, the Argentine defenders still hadn't identified where the British landings would take place. Diversions by the SAS and harassment by naval gunfire had caused them to concentrate resources around the capital Port Stanley and the settlements of Goose Green and Darwin.

D-Day was set for landings at San Carlos on Friday 21 May. Three Commando Brigade Royal Marines and Paras had transferred to the big assault ships in preparation for the landings and 4,000 men now needed to be offloaded by the smaller landing craft. The Sea King helicopters of 846 Squadron would take much of the soldiers' equipment. It would be a classic amphibious assault.

The success of the landings would be highly dependent on the weather. The ideal situation was low cloud to prevent the Argentine air force jets launched from the mainland from attacking the landing force. What the landing force got was a glorious day with clear blue skies.

*   *   *

By the evening of Wednesday 19 May, signals intelligence and an SBS patrol on the ground were reporting the presence of around forty Argentine commandos in the settlement of Port San Carlos and a further twenty commandos manning an observation post on nearby Fanning Head. Two other land-based units had threatened the intended amphibious assault at San Carlos. The airfield at Pebble Island across Falkland Sound to the west had now been effectively disabled by the SAS raid a few days earlier. Only the larger group of Argentine forces at Goose Green and Darwin to the south still remained. At dusk on Thursday 20 May, the four night-flying Sea Kings flew in a detachment from D Squadron SAS, led by mission commander Cedric Delves. They were to prevent the Argentine forces from heading north into the landing area at San Carlos.

It was also imperative that the local Argentine forces at Port San Carlos and Fanning Head were immobilised before they had a chance to call on these southern units for reinforcements. HMS *Antrim*, now returned from its success in South Georgia, was given the job of neutralising this threat. The force comprised *Antrim*'s own radar-equipped Wessex helicopter to act once again as pathfinder, an embarked *junglie* Wessex that would insert 3 Special Boat Service Royal Marines onto Fanning Head, and naval gunfire support from *Antrim*'s powerful 4.5-inch gun.

Mike Crabtree, Hector Heathcote and Corporal Kev Gleeson RM had spent much of the day in Wessex Yankee Charlie, transferring troops between *Tidepool* and *Antrim*. They had then spent a chunk of a very dark night transferring stores from ship to ship. Lifting loads high above *Antrim*'s deck, with the ship completely blacked out, required exceptional skill from Crabtree. Flying without any lighting involved relying almost entirely on peripheral vision – in the absence of an effective supply of carrots or, best of all, the night vision goggles that had proved so vital to their Sea King colleagues. A very relieved Crabtree completed the transfer and shut down, his Wessex squeezed onto *Antrim*'s deck behind the other Wessex.

The following day, Lieutenant Colonel Mike Rose, commanding officer of 22 SAS regiment, gave a briefing to the two Wessex crews on his plan to secure Fanning Head. On completion Rose diffused some of the tension in the air by buying all of the aircrew half a pint of beer each from *Antrim*'s wardroom bar; perhaps Dutch courage; perhaps final farewell. The aircrew thought it churlish to refuse such an offer and chose to disregard the normal rule about not drinking before flying. This was not going to be a normal flight.

It was already dark as the two pilots clambered up the outside of their Wessex and into the cockpit. Armed with a thermal-image camera fitted in the doorway of the rear cabin, the plan was for the Wessex to recce the Fanning Head area, locate the Argentine observation post, return to *Antrim* and begin the insertion of SBS troops. As soon as Yankee Charlie had lifted off from the deck, *Antrim*'s own Wessex was ranged on the now vacant landing spot and started up.

Once airborne, Chris Parry in the back of the *Antrim* Wessex would then use his radar to direct the troop-carrying Wessex towards the coast. The problem for Parry was that, just as he found in South Georgia, his radar was designed more for detecting submarines than for detecting land. Yankee Charlie was soon lost in the ground clutter on his radar screen. Crabtree and Heathcote quickly realised that the unexpectedly dark and solid area of sky looming in front of them was in fact the headland of Fanning Head. Unable to rely on radar control, the Yankee

Charlie crew discretely chose to ignore the directions from Parry. They would have to fly visually. While Mike Crabtree flew, Hector Heathcote squinted over his map using a blacked-up right-angle torch with only tiny pinholes of light to keep light levels low. Outside, the only visual cue was the barely noticeable contrast between the extremely dark, which was land, the slightly less dark, which was sea, and the least dark but still very dark, which was sky. It was a mission that would never have even been attempted in peacetime.

Approaching Fanning Head from the north, Crabtree's Wessex crossed the coast, climbing up over the headland and flying on down towards the little settlement of Port San Carlos. Throughout the flight, an Intelligence Corps sergeant peered through the thermal-image camera in the cabin looking for enemy activity. It was not especially reassuring to the aircrew to hear his voice exclaiming excitedly: 'Look at all those Argies down there. There's hundreds.' It fairly quickly became obvious that many of these 'hundreds' were in fact sheep.

The aircraft flew on south and passed close to Port San Carlos settlement itself where a few lights were showing. Knowing from the brief that there were very definitely enemy troops here, Hector Heathcote thought to himself: 'This is a very bad idea. I really don't want to be over the top of here at night in a Wessex with enemy troops on the ground.' Suddenly the sergeant in the back was shouting about how many troops he could see. While he was only trying to do his job, he was beginning to irritate the crew: 'This bloke does go on.'

Recce complete, it was time to return to *Antrim*, make a report, and start the business of clearing out the enemy.

Back on *Antrim*, the darkened flight deck seemed relatively well lit in contrast to the pitch-black headland.

Yankee Charlie refuelled and loaded the first 'stick' of eight SBS troops. The first attempt to launch nearly ended in disaster. After removing the nylon strops that restrained the Wessex on deck, Crabtree pulled in power to lift off. Normal maximum power in the Wessex 5 is 3,200 pounds of rotor head torque, or 'twisting moment'. Brief use of 3,500 pounds of torque was cleared for emergency only. As the Wessex became light on its wheels with normal full power applied, the flight deck dropped away in the swell of the sea, in effect kicking the aircraft in to a low hover. Crabtree was forced to pull and sustain 3,500 pounds of power in order to maintain any kind of flight. Just as it seemed certain that the aircraft would crash down over the edge of the flight deck, the deck came back up again to meet the aircraft.

Unbelievably, the tail wheel of the overloaded Wessex caught on a spotlight one foot behind the flight deck, allowing the main wheels to land back on normally. The flight-deck crew quickly reattached the nylon strops to prevent the aircraft sliding off into the sea.

The brief to the SBS had been clear. They absolutely must not exceed a total weight of 350 pounds per man. In their enthusiasm to go into battle heavily armed with extra weapons and ammunition, they had put everybody's lives at risk by loading up to around 450 pounds per man. Two of the troops were quickly offloaded and the Wessex launched successfully.

In the cockpit, Heathcote now had a single-lens night sight from the SBS team. It would be considerably less effective than the binocular goggles used by the Sea Kings. But it gave the crew a realistic chance of making a lights-off landing to a totally dark drop zone half a mile to the east of the Argentine position. Talking Crabtree down the approach to the landing site, Heathcote felt like Bernie the Bolt – *'Left a bit, right a bit.'* With the altimeter showing thirty feet above ground, the lack of distance information from the night sight rendered Heathcote's commentary less and less useful. Gleeson was hanging out of the cabin door trying to call out distance. But with the landing site completely dark, it was no good. Crabtree started to lose any kind of reference and, careering across the ground, reverted to instrument flying and maximum power just in time to pull away without crashing.

Junglies are well known for their creative and inventive ability to deal with rapidly changing circumstances. Unusually on this occasion there was a ready-prepared 'Plan B' that did not have to be made up on the spot. *Antrim*'s Wessex 3 had already loaded with three SBS troops on board. Pilot Ian Stanley, rescuer of the debacle on Fortuna Glacier, would make an instrument approach, taking advantage of his flight control system and radalt height hold. All was going well with his approach when, also some thirty feet above the ground, Stanley's aircraft became unstable. The three-foot-high lumps of tussock grass growing on the headland were confusing the aircraft autopilot. Stanley switched on his landing lights in the nick of time. It was fortunate that he did, as one of the wheels was perched over a dip. The aircraft would have rolled over on landing.

Crabtree and Heathcote were now circling nearby, their eyes well adjusted to the blackness of the night. To them the sudden dazzling and lavish display of floodlighting that lit up Fanning Head, turning a very black night into a bright white day, could not have failed to alert the Argentines. The lights were on for just a few seconds to enable a safe landing. But those seconds seemed like an eternity.

The second part of 'Plan B' was for Crabtree's Wessex

to make an approach to the troops on the ground using their torches to form a 'T' pattern. This was a well-established method of bringing troop-carrying *junglie* helicopters safely into an unlit landing site at night. Using the perspective of the T, the pilot could judge the approach angle and speed correctly. The standard T pattern requires five men holding torches. The light from the torches is just enough to enable a safe hover and landing. In this case, however, there were only three SBS troops on the ground. Nonetheless Crabtree was able to bring his aircraft in successfully to the half-T and increase the number of troops on the ground to nine. Five further round trips raised the SBS force to thirty-five troops. The aircrew were much amused by the sight of a large battery-powered loudspeaker being loaded into the cabin on one trip, presumably to warn, rather than taunt, the enemy.

With their four-and-a-quarter-hour mission complete, a relieved Wessex crew returned to *Antrim* for the night, unaware that they had been under almost continuous machine-gun fire from an Argentine observation post throughout each approach and insertion. They could not see the bullets fired directly at them because the red tracers are at the rear of each bullet. The watching Wessex 3 crew had discussed whether or not to say anything. From a distance, they could see the tracer all too clearly. They decided to keep quiet. They thought it might put the *junglies* off.

Attempts by the SBS to persuade the Argentine observation post to surrender were only partly successful. With time pressing on before H-Hour, when the assault would begin, they radioed *Antrim* to engage with their 4.5-inch guns. The dramatic airburst shells exploding high over the Argentine position and lighting up the sky above them caused the commandos to retreat. Although some withdrew in the direction of their colleagues at Port San Carlos, others disappeared into the hills to live off the land for the next two weeks. Nicknamed the 'Fanning Head mob', the remaining dishevelled Argentine troops were eventually picked up by a British patrol in the second week of June.

Although the Argentine commandos at Port San Carlos had by now alerted their colleagues elsewhere, the opportunity to reinforce the position with troops from Goose Green was lost. The capability to reinforce by air was further diminished by an air strike on an Argentine forward operating base, just to the north of Mount Kent. Guided in by directions from an SAS patrol on the ground, two RAF ground-attack Harriers from *Hermes* successfully destroyed two Argentine Chinook and Puma helicopters on the ground.

Soon after midnight, the British amphibious group arrived in Falkland Sound. With HMS *Plymouth* stationed at the mouth of San Carlos Water, the big troop-carrying ships dropped their anchors just west of Fanning Head. The huge docks at the stern of the twin assault ships *Fearless* and *Intrepid* were flooded and opened up to allow their eight landing craft to exit. The landing craft from *Fearless* were loaded with 40 Commando Royal Marines, headed for San Carlos settlement, designated 'blue beach'. The craft from *Intrepid* shuttled across to the cruise ship MV *Norland* where the soldiers of 2 Para did their best to scramble into the landing craft alongside, which were rising and falling in the ten-foot swell.

Although slightly later than scheduled, the combined landing force now set off like a long line of ducks for blue beach. As the landing craft approached the shore, they moved into line abreast for the assault. Unable to beach fully because of rocks, the troops were ordered to jump up to their waists into the freezing water and wade ashore. Mercifully, the landing was unopposed: 40 Commando dug in around San Carlos to secure the landing zone while 2 Para marched in another long line up Sussex Mountains to secure the southern perimeter of hills over-looking San Carlos Water.

Meanwhile, the landing craft returned to the ships to collect 45 Commando from RFA *Stromness* and land them at 'red beach', the Ajax Bay refrigeration plant immediately across the western bay from San Carlos settlement. In turn, 3 Para were collected from *Intrepid* and taken to 'green beach', Port San Carlos settlement, in the eastern bay. Seeing the troops land, the Argentine commando force withdrew into the hills to the east.

As dawn broke, Lieutenant Ray Harper was at the controls of his Sea King flying in ammunition and equipment for the Paras. His escort was a smaller Gazelle helicopter fitted with a door-mounted machine gun. The landing site wasn't obvious and both aircraft flew over the top. Realising their mistake they turned to withdraw at low level. The Paras on the ground had been unable to warn the approaching aircraft about the retreating Argentine commandos. The Gazelle was hit by the ground fire. It dropped quickly down and ditched into the water just off the beach. The crewman, Sergeant Eddy Candlish, dragged the wounded pilot from the wreck and waded ashore. To the horror of the watching Paras, Argentine troops continued to fire at the aircrew in the water in spite of an apparent order to cease fire. The pilot, Sergeant Andy Evans RM, died shortly afterwards. Minutes later a second Gazelle appeared and was also shot down, this time crashing upside down into the ground.

Back on *Antrim*, the sleepless Wessex crew had breakfast before coming up on deck for a surreal and stunning view of Fanning Head in daylight. It was a beautiful day with bright blue skies. There was not a breath of wind. Any tiredness was suppressed by the rush of adrenalin.

Yankee Charlie's job for the day was casualty evacuation – known as casevac. First they were to pick up Surgeon Commander Rick Jolly, their on-board medic for the day, from the assault ship *Fearless*. Almost immediately they were called to the San Carlos area to pick up a paratrooper who had slipped off the large and uneven Falkland tussock grass and jarred his back. He was put on a stretcher and taken back to *Fearless*.

While they were unloading on the flight deck of *Fearless*, they received new instructions from Tim Stanning's COMAW tasking group to go to the scene of a reported accident near Port San Carlos and pick up casualties. There was no mention of crashed Gazelles or enemy machine guns.

The Wessex flew east across the top of the settlement houses at Port San Carlos. A line of troops were marching across the fields below. 'Kev, what are these troops doing marching abreast like this?' Heathcote asked Gleeson.

As a Royal Marine, Gleeson knew exactly what was going on.

'What that means, Hector,' he replied calmly, 'is that we've just crossed the Forward Edge of the Battle Area, the FEBA. We do not want to be here.'

At the same time, another aircraft called out that they had gone too far. The Wessex immediately swung into a tight turn away from the Argentine troops who were about to open fire for a third time. Crossing the Port San Carlos River, they saw the mangled heap of the second downed Gazelle and made a hurried landing next to it. Gleeson and medic Rick Jolly leapt out from the cabin and rushed over. The pilot, Lieutenant Ken Francis

RM, was dead in the cockpit. His crewman, Lance Corporal Brett Giffin RM, was also dead but appeared to be sitting against the side of the aircraft. Despite briefings not to return bodies to the ships, the two aircrew were lifted into the back of the Wessex. It seemed the least they could do. The Gazelle's machine gun and list of coded callsigns were also retrieved before they lifted off to return to *Canberra*. As they flew back, Gleeson mentioned in a matter-of-fact way to his astonished pilots that he had joined the Corps with Brett Giffin. After shutting down, the crew were warned not to bring any more bodies on board. It was not considered good for morale.

Almost immediately after landing, an urgent announcement on *Canberra*'s tannoy warned of an incoming air raid. It was to signal the first of a dozen or so Argentine raids during the day through what became known as 'Bomb Alley'. Summoned by warnings from Argentine commandos at Port San Carlos, the small Aeromacchi MB339 jet had arrived from Port Stanley airfield and initially set itself up to overfly Port San Carlos. But the pilot changed his mind in order to avoid the glare of the sun. Approaching from the north instead, he was about to open fire on an unsuspecting Lynx helicopter when he caught sight of what seemed to be the entire British fleet in front of him. He immediately attacked the first big target, the frigate HMS *Argonaut*, with rockets and cannon fire.

On board *Canberra*, Gleeson was quick to react, grabbing a machine gun and firing wildly from the hip as the aircraft passed low overhead. All of the Wessex crew then felt the warm blast of a handheld Blowpipe missile launched near the flight deck. Those on *Canberra*'s deck cheered as the missile chased the aircraft before falling disappointingly short. The darting run by the Aeromacchi miraculously evaded a huge array of efforts to bring it down. It escaped back to Stanley after a second pass further away from the fleet. The pilot, Guillermo Crippa, was subsequently decorated for his bravery.

The crew of the Wessex were launched immediately to pick up casualties from *Argonaut* off Fanning Head. As they hovered behind the ship's boiling stern wake, Gleeson began to winch Rick Jolly down towards the deck. Suddenly they were waved off by the flight-deck crew as the words 'Air raid warning red' came over the radio. Having winched Jolly back on board, the Wessex broke off to head as fast as possible to Fanning Head.

The first wave of Argentine jets from the mainland tore into the British fleet at low level from the north. In the space of some six minutes, eight Daggers and six A-4 Skyhawks threaded their way from Falkland Sound through the entrance to San Carlos Water, strafing some targets and bombing others. The destroyer HMS *Antrim* and frigates *Broadsword* and *Argonaut* took the brunt of the first attacks, surviving the initial raids with limited damage. *Argonaut* was less fortunate second time around, damaged critically by a series of bombs dropped by two flights of Skyhawks. She was subsequently towed into the shelter of San Carlos Water.

On the ground in the relative safety of a small gully, Mike Crabtree and Hector Heathcote had a bird's-eye view of the first major air raid of the war. They watched as an impressive line of cannon shells from the first group of Daggers raked the side of *Antrim*. Minutes later the crew watched two huge plumes of water erupt either side of HMS *Plymouth* several miles off in the distance as a Mirage flashed past before heading home across Falkland Sound. The thin white line of a Seawolf missile fired from the Type-22 frigate HMS *Broadsword* intercepted the Mirage. It disintegrated in a ball of fire.

Down below, in San Carlos Water, Simon Thornewill was flying Victor Alpha, another of the seven day-flying Sea Kings whose job was to get as much ammunition, men and stores from ship to shore as quickly as possible. His instinct when he saw the first jets screaming through the valley was to keep going. But bombs were exploding everywhere and it quickly became obvious that he would also have to find his own gully, if only to avoid the deluge of fire from his own ships. As if to confirm this, a 1,000-pound bomb exploded just yards ahead of them on the beach. The huge blast of water and dirt was sufficiently close to blow out the flimsy bubble windows in the back of his aircraft. 'Too bloody close,' he thought, and headed for land.

Most of the other Sea King crews had already gone to ground. It was not so much that they were vulnerable to the Argentine attacks. Flying amongst the ships, even the biggest helicopters were unlikely to be much of a priority target to a highly strung fighter pilot focused on picking a target for his bombs within a few short seconds. It was the risk of getting in the way of the streams of machine-gun fire, rockets and missiles, pouring from the ships. Pilots tended to play it safe at first when an air raid warning was announced, going to ground early and lifting off late. But they soon began to feel their way for how to play this. More time spent on the ground meant less time available to unload ships.

On board *Antrim*, Ian Stanley's Wessex had been folded and moved off the flight deck in order that the maintainers could investigate a control fault. After finishing their night-time role to help insert the SBS team onto Fanning Head, the anti-submarine Wessex had reverted to normal pinging mode around the entrance to San Carlos Water. The task force commanders were still very nervous about the possibility of Argentine submarines. Other anti-submarine Sea Kings were out in Falkland Sound doing most of the search. The *Antrim* flight crew flattened themselves on the deck as the Daggers attacked. Ian Stanley was hit by small pieces of shrapnel in the finger and shoulder. One of his chiefs fared much worse, with wounds to the face. The aircraft was also spattered with cannon fire and associated debris.

Then came an enormous explosion from the rear of the flight deck as *Antrim* fired her rear-facing Seaslug missile in gash mode ('gash' is naval slang for rubbish). Designed to knock out high-level Soviet intruders, the missile was of little use against low-level attacks. Nevertheless, it was assumed that the dramatic *whoosh* of smoke from a missile launch would deter an incoming attacker.

Seemingly undeterred, one of the Daggers successfully dropped its 1,000-pound bomb straight through *Antrim*'s stern. The bomb bounced around inside the ship, coming to rest directly beneath the flight deck. Had it exploded anywhere near the Seaslug launch system that ran like a giant train set through the ship, *Antrim* would have peeled wide open. Instead the unexploded bomb set off small fires and left a huge bump in the flight deck.

This was the first of many Argentine bombs that failed to explode. A fuse prevents a bomb from exploding until it is well clear of the aircraft. The fuse is simply a small vane in the rear of each bomb that spins round in the wind and unthreads a screw. In attacking the ships so low, the bombs didn't have sufficient time to arm. This tiny detail overlooked by the Argentine air force undoubtedly saved many British ships and a great many more British lives.

Meanwhile down to the south of the San Carlos area, the SAS had been conducting a diversionary attack on the Argentine forces at Darwin, assisted by naval gunfire support from the Type-21 frigate HMS *Ardent* in Falkland Sound. From the six airworthy Argentine Pucaras on the nearby airstrip at Goose Green, two pairs of aircraft were briefed to search for British helicopters involved with the landings at San Carlos. Only one of the first pair actually launched, the other prevented by the naval shelling. This first airborne Pucara was shot down by a Stinger missile fired by an SAS trooper. Subsequent launches by Stinger against other aircraft were unsuccessful. The second pair of Pucaras was bounced by a trio of Sea Harriers from 801 Squadron led by Lieutenant Commander Nigel 'Sharkey' Ward. The pilot of one Pucara ejected at low level after being strafed by Ward. The other Pucara escaped in low cloud back to Stanley. Later in the day the remaining two Pucaras from Goose Green also returned to Port Stanley. Two of these three remaining airworthy Pucaras were destroyed by air attacks and naval gunfire within the next few days.

By now, Mike Crabtree and the crew of Yankee Charlie had realised that spending too much time on the deck of *Canberra* waiting to be hit by an incoming air raid was a bad idea. So as the day progressed, they kept to the hills as much as possible and accepted most of their instructions over the radio. One such instruction was to return to the scene of their night insertion on Fanning Head in order to relieve the SBS troops of their Argentine prisoners and transfer them to *Canberra*. Having just had to recover the bodies of the Gazelle crew killed by the Argentine troops, there were very mixed emotions indeed about allowing Argentine soldiers from the same unit into the same cabin space.

Mike Crabtree landed the aircraft near the group of SBS and prisoners on top of the headland. He noticed that Mike Rose, SAS commanding officer, was standing with the SBS men. After loading four weary-looking prisoners into the cabin, Rose signalled for Kev Gleeson to come out from the aircraft.

In the cockpit of the Wessex, a terrible realisation suddenly dawned. The two pilots turned to look at each other and pointed down below. The four Argentines had been left completely alone in the back of the Wessex with a fully loaded cabin-mounted machine gun at their disposal. In their sights was the head of the SAS, their own aircrewman and several SBS troops. Not wishing to alert the Argentines to the opportunity, a frantic Mike Crabtree and Hector Heathcote waved fruitlessly at their aircrewman, who was by now poring over a map with Rose. Eventually, Kev Gleeson looked up and noticed the waving arms. He returned immediately to find the prisoners still slumped in the back. It was a surreal moment in a day that was full of them.

It was now late afternoon on 21 May and the Wessex was heading for a gulley as another air raid flashed through. By now the crew had worked out something of a routine whereby they would deliberately land with the right wheel slightly higher up the slope. With the rotor blades tilted upwards on the right-hand side of the aircraft, Gleeson had a clearer view of the action with his cabin-mounted machine gun. One particular gulley on Fanning Head allowed them a view both of the amphibious and auxiliary ships in San Carlos Water to the south-east and the warships out in Falkland Sound to the south-west.

As the Wessex waited on the ground, Gleeson pointed out to the right as several Mirage jets swooped in for a further attack. As Gleeson prepared to open fire on the leading jet with the gimpy, Rick Jolly could see the trailing aircraft detach itself from the group and head directly towards the Wessex. Brief flashes from the Mirage told him all he needed to know. The Wessex was about to be hit by cannon fire. With no time for warning, and not being plugged into the intercom at the time, his only thought was for self-preservation. He leapt from the cabin and made a run for it. As Jolly buried himself into a ditch, the Mirage launched its cannon attack on the Wessex and then banked away hard to continue with an attack on the British shipping further down the coast.

It soon became clear to the crew that they were missing something. Gleeson announced sardonically to his pilots: 'Oh, the doc seems to have jumped out of the aircraft.' There had been no warning or explanation. Jolly had simply jumped out and run off before inexplicably diving headlong into a grassy ditch. Just as Gleeson added the afterthought 'No idea why . . .' the ground all around the Wessex erupted into the air. Clods of earth and grass exploded violently up through the rotor blades, onto the windscreen and all around the aircraft. As the mud and debris settled, straggly bits of what looked like metal fibre floated slowly down. It looked suspiciously like chaff, the aluminium strips used for deflecting radar. 'We've been shot at by our own bloody ships,' exclaimed Crabtree.

After a few seconds in the ditch, Jolly looked up astonished to see the Wessex still there and not obliterated. He scrambled to his feet and back into the aircraft, feeling both shocked and sheepish. He assumed the crew had known exactly what had happened. It was best to say nothing and hope that they would forgive his rapid exit.

'Oh, you back with us then, doc?' asked Crabtree coolly. Jolly assumed this was *junglie* nonchalance in the face of extreme danger. In fact neither pilot had any idea what had happened. It was a full year later before Jolly revealed the truth to a horrified Heathcote.

For the Mirage, the Wessex had been an opportunity target en route to bigger and better things. Unbelievably, the cannon fire from the jet appeared to have straddled the Wessex on either side. Had the attacking Mirage pilot been any less accurate, whether his attack had been angled or lined up a few feet off centre, it would have been curtains for the Wessex and her crew. To say they had a lucky escape is something of an understatement.

The courageous Type-21 frigate HMS *Ardent* and her crew had spent the day providing naval gunfire support against the Argentine forces in Darwin and Goose Green, successfully restricting the launch of Pucara ground-attack aircraft from the airstrip. The downside was that she was horribly exposed in the open water of Falkland Sound. As the day wore on, *Ardent* became the obvious target for a series of attacks by the Argentine jets. A lone Argentine air force Skyhawk splashed a bomb harmlessly into the sea beside the ship at around midday. A second flight of four Skyhawks en route to the frigate minutes later was intercepted over West Falkland by two 800 Squadron Sea Harriers, with the loss of two Skyhawks.

The third attempt by the Argentines to sink *Ardent* an hour and a half later faltered briefly as four Daggers were again intercepted, with the loss of one further aircraft. However, the remaining three evaded the cannon fire of the pursuing Sea Harriers for a clear run in low over Falkland Sound. The three Daggers swept in towards the ship and deposited a series of bombs. The first bounced short of the ship and up into the stern. The second bomb exploded on impact with the flight deck, destroying the Lynx helicopter and hangar and killing the flight crew. Heroic Flight Commander John Sephton and his team were last seen blazing away with rail-mounted machine guns. Sephton was awarded a posthumous Distinguished Flying Cross. The third bomb missed altogether.

Two more flights of three Daggers followed this attack almost immediately. Mercifully for *Ardent*, the first flight headed for the warships guarding the entrance to San Carlos Water, causing only shrapnel damage. The second flight headed directly for *Ardent*. All three were intercepted and splashed by 801 Squadron Sea Harriers. But there were simply not enough Harriers to go round. As *Ardent*'s damage control teams struggled to deal with the catastrophic scenes, two further flights of three Argentine navy Skyhawks headed towards the ship. Two bombs from the first flight hit the already damaged stern. It was little consolation that all three Skyhawks were subsequently destroyed, two by Sea Harriers and one by a combination of small-arms fire from *Ardent* and cannon fire from one of the Sea Harriers. Bombs from the second wave of Skyhawks missed altogether, too late to save the mortally damaged ship. Twenty-two sailors and airmen died that day, killed in action or lost to the sea.

The last thing Chief Petty Officer Ken Enticknap remembered before the final strike by the A-4s were the words 'take cover' shouted over the ship's tannoy. He had already been trying to deal with the damage from the previous attack. He regained consciousness to find the air black with thick acrid smoke. His left hand was badly damaged and he was trapped under a girder. Able Seaman John Dillon had been similarly knocked unconscious and trapped under falling debris. Coming around to the sound of screaming and the sight of thick black smoke, Dillon dragged himself out, realising that he had also been wounded by shrapnel in the back.

Responding to Enticknap's appeal for help, Dillon slowly managed to lift the girder enough for the other man to crawl free. They stumbled forward together through the smoke towards what looked like a raging fire. All of a sudden a huge expanse of sea and sky appeared through the smoke in the side of the ship where the bulkhead had been blown off. They gasped deep breaths before Enticknap fell into a hole in the decking. With his strength fading, Dillon lifted Enticknap out of the hole. As they stood overlooking the sea, they put on their lifejackets. With his jacket inflated, the badly injured Enticknap jumped the twenty feet into the sea. Dillon couldn't inflate his jacket but realised that he had no choice but to protect his injured colleague. He followed into the water. Adrenalin prevented either of them noticing the icy temperature of the water. As Dillon grabbed Enticknap to swim away from the side, Dillon couldn't believe his eyes. The stern of his former ship was a chaos of mangled metal, fire and smoke. In contrast, the front of the ship seemed remarkably undamaged. Men in orange survival suits stood against the railings pointing and waving madly at the two men in the water.

From their vantage point in the gulley on Fanning Head, Crabtree and Heathcote had seen the smoke begin to spew upwards from the stricken Type-21 out in the distance in Falkland Sound. Yet with air attacks still in progress, they felt apprehensive about rushing to aid the ship. Their dilemma was resolved as they saw *Plymouth*'s Wasp, flown by Lieutenant Commander John Dransfield, fearlessly crossing below them having collected wounded sailors from the now disabled frigate *Argonaut*. Without further thought, they headed off towards *Fearless* for an urgent refuel. While on deck, Rick Jolly rushed out and grabbed two winchable stretchers and threw them into the cabin. The Wessex lifted off immediately and headed south up over the Sussex Mountains and past the troops of 2 Para who were now digging themselves in. The normal maximum speed of a Wessex 5 is 120 knots. As Heathcote tipped the aircraft into a full power shallow dive, they reached 145 knots in their desperation to reach the scene as quickly as possible. Heathcote flared the aircraft into a hover just short of the tangled mess of metal, fire and smoke, having passed through an acrid pall of black smoke. The frigate *Yarmouth* was backing up her stern alongside *Ardent*, which was now tilting unnaturally over to one side.

At the front of the ship, the men in orange suits were waving frantically in the direction of the sea just below the Wessex. Immediately both pilots spotted Dillon and Enticknap in the water. At this point Heathcote became very aware of his inexperience as he struggled to maintain a stable hover. Hovering over the glassy and fuel-slicked surface of the sea was extremely difficult with so few visual references on the water below him. Handing over to the more experienced Crabtree quickly brought things under control. Meanwhile Gleeson had lowered the orange rescue strop on the winch down to Dillon, now struggling in the freezing water without an inflated lifejacket.

Crawling over to the doorway, it was immediately obvious to Rick Jolly that the man in the water was too weak to attach himself and was about to drown. With the perceived shame of running away from the Wessex still fresh in his mind, he knew this was his moment to make amends. Signalling his intent, he could see Gleeson talking to the crew as the strop was raised back into the aircraft. With a nod from Gleeson, Jolly attached himself and was lowered towards the drowning man. It was hard to know which was more unpleasant: the horrible jolt from the discharge of static electricity as his feet hit the water or the shock as his body submerged into the bitter South Atlantic water. The water temperature was just three degrees above zero and was fast numbing his body and draining his energy. Adrenalin kicked in as he grabbed the desperate man and locked his hands around his chest in a bear hug. As Crabtree gently lifted the helicopter, the two men rose, dripping from the sea. Gleeson winched them upwards towards the cabin. With small delicate movements on the winch control and strong arms to haul his load on board, Jolly and Dillon collapsed on the floor of the Wessex. A quick compression of Dillon's chest produced two vomited bursts of sea water. He was alive.

Gleeson now looked at Jolly expectantly. With a thumbs-up, Jolly was lowered once more towards the sea. As the medic span around on the winch, it was like watching a crazy revolving film show. Burning *Ardent*. *Yarmouth*. Falkland landscape. Then back to the sickening sight of *Ardent* again. The spinning stopped with the second dose of static shock followed by icy numbness as he entered the water. This time there was no way he had sufficient strength to hold onto the second man. Kicking through the water, he fastened Enticknap's lifejacket onto the winch hook above his own strop. Thankfully the lifejacket held without tearing as the two men were lifted once more to safety. With the wounded and freezing men safely on the floor of the Wessex, Gleeson closed the door and put the cabin heaters on full blast as the aircraft sped back north to *Canberra* in San Carlos Water. Behind them in Falkland Sound, the remaining survivors from the still burning HMS *Ardent* abandoned ship, clambering directly across onto HMS *Yarmouth*.

Ardent sank the following day. Altogether twenty-two men had died in the attack. For their courage, Dillon was later awarded the George Medal and Enticknap the Queen's Gallantry Medal.

With darkness falling, there were no further air strikes on that dreadful day. Crabtree, Heathcote and Gleeson had flown more or less continuously for thirteen and a half hours since their glass of beer with Mike Rose the previous afternoon. An utterly exhausted Wessex crew shut down on deck and called it a day. A long night still lay ahead for Rick Jolly, however. He was told to get his men and medical equipment off the ship and onto land to set up the field hospital in the old refrigeration plant at Ajax Bay. The Wessex crew were already asleep when the *Canberra* sailed out of San Carlos towards the safety of the carrier group to the east of the Falklands.

The epic D-Day duel had cost the Argentine air force five Daggers, five Skyhawks and two Pucaras in exchange for the destruction of HMS *Ardent*, the loss of two Gazelle helicopters, serious bomb damage to HMS *Argonaut* and *Antrim*, and cannon damage to HMS *Brilliant* and *Broadsword*.

But the British had successfully landed on East Falkland with the 4,000 men of 3 Commando Brigade.

Chapter 8

'Air raid warning red, SCRAM!'
22–24 May 1982

After the drama of the first day landings, low cloud and light rain on the second day gave the British ships unloading in San Carlos Water respite from air attack.

From Falkland Sound two fingers of water jut inland, surrounded on all sides by hills – Fanning Head to the north, the Sussex Mountains to the west and south, and further hills to the east behind Port San Carlos and San Carlos settlement. This bubble became a hive of activity, with landing craft shuttling men and stores from the larger warships and supply ships. Sea Kings continued to lift huge quantities of stores and ammunition from ship to shore, helping to establish the British foothold on Falklands soil. But the badly needed Wessex remained underused, and in some cases, unused, scattered in dribs and drabs among the task force ships.

Pete Manley stood on the flight deck of the Royal Fleet Auxiliary supply ship *Stromness* sailing towards San Carlos Water. He had been ordered to get his Wessex gunship, Yankee Sierra, onto land as quickly as possible. The journey south on the giant container ship *Atlantic Conveyor* had taken just eleven days from leaving Ascension to joining up with the task force in range of the Falklands. His cocktail party on the tail ramp had never materialised. *Conveyor* and its huge quantity of supplies was now being held back for a few days because of the ferocity of the air raids in San Carlos. But a helicopter gunship might come in useful for the land forces.

In gunship role, the Wessex could carry either twenty-eight 2-inch rockets, fired by the pilot from the right-hand seat, or a pair of wire-guided AS12 air-to-surface missiles fired by the missile aimer from the left-hand seat. In the cabin behind and below the cockpit were two gimpy machine guns, mounted on either side of the aircraft and fired by the aircrewman. Even fully armed, there was still space in the back for eight or more troops, depending on how much fuel the aircraft had on board. Accompanying Manley were co-pilot Sub-Lieutenant Ric Fox and aircrewman Colour Sergeant Dave Greet RM.

As *Stromness* eased its way quietly into San Carlos Water, Manley realised that it would be a whole lot safer to be based on land than on a floating ammunition ship. Radio traffic between the ships was frantic with signals and orders. So it took some while for Manley to establish authorisation to clear the deck and support the troops of 45 Commando based at Ajax Bay red beach. Within minutes he and the crew were very relieved to flash up Yankee Sierra on the flight deck and head off towards the south-west of San Carlos Water. As they approached the big warehouse of the Ajax Bay refrigeration plant, lines of trenches dotted the hillside like dominoes as the British troops dug in. Manley lowered the gunship gently down onto the grass near the warehouse and pulled the throttles closed. Keeping one engine running, he brought the rotors to a halt. The crew climbed out to look around. A bemused Royal Marine sergeant wandered over and asked what they were doing. 'We were wondering if we could help you chaps out,' replied Manley cheerily.

What followed was typical *junglie* pragmatism. The aircrew needed a base and food. The Royal Marines of 45 Commando needed help lifting their equipment, air-defence missiles and ammunition higher up the hillside. For several hours that day and the next, Manley and his crew operated as a rogue helicopter without any obvious input from the landing force commanders just across the bay on HMS *Fearless*. In any case, despite offering assistance to any and every ship in San Carlos Water, the loads of ammunition and stores sitting on most flight decks were made up for the bigger Sea Kings, too big for the Wessex to lift. Ships mostly made use of the rogue Wessex as a taxi service for ferrying senior officers around the bay. Getting people or messages to or from a ship often proved challenging because the flight decks were so clogged with netted pallet loads. A great deal of initiative was called for, plus a bending of the usual rules for ship-to-helicopter operations. Pilots saved time by hovering unconventionally above the bridge wing or the front of the ship and using their winch.

Within a few hours of doing whatever jobs they could find, it was getting dark and they shut the helicopter down on the hillside behind Ajax Bay. Like the troops further up the hill, Manley and his crew simply grabbed their sleeping bags and roll mats from the back of the Wessex and bedded down outside in the open air, between clumps of gorse. It was bitterly cold.

*   *   *

Sunday 23 May was a classic Falklands day. The light rain had cleared, the air was cold and bright, the skies were blue and the inlet of San Carlos Water was glassy calm. The Ajax Bay warehouse was now being set up as the main field hospital, with huge red crosses painted over the roof and walls and acquiring the name 'the red and green life machine'– red for Paras, green for Marines. Medics would always be a good source of food. Although a limited supply of bacon and eggs in the field kitchen soon ran out, replacements of porridge, corned beef concoctions, anything involving curry powder, and an endless supply of tea meant there was always something to fill the grateful scavenging aircrew.

In the early morning light, Fox and Manley began their pre-flight walk round of Yankee Sierra, which included a check of the various oil and fluid levels. One of the hydraulic fluid levels was low, suggesting a possible leak. Either way it needed replenishing. For helicopters, hydraulic systems provide the power assistance that translates the pilot's movement of the flying controls in the cockpit into the pitch control movement on the rotor head in order to alter the angle of the rotor blades. Since the main blades have to lift the helicopter off the ground, it would be physically impossible for any human to move the controls without a hydraulic boost. In the Wessex, as in all large helicopters, there are two hydraulic systems in case one fails. Failure of both systems would mean the blades doing their own thing, leaving the flying controls thrashing about in the cockpit and the helicopter totally out of control.

With their engineering support 200 miles away out at sea on *Atlantic Conveyor*, the crew had to sort out the problem themselves. Manley figured that topping up the hydraulic system couldn't be that hard. So having bartered a can of fluid from the Marines in exchange for a couple of Mars bars, the three of them set about replenishing the system. One topped up the fluid, one loosened the nut on the relevant drain, and the other pumped the fluid through. Crossing their fingers that it really was as easy as that, the rogue helicopter was able to resume its ad hoc role under the clear blue skies of San Carlos.

Unfortunately the beautiful skies also meant a renewed opportunity for the Argentines to resume their attempts to thwart the British landings. Over the next two days, some thirty-two Argentine jets – Skyhawks and Daggers – found their way to San Carlos. Minutes before each approaching attack, one of the British ships would radio a warning 'All stations, air raid warning red', at which point helicopters buzzing around the bay headed ashore for the nearest gulley and shut down. The trick was to get behind a ridge so the helicopter was out of the line of direct fire from the ships. But neither did they want to stray too far inland, not knowing enemy positions surrounding the San Carlos bubble.

Just as Crabtree had done two days earlier, Manley found himself a particular favourite gulley into which he could dump the Wessex and pull back the throttles. After bringing the rotors to a halt with the brake, one engine was left running in order to avoid relying on unpredictable batteries and damp cables for the next start-up. Meanwhile, the crew clambered out as fast as possible, grabbing bergens and machine guns and flattening themselves on the damp ground away from the aircraft.

From their positions lying prone, the Wessex crew had a bird's-eye view of the action in San Carlos Water. Aged twenty-three, Ric Fox had just completed his first tour as a Wessex pilot, including five stints in Northern Ireland. Being at war felt surreal, weird, incredible; like watching a movie.

It was just after midday when the first two pairs of Skyhawks sped across the open water of Falkland Sound, overflying a Lynx helicopter belonging to the Type-21 frigate HMS *Antelope*, and setting themselves up for their run-in over San Carlos Water. Ric Fox heard the roar of the jets long before he could pick out their camouflaged grey shapes. A web of orange tracer bullets from the ships gave the first clue where to look. Plumes of water from bombs made it easier to pick out the attacking aircraft. Skimming the top of the hills and flashing down between the British ships, the first pair dropped their bombs on *Antelope* before being rocked by exploding missiles launched from other warships. The roar became a horrible screech as the jets circled around at low level for an ineffective second pass and escape to the north. Blasting away at the enemy with machine guns had little effect, but it felt better than doing nothing.

The second pair of Skyhawks attacked *Antelope* again. Fox and his colleagues watched mesmerised as a land-based Rapier missile tracked towards one of the jets, remorselessly catching up and enveloping the aircraft in an orangey-red explosion that quickly decayed into a trail of black smoke. There was no great celebration at the destruction of the Argentine aircraft. No whoops of joy. That was that. Minutes later, three more jets swept in from the west at low level and away across the bay.

The initial outcome of these attacks was confused and unclear. As well as losing one Skyhawk in the first wave of attacks, it later turned out that another aircraft from the second wave had crashed on landing back in Argentina. But it didn't take long for the success of their mission to become very apparent indeed. Even though the seven Skyhawks had dropped their bombs too close to their targets to allow the bomb fuses to unwind, two unexploded bombs were left behind buried deep within *Antelope*.

After relative calm returned and the bustle of activity resumed in the bay, the crew looked at each other and decided to crack on. Starting up the Wessex, they heard the radio request to assist in the evacuation of *Antelope*. As they approached the ship, lifeboats and other landing craft were already moving people off. The flight deck was crammed. Along with other helicopters in the area, the Wessex played its part in winching survivors to safety and transferring them to other ships. Later on the crew dropped a bomb disposal team onto the now abandoned flight deck.

British loss of life might have been far worse that day. It wasn't merely down to the failure of the Skyhawk bombs to fuse before slamming into *Antelope*. A flight of Argentine Daggers was intercepted by Sea Harriers over West Falkland before they even reached the British amphibious group. One aircraft was despatched with a Sidewinder missile and the rest turned back. In the evening, a further Argentine attempt to launch an Exocet attack on the fleet out at sea was aborted when the attacking Super Etendards failed to find their expected target.

Antelope was now anchored overnight in the sheltered waters of San Carlos while two engineers bravely attempted to defuse the unexploded bombs. A small charge meant to disarm the fuse inadvertently set off one of the bombs, killing one engineer and seriously wounding the other. The appalling 'crump' echoed around the bay. The sleek frigate broke her back spectacularly and sank, leaving only her bows and stern jutting above the waterline the following morning in a V-shape, from which a tube of black smoke billowed upwards.

Flying around San Carlos Bay, it was hard to ignore the morbid sight of the sunken *Antelope*. As the day wore on, the angle of the V became more acute. Eventually the ship disappeared beneath the surface altogether. *Antelope* was the third British warship to be sunk. She wouldn't be the last.

Sub-Lieutenant Dave Ockleton was one of those who had been watching the explosion from the nearby ferry MV *Norland*. He had been on deck as the first wave of Sea Kings got airborne from *Norland* and *Canberra* on the first morning of the landings. From the bridge wing he had watched the early Argentine air raids. The very first two Skyhawks had instantly earned his respect as they darted between the British ships. One red and white, one camouflaged, they were incredibly manoeuvrable. In the eerie silence after the raid, he looked up to see four lights in a square pattern immediately above him. They floated silently over the ship like a UFO before exploding violently.

The lights were the rockets on a Seacat missile, fired from a neighbouring ship. The missile was just yards away when it detonated. It felt like his nose was being parted from the pressure of the blast. After another raid, his eardrums felt shattered as a Mirage swept past. It wasn't the Mirage that made the big noise. Ockleton turned behind him to see one of the *Norland* chefs aiming a rifle at the jet. His face was less than six inches from the line of the bullets.

Ockleton had finally been put to good use – looking after Mike Crabtree's Argentine prisoners from Fanning Head who had been brought to *Norland*. He had escorted them down to cabins on the lorry drivers' deck. A rating was posted with orders to shoot anybody who stuck their head out into the corridor.

Norland then sailed out of San Carlos overnight only to return a day later to unload more troops and equipment. Having been left alone on the first day, the ship now became a more obvious target on her second visit. Two Skyhawks came at the ship head on. These were the same jets that had attacked and mortally wounded *Antelope*. From the bridge wing, Ockleton watched the first Skyhawk let loose with a cannon attack on *Norland*. The second dropped two light green bombs; both missed the ship but created huge explosions in the water. There was a flash as one of the Skyhawks was hit by a Rapier. The metallic tinkling of the debris sounded like rain on the side of the ship. Steve O'Shea, an engineer on the flight deck received minor wounds from the falling metal.

Dave Ockleton had made it to the Falklands. He had been in the thick of the action. But it had been an incredibly frustrating few days for him and his handful of colleagues. They were the spare Wessex pilots and aircrewman from 848 Squadron. Their frustration was that they had no helicopters to fly.

Early on the morning of Tuesday 24 May, RFA *Resource* eased quietly into San Carlos Bay and dropped anchor. From the darkness of the bridge, Jack Lomas wondered whether the burning glow to the south of them was fighting ashore. It wasn't until dawn broke on another beautiful Falklands day that it became very obvious this was a ship on fire, Lomas's second after HMS *Sheffield*. He had not been briefed to disembark with his two Wessex that day. The plan was to unload some of *Resource*'s ammunition by boat, some by Sea King from the flight deck, and then withdraw to the relative safety of the battle group out sea. However, the prospect of sitting on a floating bomb all day appealed as much to Lomas as it had to Manley two days earlier on *Stromness*. Lomas briefed his team to prepare both aircraft for launch. He would sort something out with the operations team on *Fearless*.

The sun came up on another stunning clear day. Lomas knew it wouldn't be long before Argentine jets continued their attempt to disrupt the British landings. High up on *Resource*'s flight deck, he watched as his team went about their work. All of his engineers had been equipped with rifles or machine guns in anticipation of enemy attack. The flight-deck telephone rang from the bridge warning of an incoming air raid. 'Right!' shouted Lomas at his team. 'If they come past us, shoot six aircraft lengths ahead, get some lead into the sky, and don't bloody shoot any of our own ships.' The prospect of sailors with guns amused and horrified aircrew in equal measure.

The first raid of the day was a determined effort by the Argentine air force to swamp the British defences, with two flights of four Daggers attacking simultaneously. One flight was virtually wiped out in a remarkable interception. Two Sea Harriers splashed three Daggers out of four with their Sidewinder missiles as they crossed West Falkland. The fourth Dagger fled. However, the second flight of Daggers swept low up through San Carlos Water.

Pete Manley, Ric Fox and Dave Greet were already airborne and trundling past the smoking sinking wreck of the *Antelope* as the air raid came through. It may have appeared that their Wessex was nonchalantly getting on with the job regardless. In fact, the crew of Yankee Sierra were desperately trying to get out of the way.

On board the flight deck of *Resource*, nobody quite knew in which direction to look at first. Eventually somebody spotted the jets approaching from the south. 'Heads up, they're coming, weapons free, fire when they get close,' shouted Lomas. There was a brief pause, almost as if everybody was thinking the same thought. Aeroplanes. Be careful. We don't shoot at aeroplanes. It wasn't until Lomas himself drew his 9mm pistol and started firing that the rest of the team followed suit. On board every ship in San Carlos Bay, soldiers, sailors and airmen were firing away in all directions as the enemy jets swept through at low level between *Resource* and the command ship *Fearless* and away to the north after another ineffectual attack. It sounded like Chinese New Year as every weapon across the bay lit up. Lomas realised immediately that the biggest danger to the Wessex crews was being shot by our own side. And in that moment, he also knew that it would be ridiculous to hang around on the ship for one moment longer than necessary.

Some of the tents and equipment needed to set up a forward operating base were ready to be taken ashore from *Resource*. A flurry of calls to ships in the bay revealed further equipment that could be borrowed. The two Wessex began their disembarkation immediately, aiming to set up their forward operating base 'Whale', at Old Creek House, an even tinier settlement to the north of San Carlos and alongside some of the Sea Kings.

An unexpected source of camping supplies turned out to be one of the other Type-21 frigates, HMS *Arrow*, sister ship of *Antelope* and *Ardent*. The flight decks of all these frigates were usually restricted to the smaller Lynx and Wasp helicopters. But with no movement of the deck in the calm sea, the much bigger Wessex could just about squeeze all three wheels on with a matter of feet to spare between blades and the ship's aerials, if the pilot was careful. To protect the deck from overstressing, the pilot maintained power and kept a wheels-light hover: just touching the aircraft wheels onto the deck made loading and unloading people and stores into the cabin a lot safer and more stable than doing so in a low wobbly hover.

It didn't always work out. Sub-Lieutenant Steve Judd later tried this trick on HMS *Arrow* only to misjudge the distances and strip the tips off all four rotor blades on the ship's aerials. To the great amusement of the other helicopter crews operating in San Carlos, *Arrow*'s flight-deck director then casually announced over the emergency frequency: 'Would the Wessex pilot who has left his rotor tips on our deck care to check his aircraft and come back and collect them.'

As punishment for his indiscretion, Jack Lomas sent Steve Judd onto *Fearless* to find a way of bringing back four new blades from the spare Wessex in the ship's hold. To his credit, Judd persuaded the engineers on board to unbolt the blades, and a passing helicopter to carry them over. The Wessex was back up and running by the following morning.

Having landed at FOB Whale, their new base south-east of most of the ships, Lomas needed to change seats in order to sort things out on the ground. Not wanting to shut down, he and Knight left the aircraft running completely on its own without anybody in the cockpit. Just over the bay, they could clearly see their mother ship *Resource*. At another time it would have been a glorious sight on a beautiful day. But any such thoughts were broken by an urgent voice on the UHF radio: 'Air raid warning red, air raid warning red, SCRAM, SCRAM!'

On board *Fearless*, the aviation staff had noticed that helicopters were either ignoring the air raid warnings and going to ground too late, or assuming attack was imminent and going to ground too early. Lieutenant Commander Ed Featherstone had invented a brilliant warning system that kept time on the ground waiting for a raid to pass to a minimum. Early warnings were coming from a range of sources. British submarines west of the Falklands could detect Argentine jets as they flew out from the mainland. As they coasted in over West Falkland, they could be heard or seen by the SBS patrols which had been inserted by the night-flying Sea Kings and were now hidden in the barren terrain. Sometimes the Royal Navy warships posted to the north and south of the islands could also detect the raids on their radar. Closest of all, look-outs on the Sussex Hills above San Carlos could see the jets as they approached.

The earliest warning on the radio net, transmitted as 'Air raid warning yellow', meant that enemy jets were some fifty miles from San Carlos. These transmissions had little effect on operations other than as a general warning. Once the intruders were closer to fifteen miles and an attack was imminent, 'Air raid warning red' would be called. Helicopter pilots would then know they had to make a quick decision about whether to break off what they were doing and head for a gulley or shut down on a flight deck. As the attack materialised, 'Air raid warning red, SCRAM!' told crews that jets were coming over the hills. Being airborne when you heard the words 'SCRAM, SCRAM!' meant you were at serious risk of being shot down by your own side. There was one more important protection to prevent confusion. It was only ever Ed Featherstone's voice on the radio.

With Yankee Tango on the ground in the gulley, Knight climbed out of the left seat and ran around the front of the aircraft, up into the right seat vacated by Lomas. At least the helicopter had not tried to fly itself away with the sole passenger, aircrewman Petty Officer Arthur Balls, in the rear cabin. Even above the huge noise of the rotor disc and two Rolls-Royce engines, Lomas clearly heard the roar of the first of five Skyhawks screaming overhead. The underside of the jet was a beautiful duck egg blue against the dark blue sky. But where were the Harriers?

Up in the cockpit, Knight had just finished strapping himself in as a Skyhawk flew over. Almost immediately, there was a sudden loud bang to his left. The windscreen imploded. Knight looked down to see a flattened bullet sitting innocently on the left seat. 'I've just been shot!' he called down to his aircrewman.

'What, what? Don't be so stupid,' cried Balls.

'No, not me, we've just been shot. I've got a big hole in the windscreen. Poke your head up and see.'

As soon as Balls pushed upwards on the left cockpit seat, glass tinkled down into the cabin by his feet. The bullet had smacked into a metal spar just by Knight's left shoulder. Had he remained in the left seat, the bullet would have hit him. Looking out towards *Resource* across the bay, they both realised they'd been shot by their own side. 'It's our bloody ship!'

The main reason for the machine gun in the cabin of a Wessex was to shoot back at an attacking jet. But since the arc of fire was limited, so that the bullets didn't go up through the rotor blades, it was never used in anger. This is 845 Squadron aircrewman Arthur Balls.

Over on the other side of the bay, just a few hundred yards away behind the Ajax Bay warehouse, Manley and his crew had responded to the cry of 'Air raid warning red, SCRAM!' by shutting down Yankee Sierra to one engine. As they ran from the aircraft, a Skyhawk flashed down the gulley heading straight towards them. 'Ric, check your three o'clock,' shouted Manley.

Caught out in the open, Fox just had time to look out to his right as the jet passed no more than twenty feet above their heads going flat out. The pressure wave blew both of them to the ground and the noise was deafening. Almost immediately they heard cannon fire from the ships splitting the air above their heads, followed by a huge bang as a Seacat missile exploded having missed its target. Fragments of the missile crashed down fifty yards away, perilously close to the Wessex, whining away on one engine on its own.

Back on *Resource*, Knight shut down the damaged Yankee Tango and asked the engineers for some sort of battle damage repair to the windscreen. He wandered off to find a very apologetic bosun's mate who had been operating the offending gun on the starboard side of the ship: 'I'm really sorry, it won't happen again.'

Having smoothed things over, Knight returned to the aircraft after grabbing a sandwich and cup of tea. He was surprised to find that instead of replacing the shattered windscreen, the screen had simply been covered on both sides in fablon, a sticky-back plastic sheeting normally used to protect maps from the rain. Yankee Tango's windscreen had certainly been repaired. It was just impossible to see anything through it.

Knight's colleague, Sub-Lieutenant Noddy Morton, was expecting to take the aircraft for the afternoon. 'I'll wait for the other one if you don't mind, Oily,' he said. For the rest of the war, Yankee Tango became the aircraft nobody wanted to fly.

There was to be one further air strike on this day by a flight of three Skyhawks. Avoiding interception by the Sea Harriers, the flight swept up San Carlos Water chased by a wall of lead and missiles from the British ships. Two of the Skyhawks managed to release their bombs into the landing ships logistic, RFA Sir *Galahad* and *Sir Lancelot*. Both ships had already unloaded much of their stores. However, the attack put them temporarily out of action. Some of the crew were evacuated while the unexploded 500-pound bombs were defused or hauled overboard.

After their twenty-one-hour marathon adventure before and during D-Day, a shattered Crabtree, Heathcote and Gleeson were relieved to park Yankee Charlie for the night high up on the helicopter deck of *Canberra* and get some rest. However, naval command insisted that the 'great white whale' *Canberra* withdraw from the immediate danger zone of San Carlos as soon as possible. As the crew of Yankee Charlie woke up early the following morning, expecting to continue tasking around the beach-head, it was somewhat disconcerting to find themselves steaming back out to sea and away from the action. Unable to establish any kind of authorisation to move on, they were forced to spend a frustrating two days twiddling their thumbs on board.

Heathcote made good use of his time chatting to Lieutenant Bob Horton, pilot of the Sea King that had crashed into the sea two days earlier with such appalling loss of life after reportedly hitting an albatross. Horton was convalescing with a broken ankle, the result of kicking out his cockpit window underwater in a desperate bid to escape from his rapidly sinking helicopter.

Eventually, after a frustrating two days, Crabtree finally managed to get authorisation to return to their parent ship RFA *Tidepool*, where the other half of his flight and their maintenance crew awaited. Although there was some uncertainty about the exact location, they needed no encouragement to set off. Without any means of refuelling from *Canberra*, they would have to make do with the little over an hour of fuel available on board, equivalent to some 120 miles range. It should be more than enough.

Visibility was poor as they set off, almost immediately switching to instrument flying whereby the pilot relies entirely on his cockpit instruments. They skimmed in and out of wispy cloud at 400 feet above the sea, beginning to wonder whether this was such a great idea after all. The odds of hitting *Tidepool* without radio contact were almost nil. The fuel gauges wound slowly down as they passed the point of no return. They were now committed to continuing. They had to find *Tidepool*.

Crabtree broke radio silence: 'Nine Delta Alpha Four, this is Yankee Charlie, inbound and requesting urgent vector.' One or two short replies from *Tidepool* would do the trick. The crew could then use their ADF direction-finder needle to home the aircraft onto the source of the radio signal and find the ship. But there was only silence. Two further calls produced no reply. The situation was beginning to look critical. Heathcote felt down for the connectors between his lifejacket and the liferaft contained in his detachable seat.

'Nine Delta Alpha Four, Yankee Charlie, you can tell us where you are, or you can come and collect us when we ditch.'

They were now down to twenty minutes of fuel. There was a collective outtake of breath as *Tidepool* replied giving them a closing vector. Minutes later – a wonderful sight – the huge shape of the ship with its high bridge and refuelling gantries, emerged out of the gloom.

Chapter 9

Coventry and Conveyor
25 May 1982

Argentina's National Day, Tuesday 25 May. The war of attrition was putting pressure on both sides to act decisively. The British were losing ships. The Argentines were losing aircraft. The beachhead at San Carlos was well established, but still needed significant strengthening. The giant container ship Atlantic Conveyor *was due to offload its stores and helicopters next. Its arrival was the key to an early break-out.*

The British knew the Argentines would want to use their National Day to inflict a mortal blow to the task force. The British had already lost three out of only twenty-three available frigates and destroyers. Several more warships were badly damaged. Since the landings, they had lost another Sea Harrier to an accident at sea, an RAF Harrier shot down during a ground attack on Port Howard in West Falkland. By way of reply, the Sea Harriers had knocked down thirteen Argentine air force and navy attack aircraft, with a further four brought down by ground fire, Rapier and Broadsword's *Seawolf missiles.*

* * *

Around San Carlos, the troops of 3 Brigade were well entrenched on the ground: 3 Para at Port San Carlos green beach, 45 Commando at Ajax Bay red beach, 40 Commando at San Carlos blue beach, and 2 Para up in the Sussex Mountains to the south of San Carlos. To break out from the San Carlos area and head the thirty miles or so east toward Stanley, the British needed additional support. But their supplies, stores, ammunition and equipment were still being unloaded, and all too slowly, inhibited by the ferocity of the daytime air raids from the mainland. A huge volume of stores and helicopters awaited out at sea on *Atlantic Conveyor*, while the second wave of troops from 5 Brigade was still several days away, southbound on the cruise ship *QE2*.

The fuel tanker *Tidepool* sailed into San Carlos Water on the morning of 25 May, bringing Mike Crabtree and his flight of two more Wessex. The five Wessex of 845 Squadron were still outnumbered by the ten more powerful Sea Kings of 846 Squadron. After losing three Sea Kings to crashes and the Chile mission, now another was grounded following a misjudged landing near Fanning Head that had broken off the tail. Six were employed lifting endless loads from ship to shore. The other four continued their night-flying role in support of the special forces patrols around the Falkland Islands.

Either way, more helicopters were urgently needed to speed up the advance out of the beachhead, across East Falkland, and on towards the capital Port Stanley. Six more Wessex and four heavy-lift Chinooks were expected to arrive the next day with *Atlantic Conveyor*. The ground forces were relying on them.

Argentine National Day had started well for the British. Defence against air attacks had relied heavily on three continuous and overlapping Sea Harrier patrols to the north, south and centre of West Falkland. The major limitation was the ninety-minute endurance of the Sea Harriers, which included transit time to and from the aircraft carriers *Hermes* and *Invincible*. The Royal Navy was understandably nervous of bringing the carriers in too close to the islands. Sink one or both carriers and the British air defence would be in disarray, rendering the task force impotent.

As the outer layer of the Navy's strategy of defence in depth, the Sea Harriers were extraordinarily effective. The Argentine air force pilots were well aware of the stunning success of Lieutenant Commander Sharkey Ward's Sea Harrier trials unit in aerial dog fights against American F-5 Freedom Fighter and F-15 Eagle jets back in the UK. This fearsome reputation caused dozens of Argentine attackers to turn back simply on detecting the sweep of Sea Harrier's Blue Fox radar. Those prepared to ignore this deterrent ran the gauntlet of the lethal Sidewinder missiles and cannon carried by the 'black death'. The problem was that the long transit to and from patrol left the Sea Harriers with little time on task and the landing force with holes in the outer defence.

Local air defence around San Carlos relied on the 'goalkeeper' ships, sitting bravely exposed out in Falkland Sound as bait, inviting attack. In the role of goalkeeper, *Broadsword* had already notched up one Dagger on the first morning and a possible Skyhawk two days later, claimed jointly with the land-based Rapier. Rapier's own performance had been far less impressive than advertised.

The Royal Navy were also applying their strategy of positioning a Type 22–42 combo as a missile trap way out to the east, at worst to provide early warning and at best to lure and destroy the incoming attack altogether. Attacking jets would first have to avoid the Sea Dart missiles fired at them from the Type-42 destroyer forty miles away. Any that survived would then have to get past the Seawolf missiles fired at them from the Type-22 frigate at close range. Seawolf had already knocked down four Argentine jets. Sea Dart was yet to have its first success.

That morning, the Type-22 HMS *Broadsword*, and Type-42, HMS *Coventry*, were positioned on picket duty north of East Falkland. It was most likely an Argentine Hercules transport plane that first spotted the two ships on radar and reported their position back to the mainland. Soon afterwards three Argentine Skyhawks took the bait. The first Sea Dart launched from *Coventry* at long range knocked out one of the jets. The other two jets turned and fled. The 22–42 combo plan was working.

It was three hours before the next air strike appeared, this time heading for the San Carlos area. Sparky Harden, one of my twenty-one-year-old contemporaries, along with Hector Heathcote, had just arrived on *Tidepool*. It was his first air raid. Hearing the cry: 'Air raid warning red, air raid warning red, SCRAM, SCRAM!' during tasking, he needed no further invitation to roll his Wessex steeply onto its side and flare into a fast-stop landing. Lowering the nose of the aircraft carefully down onto the boggy Falkland soil, he pulled the throttles and started unstrapping. What seemed like seconds later, he was lying on the damp grass next to his Geordie aircrewman 'Smiler' Smiles, listening to the distant screech of jets crossing behind the hills. He watched the flash as a Rapier missile threaded its way across the sky. Four Skyhawks sped through San Carlos Bay out of sight. He couldn't see the Skyhawk that was hit, whether by cannon fire from the ships or Rapier or both. The pilot ejected into the water to be picked up by one of the Royal Marine boats.

The other three aircraft fled to the north, making the

mistake of passing within range of the two ships out to the north of Pebble Island. A second Skyhawk was destroyed by a Sea Dart missile from *Coventry*. Opportunistic, it was their second of the day.

Meanwhile Ric Fox, Pete Manley and Dave Greet had been looking for an opportunity to get on board one of the supply ships for a shower after four days of sleeping rough. During a lull in the tasking they parked Yankee Sierra on a spare flight deck and headed down below. The Chinese laundrymen promised to return their combat clothing clean within the hour. After a well-earned hot shower, they were heading into the galley area when the ship's alarm sounded: 'Action stations, air raid warning red'. Awaiting the return of their clothes, there was little they could do as the ship's crew disappeared to man their posts but help themselves to curry.

It was early afternoon when the next Argentine strike came in. This time the bait was well and truly taken. This strike directly targeted the ships *Coventry* and *Broadsword*, which had been responsible for despatching two of their aircraft that morning.

The first flight of two Argentine Skyhawks sped low out of the distant horizon of Pebble Island, fifteen miles to the south of the ships. High above them, two Sea Harriers on Combat Air Patrol were given directions to intercept them. The leading Sea Harrier was just three miles behind the Skyhawks when he was ordered to break off the attack and leave it to the ship's own missiles. *Coventry*, steaming ahead of *Broadsword*, was the better placed to acquire the low-flying jets. But the radar for her Sea Dart missile failed to get a lock. It was *Broadsword*'s turn. Her radar now locked on to the approaching jets. Just as Seawolf seemed ready to claim its fifth and sixth victims, the computer system inexplicably froze, leaving both ships with only cannon and small-arms fire for defence. The Skyhawks swept towards *Broadsword* and released their bombs.

In the flight-deck hangar of *Broadsword* were two Lynx helicopters, one previously damaged in rough seas, the other the victim of cannon damage from a Dagger attack in San Carlos Bay three days earlier. Outside on the flight deck itself was ranged a third Lynx, borrowed from *Broadsword*'s sister ship HMS *Brilliant*, and the only one of the three in good working order. Just inside the hangar stood Sub-Lieutenant Ray Middleton, another twenty-one-year-old contemporary of mine who had been fast-tracked through training onto the Lynx. His father was Lyn Middleton, captain of the aircraft carrier HMS *Hermes*, some 200 miles to the east.

The flight deck of *Broadsword* was not a good place to be on this day. Middleton Junior watched open-mouthed as bombs left the fast approaching Skyhawk. The jet was so low that the first bomb didn't even enter the water. It just bounced back off the sea with a giant splash and straight through the front of the Lynx, taking the helicopter nose with it. Middleton picked up the hangar telephone to report to the bridge. He found himself completely unable to speak due to shock.

Apart from destroying the front of the Lynx helicopter, the attack by the first two Skyhawks was wholly unsuccessful. Three of the remaining four bombs had missed altogether. The second Skyhawk attack swept in behind them moments later. The frustrated Sea Harriers above now turned their attention to this second pair, only to be ordered once again to break off their intercept.

This time *Broadsword* picked up the attacking jets with her radar and was ready to fire her Seawolf missiles. Usually, the best way to operate the combination of

Coventry's long-range Sea Dart missiles and *Broadsword*'s Seawolf missiles was to keep both ships as close together as possible. Both ships were manoeuvring hard from side to side. However, to *Broadsword*'s dismay, *Coventry*'s manoeuvre took her straight across the bows of *Broadsword* and broke the Seawolf radar's missile lock. *Coventry* was now horribly exposed, firing off Sea Dart in desperation. This time three of the four bombs smashed into *Coventry*'s port side, exploding deep within the ship and killing several of the ship's company. *Coventry* was instantly crippled by the huge explosions, which cut off all power supplies and communication within the ship and filled it with thick black smoke.

Coventry began to list badly as water filled the holes in her port side. There was no need for any announcement. The crew began to abandon ship into their liferafts. Every helicopter operating in the San Carlos area was immediately instructed to head north-east to assist in the rescue. Anti-submarine Sea Kings from nearby Fort Grange were also sent to help. Even some of the night-flying Sea Kings were woken up and scrambled, at subsequent cost to that night's planned special forces insertions.

Simon Thornewill in Victor Alpha was soon leading a gaggle of five Sea Kings past Fanning Head and out to the north-west over the sea. Away from the protection of the San Carlos hills, he was very aware of how exposed they were. A further air strike would make them sitting ducks. Worse, none of the crews were wearing immersion dry suits to protect them if they were shot down and went into the water.

The first Sea Kings on site were confronted by the shocking sight of a large British warship lying at an acute angle, smoke pouring from her superstructure. Orange rafts and men in orange once-only survival suits bobbed up and down in the water, drawn into the ship's side and unable to escape. Helicopters began to gather on the scene. Chief Aircrewman Alf Tupper was lowered down from his Sea King into one liferaft to help winch the survivors up into the helicopter. The rafts were full of very frightened sailors, most of whom were soaking wet and frozen from their unexpected swim in the icy South Atlantic. Some crew members were also burned or wounded. The same sorry story was encountered by other Sea King aircrews dropped into other liferafts. As the survivors were winched up into the aircraft one by one, so much water drained into the Sea Kings' cabins from the once-only suits that pilots could feel it sloshing around and destabilising the aircraft.

Each Sea King took on board twenty or so survivors before heading back to San Carlos, or transferring them to the nearby *Broadsword*. With *Broadsword*'s flight deck out of action, blocked by the bomb-damaged Lynx, a clear area was urgently needed onto which to offload some of *Coventry*'s survivors. The hangar roof now became an impromptu flight deck, too small for landing but big enough for winching.

The round trip, from San Carlos to the stricken *Coventry* and back, was forty minutes. For a Sea King this posed no problem. For a Wessex, the reduced endurance meant thinking very hard about fuel. Heathcote and Gleeson had been transferring tents and other maintenance equipment from *Tidepool* to their new forward operating base when they heard the call on the radio. Heathcote was flying alone because simple operations within the San Carlos made much more sense to fly single pilot, allowing the aircraft to lift a further 200 pounds of fuel or load. With a little over an hour's fuel remaining, they agreed they should 'leg it'. Within a few minutes, they had second thoughts and turned round for a quick refuel on *Tidepool* before setting course for HMS *Coventry*.

Oily Knight and his aircrewman Arthur Balls had also been doing an offload in San Carlos. They had broken off as soon as they heard the request for further aircraft over the radio. Not knowing exactly where to go, they followed the direction taken by the Sea Kings ahead of them in the distance.

By the time they arrived, *Coventry* was floating on its side with *Broadsword* still in attendance, its Lynx sitting forlornly on the flight deck with serious damage to the aircraft nose; it was clear the Lynx wasn't going anywhere. Two other Sea Kings were winching survivors from the water. A few people in their orange lifesuits were trapped right up against the side of the upturned hull, unable to get away. Although there was now no sign of smoke, Balls warned Knight that the ship might go up at any moment.

Transferring people to and from any ship without a serviceable flight deck requires quick thinking from all of the crews. This was especially true when the ship is listing at an angle. Because of the direction of the wind, it seemed best to position the Wessex over the hull of the ship and actually land both front wheels on the upturned hull, leaving the tail suspended over the water behind the survivors. Knight reckoned he could claim this as a deck landing for his pilot's log book.

Balls left Knight to get on with his unorthodox deck landing and concentrated on winching survivors up from the liferaft below him which had become trapped between the bridge front and the foc'sle. The first man to be winched up was being manhandled into the dangling orange strop. But it had been put on the wrong way round, across his chest instead of around his back. Despite shouting and waving at the survivors below to turn the strop around, Balls eventually thought *sod it* and winched him up as it was. Facing inwards instead of outwards made it far harder to get the passenger through the doorway. But there was a reason why the strop had been put on the other way. Viewed from the front, the sailor looked fully dressed and normal. But from the back, it took Balls's breath away. There was nothing. No clothing, no skin. Just a mess of burnt flesh. Even above the roar of the hovering Wessex, Balls could hear the man screaming in agony. He had never felt so helpless. But he had to get on with winching the others. Many other casualties also had burns or broken limbs. The cabin quickly became a scene of mayhem. 'I need to ease the crowding. Let's get some of these guys onto the other ship,' he told Knight.

Knight eased the Wessex away towards *Broadsword*, waved in by the Lynx aircrew who were now making themselves useful on the hangar roof. Time was pressing because of their lack of fuel and the urgent need to get the wounded back to the field hospital at Ajax Bay. It would be much quicker if they didn't have to winch anyone down. Parking one wheel on *Broadsword*'s hangar roof for added stability, Knight skilfully swivelled the Wessex around in the hover so that the less seriously injured survivors could simply jump out onto the roof. The other two wheels were suspended in mid-air. 'Another deck landing,' concluded Knight, before clearing away and accelerating towards San Carlos.

Heathcote and Gleeson arrived just in time to watch the other Wessex balancing precariously on the side of *Broadsword*'s hangar. After D-Day in San Carlos, where he had the impression of seeing very few helicopters at all, Heathcote was surprised to see so many Sea Kings now buzzing around HMS *Coventry*. Hands waving from a liferaft showed them their immediate task. It was just a few days after the rescue from *Ardent*, where hovering fifteen feet over a glassy sea had proved so difficult. This time the surface choppiness and bubbles gave Heathcote a lot more to use as visual references, making hovering above the liferafts a little easier. Gleeson kept up a constant chatter of instructions as he winched survivors into the aircraft. In all the urgency to recover people from the sea and liferafts, Heathcote barely noticed that *Coventry* had rolled slowly over, and was completely inverted.

It was almost one hour since the attack by the Skyhawks. With the additional fuel giving them more time in the air, Heathcote and Gleeson filled their cabin several times, winching survivors down to the hangar roof of *Broadsword*. Making a final sweep of the area, eventually they returned to *Tidepool* back in San Carlos Bay, lost in their own thoughts of what they had just witnessed. Far from receiving a hero's welcome on return, Heathcote received a bollocking from Crabtree for pushing his luck and heading too far out into the unknown on his own.

Nineteen men died in the attack on HMS *Coventry*. A disastrous afternoon for the British forces was about to get a whole lot worse.

Out to the north-east of the Falklands, the battle group positioned itself to despatch *Atlantic Conveyor* into San Carlos to offload the vital helicopters and huge volume of stores. All of the Harriers had left the ship noisily several days earlier and were now operating from the carriers *Hermes* and *Invincible*. Two of *Conveyor*'s helicopters – one of the heavy-lift twin-rotor Chinooks and Yankee Delta, one of the Wessex that had transferred from

RFA *Fort Austin* via *Hermes* – were now airborne on check test-flights

In the cabin of the Wessex sat Royal Marine aircrewman Corporal Ian 'Gus' Tyrrell. He had spent most of the morning wandering around *Hermes* in search of a spare part that was common to both Sea King and Wessex. Somehow finding his way through the maze of corridors, the Sea King engineers told him that they couldn't help after all. The search was in vain. As he wandered empty-handed back up to the flight deck to hitch a lift back to *Conveyor*, his mind switched to the exciting prospect of landing on the Falklands timetabled for the following day. Almost without thinking he paused by the ship's main notice board. Amongst various bits of paper was one headed 'Casualty List'.

He didn't really expect to see any names that he knew. So it took a while to filter in. The name at the top of the list was Corporal M. Love, 846 Squadron. Michael 'Doc' Love had been killed in the terrible Sea King accident a week earlier. The news had been kept from Gus Tyrrell deliberately, though it was inevitable that he would find out somehow. Love and Tyrell were not only best friends and fellow Royal Marine aircrew, but Love was engaged to the twin sister of Tyrrell's wife. They were about to become brothers-in-law.

Back on board *Conveyor*, Tyrell spent most of the afternoon in a daze, writing a letter to his wife's twin sister. Maybe he was sent up for the early evening test flight to get his mind back onto the job. Maybe, more prosaically, it was just that the duty crew who should have been airborne had pulled rank and sent him and pilot Kim Slowe up in their place. The flight clashed with dinner time and the free beers on offer as a farewell from the *Atlantic Conveyor* officers.

* * *

That evening, David Baston and Nick Foster and most of the embarked aircrew were enjoying the hospitality of the Cunard ship's officers, excited in anticipation of testing their skills in action in San Carlos. It was still light as Nick Foster wandered out onto the bridge wing and chatted with merchant seaman Ian North, captain of *Conveyor*, and universally known to all as Captain Birdseye, due to his bushy white beard.

'Don't you worry about it, lad,' said North, detecting some nervousness from Foster about going ashore the next day, 'I was sunk twice in the last lot. You'll be OK.'

An announcement over the ship's tannoy reminded of the final opportunity to take unwanted kit to the 'op baggage' store by 19:45 hours. Foster finished his beer in order to ensure his officers' whites and other non-combat clothing would be returned to the UK. A voice behind him said: 'Come on Foster, have another beer. Are you man or mouse?'

'No, no. I've only got five minutes to get all the way down.'

But Foster needed little encouragement to stay for a fresh tin. The extra Double Diamond probably saved his life.

Thirty-five miles away, two newly refuelled Super Etendards of the Argentine air force had picked up radar returns indicating they had a big target in front of them. It must have looked like one of the British carriers. Just ten minutes after *Coventry* had capsized, Argentine jets had another British ship in their sights. The Argentines only had five Exocet missiles. They had sunk HMS *Sheffield* with one of the first two. The Super Etendards were now heading inbound towards the British task force with two of the remaining three.

Dropping down to low level, the pilots released their

load. The missiles looped away from the jets in a cloud of white smoke before settling down to skim over the water towards the British ships at supersonic speed. The Super Etendards wheeled away, their job done.

It was the Type-21 frigate HMS *Ambuscade*, sister of *Ardent* and *Antelope*, that first detected fast-moving inbound targets, flashing an immediate 'handbrake' warning to the rest of the fleet. On the bridge of *Conveyor*, the action-stations warning bell sounded. Officers and senior ratings dropped their drinks and ran out to the bridge wings in time to see nearby helicopters and ships excitedly firing off rockets and chaff. The Exocets bore on remorselessly, perhaps deflected through the chaff cloud decoys, but then immediately scanning the horizon to acquire a new target.

On board the Wessex Yankee Delta, Tyrrell and Slowe had finished their test flight. They heard the shrill warning 'Air raid warning red' over the radio as they began their final approach to *Conveyor*. The sky was overcast, the sea choppy with a low swell, not especially rough.

Tyrrell sat in the doorway of the Wessex with his camera in hand. He was pleased that he now had good snaps of some of the warships. He was getting ready to take one more of the forward flight deck of *Conveyor* as the Wessex came in to land. A thin dark shape hurtled low towards him across the water, flame jetting from its rear. It was going to pass directly beneath them. His camera was already in hand. All he had to do was point it at the missile and flash off a couple of quick photos as the missile sped below and out of sight.

The brown and red shape made a huge *whump!* as it struck the port quarter ten feet above the waterline and forty feet below the mess where the officers had been drinking beer. A second massive bang followed immediately after the first. Maybe it was the second Exocet. Maybe it was an echo of the first explosion within the giant hold. Nobody could tell.

The immediate effects of the blast were more apparent inside the ship than out. To Nick Foster, flat on his face on the bridge floor, the sound was like a 4.5-inch gun firing from a frigate. The impact made the ship shudder horribly. Even high up on the bridge, the sharp smell of cordite filled the air within seconds. Foster winced as if he'd swallowed lemon juice.

Down below beneath the aft flight deck, Lieutenant Ian 'Lapse' Chapman, another of the Wessex pilots, was in a meeting room discussing disembarkation plans. The terrific explosion and flash knocked him and his colleagues off their feet. Smoke spread throughout the ventilation system with extraordinary speed. Wondering what was happening, Chapman pulled out his torch and told the others to follow him. Crouching to avoid the worst of the dense black smoke, he took a deep breath and bravely climbed the exit ladder up through the pitch blackness where there should have been daylight.

It was now obvious to all what had happened. Exocet. Over the ship's tannoy came the urgent but redundant warning 'Hit the deck, hit the deck'.

From outside, it was hard for Slowe and Tyrrell in their Wessex to believe what they were witnessing as they approached the port side of the ship. There was initially very little smoke coming from the missile strike, but hovering alongside the ship, the gaping hole just above the waterline was very obvious. From the Wessex doorway Tyrrell snapped more photos.

They heard the radio report of a man overboard at the same time as figures on the flight deck started waving down into the water near the missile's entry hole. In the swell, it was hard to spot the casualty. But a quick-thinking serviceman had thrown a liquid oxygen container into the freezing water to mark the position. Tyrrell immediately began to talk Slowe across to a hover over the floundering man, at the same time lowering the orange rescue strop down on the winch wire. In the freezing South Atlantic water, the man struggled to fit the strop properly over his head and around his back. The first attempt ended frustratingly with his body lifted halfway out of the water, only to drop straight back through into the sea. The lightweight strop flitted about in the downdraft. The second attempt was better, if unorthodox, as the man finally grabbed the strop and wrapped it around himself. He hung suspended like a rag doll as he was winched up into the cabin.

Tyrrell hauled the soaking body into the cabin and slid the door shut. The man, an RAF sergeant, was suffering from the onset of hypothermia. He quickly folded up the troop seats and shoved the man up against the cabin heaters that Slowe had switched to full blast, as the helicopter headed off in the direction of *Hermes*.

Making his way to the bridge, David Baston found *Atlantic Conveyor*'s attached senior naval officer, Captain Mike Layard. They looked down onto the huge forward deck spread out in front of them. A Wessex stood ranged between the stacked containers pointing aft and ready to go. They briefly discussed the possibility of getting the Wessex airborne. But with smoke and flames billowing from below and to their left, the ship's company had been split in two, one forward on the flight deck and one aft from the superstructure. It would be extremely dangerous for any pilot up on the island to get forward to the helicopter.

Royal Navy and Royal Fleet Auxiliary ships are all equipped with firefighting and damage control systems specifically designed to contain major damage. As a merchant ship *Atlantic Conveyor* had none of these. It was becoming obvious that everyone would be leaving imminently. Baston ran down to his cabin and put on his goon suit, the waterproof flying overalls that would protect him in the freezing water.

By now, Slowe and Tyrrell had returned from *Hermes* after dropping off their casualty. People were clambering down ladders attached to the stern of *Conveyor* and into liferafts suspended close to the ship's side at an uncomfortable angle. The ropes holding the liferaft weren't quite long enough for the fifty-foot drop. The frigate HMS *Alacrity* had positioned herself close in and was beginning to draw some of the liferafts across.

Slowe adjusted his approach to make for the group of men on the clear area of the flight deck, right up forward. As Tyrrell began paying out the winch, he realised it would be far quicker to land. Smoke shrouded the back end of the ship but the flight deck seemed clear. Both of them were well aware that the bomb store lay immediately underneath the flight deck. Neither mentioned it.

Maintainers and flight-deck crew watched anxiously as the helicopter came in to land next to them. As soon as the wheels touched, Tyrrell held up both hands. 'Ten,' he mouthed, waving them in. With the fuel they were carrying, he reckoned that was all they could take.

'Take in three more,' Slowe told him.

The ship was on fire. With all the seats up they could make extra space for casualties.

As Slowe increased power to lift off, the men still on the deck leant into the gale-force downdraft created by the helicopter. He was acutely aware he was leaving them behind. Realising he had power to spare, he immediately dropped the Wessex back onto the deck.

'I can do two more.' Tyrrell held up two fingers to wave in the extra men.

Yankee Delta finally lifted clear of *Conveyor* with fifteen passengers crammed into the cabin. As the Wessex circled around to head for *Hermes,* Tyrrell watched a dark blue anti-submarine Sea King approach for the next pick-up. 'Best we don't tell them what's underneath,' he said to his pilot.

Slowe now set up his approach to land on *Hermes*. But with the extra passengers, the Wessex was way over its normal maximum weight. Once in the descent, they would be committed to land. Tyrrell stood in the doorway giving a running commentary on their approach. Because of the weight, they were unlikely to be able to hover. Slowe radioed his final approach to the carrier. 'Yankee Delta, we're really heavy with survivors. Request you clear space for us to do a run-on landing.'

'Roger.'

Just as they were fifty feet from the deck, the *Hermes* flight-deck director crossed his hands above his head. It was a wave-off. It didn't matter why. They were now being refused permission to land. The ship might have been about to turn. Harriers might be about to land. There might be some other emergency. But whatever the reason, it was too late. The helicopter was committed to its descent. They would either land on the ship or ditch in the sea. If they made it in one piece, they would have to deal with the consequences later.

'Yankee Delta, I'm committed,' radioed Slowe.

The ship didn't seem to be turning. He ran the Wessex onto the aircraft carrier's deck and braked to a halt. The survivors spilled out of the cabin and onto the flight deck. The flight-deck crew marshalled them towards the superstructure where they could be gathered up. The wave-off now seemed forgotten. As soon as the survivors were clear, Slowe lifted off again and returned towards *Atlantic Conveyor*. The light was now beginning to fade.

Rushing up to *Conveyor*'s bridge, Lieutenant Nick Foster grabbed one of the orange survival suits and was about to put it on. The Exocet had hit the ship thirty minutes earlier. Smoke and flames were spreading from beneath them and there were intermittent explosions somewhere down below. Foster wondered when the weapons at the front of the ship would blow.

The two captains, North and Layard, were standing out on the bridge wing. 'What do you think about going down and flashing that up and getting airborne, Nick?' asked Layard.

Foster looked down at the Wessex beyond the swirling smoke. 'Sir, if you're ordering me, I'll do it.'

Even if he could make it through the smoke to get to the aircraft, he worried that the thing might not start, leaving him stranded on the front deck. He'd also have to take off the four strops that held the helicopter on the rolling deck before he climbed up to get the rotors started. Not a good idea.

'If you're just asking, sir, then I'll decline.'

'I'm just asking.'

Foster overheard the two captains discussing the worsening situation. They agreed it was time they left. North calmly picked up the tannoy microphone. There was no sense of panic in his voice. 'The fire is out of control. We are going to abandon ship. Make your way to the starboard side where there are ladders and liferafts already deployed.'

Nick Foster headed back down to his cabin only to find David Baston complaining that he couldn't get the zip up on his goon suit.

'What's wrong with this?' he said, tugging at it frustratedly.

'Try reading the name tag, David. Look – Lieutenant Foster, not Lieutenant Commander Baston.'

'Bugger,' said Baston.

Once safely zipped up in the right suits, both men put on their lifejackets and fighting order. Grabbing rifles and 9mm Browning pistols, they headed down to deck level. As they ran down the stairway, they checked the others had heard the message to leave.

At deck level, ship and flight crew were already scrambling down the long drop to the liferafts below. There was a lot of smoke. Explosions were becoming more frequent, now directly below their feet.

Perched on the side of the ship in his goon suit, Foster felt remarkably relaxed about the surging water far below. Years of underwater escape drills in the dunker back at Portsmouth gave him confidence as he guided some of the younger men over the side and down the ladders. Close by, *Alacrity* was vainly firing jets of water into *Conyeyor*'s smoking hull.

As Baston clambered over the side and down, behind him, on the rear flight deck, he heard the whine of a power unit starting up of its own accord. 'Bloody hell, it must be hot to set that off,' he thought.

Halfway down the rope ladder, he realised there was no more ladder beneath him. It must have been sliced away when *Alacrity* bumped up alongside. Nearby explosions were blowing small holes in the ship's side. Baston let go of the rope and dropped into the water, to be hauled into a liferaft by one of his aircrew. As the only one with a knife, he then hopped around the dangling liferafts cutting them free.

Foster watched in horror as the ship's Chinese

laundrymen jumped over the side with their lifejackets already inflated. The two men vanished immediately beneath the surface, leaving the buoyant jackets floating pathetically.

'Time for me to go.'

Just as he began to clamber down one of the ladders, there was a huge explosion right next to him. A hole appeared in the side. The gas bottles inside the ship were exploding in the heat. He saw another ladder further down the deck and decided to try it. As Foster ran, he could see nobody else around. It looked like he was last on board. Smoke and flames were getting worse. Halfway down this ladder, another canister exploded, this time directly beneath him, blowing the bottom half of the ladder away. There was just enough rope to get a little further down. Seeing a liferaft now eight feet below him, he let go, and landed in it, to the displeasure of its occupants. He hadn't even got his feet wet.

Just as had happened with *Coventry* hours earlier, the liferafts now found themselves being sucked back towards the crippled ship in the swell. Only this time the rounded shape of the giant container ship high above them was sucking them underneath the overhanging stern. It was terrifying, but far worse for those in lifejackets still in the water. The two captains were submerged by the dark hull. Miraculously, Mike Layard surfaced right next to Nick Foster who grabbed him and hauled him on board. Ian North was never seen again.

A body, one of the ship's officers, floated past the liferaft. There were flecks of foamy vomit around his mouth. Unable to lift him on board in his water-filled survival suit, Nick Foster clung onto him. Maybe a kiss of life might have saved him, maybe not. He was dead by the time they reached *Alacrity*.

With cold fingers, and bodies frozen by the water and pulling on the thin ropes that held the liferafts, climbing the scrambling nets was now a major hurdle. David Baston had reached the top of the netting when somebody trod on his frozen fingers. He fell back into the water. Hands grabbed at him from the liferaft and helped him up successfully a second time.

After a final check for people on the forward deck, Kim Slowe and Gus Tyrrell flew back to *Hermes* only to be told to hold off during a Harrier strike on Port Stanley. Apart from being allowed to land for fuel, it was two and a half hours later into the night that they were finally cleared to shut down. They passed the time chatting about life back home. Separated from their shipmates, little did they know that they had been recorded as MIA, Missing in Action.

When they did finally land and shut down on *Hermes*, they were taken from the aircraft and treated as survivors. Gus Tyrrell had to hand in his camera and his valuable photos. Both of them had to give in their flying clothing for use as spares. They decided to pass on film night; the movie showing on *Hermes* that evening was *The Poseidon Adventure*.

The Wessex aircrew from *Atlantic Conveyor* never actually made it to land, although they came close. HMS *Alacrity* spent the next two nights conducting runs up and down Falkland Sound. The day after the Exocet strike, the ship's off-duty crew and some of the *Conveyor* survivors assembled on deck for the burial of the three bodies they had recovered at sea. It was a deeply moving occasion. The following day, Thursday 27 May, the survivors transferred to the tanker *British Tay* to sail to Ascension Island.

Their eventual return to the UK was a classic story of

inter-service rivalry. The RAF survivors from *Atlantic Conveyor* were given new uniforms for their triumphant return to Brize Norton. They were to leave the RAF VC-10 aircraft first for the waiting media. But when they saw the smartly dressed young men emerge, the welcome band stopped playing, disappointed that this was merely the aircraft crew. Then the Royal Navy aircrew and engineers emerged, unshaven and dishevelled, the image of true survivors, to roars of applause. It wasn't the stage-managed RAF return that made all the papers. It was the photo of Royal Marine Gus Tyrrell's welcome hug from his wife.

The fires burning inside the stern section of *Atlantic Conveyor* eventually reached the bomb store underneath the forward flight deck a day after the double Exocet strike. The explosion blew off the nose of the ship. The giant stern and superstructure sank into the darkness of the South Atlantic the following night.

As well as the tents and portable runway, ten helicopters were lost – three Chinooks, six Wessex and a Lynx. Two helicopters survived. Another crew could be found to fly the Wessex. But the unique capability of the Chinook to carry huge loads made it an exception. The sole surviving Chinook was too important to lose. The RAF crew stayed behind on *Hermes* with the intention of disembarking to San Carlos as quickly as possible.

Twelve men died as a result of the missile strike on *Atlantic Conveyor*. They included two young 845 Squadron engineers, Air Engineering Mechanic Adrian Anslow and Leading Air Engineering Mechanic Don Pryce. Most shocking was that nine of the deaths happened in the water and only three on board. There were plenty of liferafts. There was plenty of time. It seemed so avoidable.

Chapter 10

Break-out
26–29 May 1982

The loss of Atlantic Conveyor *was a stunning blow to the forces on land. Three Commando Brigade had been relying on the extra helicopter support to airlift them nearer to the capital Port Stanley. They would now have to do it on foot.*

The loss of HMS Coventry *was an equally stunning blow to the forces at sea. Four out of twenty-three British warships had now been sunk. Several others were badly damaged.*

Fearing stalemate, the politicians and military commanders back in the UK now demanded progress on land and some sort of victory. On Wednesday 26 May, invasion commander Brigadier Julian Thompson gave the orders to move out. Three Para and 45 Commando were to head for Stanley. Two Para were to take Goose Green.

After such terrible losses it was hard to imagine that Tuesday 25 May would prove to be such a turning point in the war to regain the Falkland Islands. The British forces were now firmly established on their beachhead at

San Carlos. Although it wasn't appreciated at the time, the Argentine air force and navy had suffered such traumatic losses themselves – losing ten Skyhawks and sixteen Mirages – that further air attacks on the islands would become sporadic. Argentine ground forces at Goose Green had been successfully constrained, and the destruction of their helicopters by the ground-attack Harriers had made it all but impossible for them to reinforce troops by air. Argentine forces no longer had the means to dislodge them.

Concerns had already been growing in London that the British advance had become bogged down at the beachhead. There were also worries that, in the absence of any sort of land battle, an enforced international settlement might leave the British stranded without securing the islands. Little of this was communicated to the forces on the ground. What was conveyed was an assumption that, having landed, the British troops should move out towards Stanley immediately. It was an utterly impractical expectation, given the nature of the terrain and extent to which the logistical supply line was already stretched.

Brigadier Julian Thompson was under no illusions that the landing forces needed to have a strong base from which to extend. Only after unloading stores, ammunition and supplies could the vital few helicopters be released to move the troops forward. It was frustrating to all that the build-up of the Brigade Maintenance Area was slower than expected. Part of the reason was that supply ships were remaining in the San Carlos anchorage for the minimum time, sometimes lingering only during daytime. Also, as Tim Stanning had wryly forecast during the planning stage at Ascension, the number of helicopters able to operate was limited by the number of available decks. The loss of so many helicopters with *Atlantic Conveyor* now made it virtually impossible to move 3 Brigade by air. With the next wave of support helicopters still en route from the UK, Thompson now had little choice but to instruct his commanders to move out east, on foot, across the Falkland bog. He was also given clear instructions from London to engage the Argentines in order to achieve some sort of land victory. The Argentine forces at Goose Green held no strategic significance and were to have been sidestepped by the British in their move towards the main objective of Port Stanley. However, Goose Green, some twelve miles south of the beachhead, was also the obvious target for the politically desirable land battle. Thompson held a meeting with his commanders on Wednesday 26 May and instructed 2 Para to proceed immediately.

There were still only fifteen troop-carrying helicopters available on the Falklands, ten Sea Kings and the five Wessex.

Because the larger Sea Kings were operating as a squadron, the jobs they were assigned to do could be coordinated. However, the Wessex were operating without any sense of coordination, mostly making it up as they went along. Pete Manley and his Wessex gunship had set up shop at Ajax Bay on the day after the landings. Without maintenance or support, he had been operating largely on his wits and negotiating skills. Mike Crabtree and two more Wessex joined him there three days later.

Rather than running around picking up odd jobs, it made sense to coordinate what they had to do. So on the morning of Wednesday 26 May, Manley got himself dropped off onto the command ship HMS *Fearless* to go and speak to helicopter tasking commander, Tim Stanning. Walking into the operations room, he was delighted to see Jack Lomas, who had come on board for exactly the same reason. 'Jack's here,' thought Manley. 'Dave Baston's gone home. So where's the boss?'

It was the first time he'd wondered where his commanding officer might be. In fact Lieutenant Commander Roger Warden was stuck 4,000 miles north, running the resupply operation at Ascension Island. Lomas was now the senior Wessex flight commander on the Falklands. 'You'd better get everyone to come over and join us. We're on the other side of the bay,' said Lomas.

When they arrived two days earlier, Lomas and his two Wessex had joined up with the Sea Kings at Old Creek House, some two miles north of the settlement at San Carlos. Now with five Wessex together in one place, 845 Squadron was beginning to feel a bit more like a single unit once more. Royal Navy *junglie* squadrons are accustomed to operating helicopters out in the field, living in tents, being flexible, making do, and playing at soldiers. But two and a half years on exchange with the Army Air Corps in Germany had shown Lomas that it could be done so much better. He needed somebody who could kick arse and concentrate on the military side of things, somebody who didn't have to worry about flying or aviation or engineering. That was why he had brought along Warrant Officer Tommy Sands RM. Sands had already proved his worth as an additional unofficial aircrewman on the way south. Now it was time for him to do his day job.

The threat of intruders on the ground was very real. Some of the Argentine commandos who had been driven off Fanning Head on the night of the landings had not yet been captured. They were still at large north of Port San Carlos. Just a day earlier, an Argentine marine corps officer had been picked up by a patrol in the hills just behind the Wessex base. It made aircrew wary of wandering too far away.

The threat of bombing from the air was also real but a lower priority threat. Had the aircraft remained on the ground for long during the day, they would have been dispersed to protect them from air attack. But as darkness fell, it made more sense to keep the aircraft fairly close together in order to keep a tight perimeter.

A whole host of security procedures needed to be implemented. Sands insisted on a general stand-to at dusk and dawn in anticipation of enemy attack. The exception was for senior engineer Chief Petty Officer Stewart Goodall, who was given leeway to continue aircraft maintenance during these times, provided his engineers kept their rifles at hand. He even interrupted a casual conversation between Jack Lomas and Mike Crabtree out in the open, giving them a stern warning that the two flight commanders needed to be separate from one another.

A sentry roster was set up to man the machine-gun posts. Nerves ran high on watch at night. Arthur Balls and Steve MacNaughton had already spent an entire four-hour watch lying shoulder-to-shoulder, staring out into the darkness without speaking a single word. Early on their first morning in the camp, Crabtree and Heathcote wandered casually back into the main part of the camp from their two-man tent. They didn't hear the sentry call out in the dark 'Who goes there?' They did, however, hear the sound of a machine gun being cocked. It encouraged them to be a lot clearer about identifying themselves.

Nervous tension in the camp also produced its lighter moments. The communal fire used for the evening meal had somehow reignited itself during the night, providing a nice flickering target for any Argentine observers. The aircrew sleeping in the ten-man tent rushed outside,

woken by the sentry ringing through on the field telephone. The fire was quickly extinguished with four
streams of aircrew pee.

However, *junglie* pragmatism on the ground was not
shared by all. On the afternoon of 26 May, they were also
joined by a large visitor in the shape of Bravo November,
the huge double-rotor RAF Chinook helicopter. Having
lost all their support equipment on *Atlantic Conveyor*, the
Chinook crew had parked up for the night on the deck
of *Hermes*, along with the surviving Wessex, Yankee Delta.
There was no question of despatching the RAF Chinook
crew home. The huge aircraft, capable of doing the work
of five Sea Kings, was desperately needed onshore. They
had flown all the way in to San Carlos from out at sea
and would need a home.

Jack Lomas was airborne as he heard Bravo November
given instructions to join the Wessex at Old House Creek.
He had a pretty good idea that his under-equipped team
would end up looking after the RAF crew as well. 'I know,'
he thought to himself sardonically. 'Camp with Lomas.
He's got nothing either.'

On hearing that the Chinook was inbound, Lomas got
himself down to the tents to give them a warm welcome.
The only sensible option for the night was to cram the
Wessex crews into the existing tents and free up space for
the Chinook crew, led by Squadron Leader Dick Langworthy.

Lomas began to brief them about their allocated positions for stand-to and the arcs of fire into which they
could shoot.

'But we have RAF Regiment to do that.'

'Do you have RAF Regiment here?' asked Lomas.

'No'.

'Then you're defending your aircraft and yourselves.'

'That's very irregular.'

Although seeming put out at being asked to perform this unfamiliar role on the ground, they did as requested and mucked in as best they could with the few people they had. In the days that followed, the Chinook and its crew were to prove their worth one hundred times over. Lomas and the other Navy aircrew were unstinting in their praise for the RAF aircrew's flying of giant loads at low level in the mountains, often in appalling weather conditions. Their senior engineer and maintenance team, who arrived later without spares, performed brilliantly in keeping the Chinook flying all hours of the day and night. In the air, they were 'bloody fantastic', said Lomas.

Another of the great success stories of the Falklands war, Bravo November was the only Chinook to survive the sinking of the *Atlantic Conveyor* and the only RAF helicopter on the islands. The crews did their service proud. The Chinook could carry huge loads. For example, four 'bollocks' dangling underneath contained eight tons of aviation fuel, allowing our twenty-five Royal Navy Wessex to operate far more-efficiently on the front line.

*   *   *

As dawn broke on Thursday 27 May, 2 Para were already halfway from the Sussex Mountains to Goose Green, lying up for shelter in the abandoned house and sheds of Camilla Creek House. Back in San Carlos, the Royal Marines of 45 Commando were boarding the landing craft that would take them across the bay from Ajax Bay red beach to get to Port San Carlos green beach. They were then to set off on foot from Port San Carlos in parallel with 3 Para towards the settlement of Teal Inlet. It was the beginning of an epic twenty-five mile 'yomp' (for the Commandos) and 'tab' (for the Paras) across the boggy Falkland peat, carrying up to 120 pounds of unimaginably heavy bergens and weapons with them.

For the Paras at Camilla Creek House a few miles south, the day started badly. The early morning BBC World Service news had announced that British para-troops stood poised to attack the Argentine positions at Darwin and Goose Green. It was an appallingly ill-judged leak, the source of which has never been estab-lished, and an utterly irresponsible broadcast by the BBC. Two Para's Commanding Officer, Lieutenant Colonel 'H' Jones, turned on the BBC reporter Robert Fox and threatened to sue the Secretary of State for Defence if a single life was lost as a result.

In fact there had been several days of open speculation by the British media about such an attack. The Argentines were already reinforcing the garrison using their few remaining helicopters. They were right to do so. Three days earlier, under pressure from London, Brigadier Thompson had briefed Jones to conduct a raid on the Argentine forces at Darwin. D Squadron SAS were already being extracted from the area, where they had created the diversion for the San Carlos landings, and inserted by Nigel North and his Sea King night-flyers onto Mount

Kent in preparation for the assault on Stanley. Two Para were reconnoitring the route to Darwin on foot when the news came through of the sinking of *Atlantic Conveyor*. Thompson cancelled the raid, to the fury of Jones. But renewed political pressure now gave the Paras the opportunity for a full-scale attack on Darwin and Goose Green.

It's improbable that the ill-advised BBC World Service broadcast caused the Argentines to change their plans for the defence of Goose Green; the capture of a senior Argentine reconnaissance officer, out on patrol in a Landrover, revealed that the Argentines were well aware the British were coming. However, it did change the plans of the Paras, who were immediately forced to leave the shelter of their buildings and dig in. The stage was set for the first set-piece battle by a British Army unit since the Korean War battle of the Imjin River in 1951, in which, in their last stand against overwhelming Chinese forces, 620 infantrymen of the 1st Battalion Gloucestershire Regiment, 'The Glorious Glosters', were killed.

Late in the morning of Thursday 27 May, two RAF Harriers ran in low towards the airfield at Goose Green to soften up the Argentine defences. One of the Harriers was hit by cannon fire during a bombing run. They were the same Argentine air defence guns that had knocked out Nick Taylor's Sea Harrier on the very first raid. The damaged jet flew on for several miles with the engine on fire before the pilot, Squadron Leader Bob Iveson, ejected. He was picked up by a British helicopter three days later.

Until the Paras and Marines of 3 Brigade had begun their break-out from the San Carlos area, Wessex and Sea King helicopters were mostly operating within the bay and surrounding hills. Long-range sorties for the special forces by Bill Pollock's Sea King night-flyers were the main exception to this.

Aircrew referred to the list of jobs they were given to do as 'tasking'. Tasking for each day tended to start with a radio call to *Fearless*, whose staff gathered requests and allocated the helicopters according to priority. Some of the aircraft bases had an attached Mobile Air Operations Team (MAOT), for whom allocating jobs to aircraft was their bread and butter.

For the first few days at FOB Whale, Wessex tasking was received over the radio by one of the aircrew. Some aircraft were given a particular role for the day, such as HDS (Helicopter Delivery Service) around the San Carlos area or casevac between the field hospital and the hospital ship SS *Uganda* out in Falkland Sound. Other aircraft were given specific jobs. A typical start to the day might involve landing on the deck of *Fearless* and taking advantage of the opportunity to refuel. Somebody would then bring in a list of instructions to the aircrewman who would discuss it with his pilot. The aircrew would then work their way through the list until complete.

A typical task would be 'loads from *Sir Galahad* to green beach grid 123456', or 'Rapier resupply red beach grid 234567, destinations as advised'; or '40 Commando troop move blue beach two grid 345678 to Sussex Mountains'. During the day, *Fearless* might radio a helicopter to switch to another job. And if an aircraft had an empty return journey, the aircrew would always radio ahead to offer the space. In this way, an awful lot of useful additional work took place. When aircraft ran out of instructions, they would simply return to their forward base.

But tasking was also a major source of frustration. Although all *junglie* aircrew were highly proficient at moving loads and stores, they were not being used to move troops forward. *Junglies* are trained for front-line operations. The Royal Marines yomping out of Port San Carlos knew this. Both troops and aircrew wondered why at least some of the helicopters weren't giving them a lift. Jack Lomas went out of his way to find out why his boys were still spending all their time offloading ships. The response was very clear: building up beachhead supplies remained the priority. Wessex would not be released from ship control to land control until later on. The troops would have to walk.

There were also minor frustrations of working with units not accustomed to helicopters. But these rarely lasted. The Rapier air defence teams had drawn a very short straw indeed, living in miserable muddy trenches high up on the hills above San Carlos, often in cloud and freezing drizzle. Resupplying each of these cells with fuel and food was a vital task. But sending aircraft back to the same site for the fourth time because somebody had forgotten something did not endear ground troops to aircrew. Lomas made sure his aircrew and the Rapier teams both understood that aircraft were to be used for the job and not the day. Rapier resupply for weeks thereafter became a vastly more efficient operation.

Venturing too far inland was another issue for aircrew unwilling to risk an unnecessary encounter with enemy ground troops. During air raids, pilots were very aware of the tension between finding a sheltered gulley close to the beachhead but far enough away to avoid getting shot by their own side. The incident with Yankee Tango's shattered windscreen convinced crews to push outward a little further. The real threat from the ships was definitely greater than a perceived threat from the enemy, who may or may not be just over the hills.

For aircraft caught out on the Ajax Bay side of San Carlos Bay, taking shelter from air raids was much less of a problem. With both 2 Para and 45 Commando occupying the hills to the south and west, aircraft could hide as far into the hills as they liked. It was where Pete Manley and Ric Fox had holed out during the many air raids of the first few days.

With so few pilots and aircraft in the San Carlos area, single pilot operations made sense. This freed up Jack Lomas and Oily Knight to take turns running operations on the ground. It kept a few fresh pilots in reserve. And it added some ten per cent to the available payload, whether in extra fuel or extra stores. The flying was straightforward enough, but still exciting. Operating alone showed the incredible responsibility and trust placed in the skill and capability of twenty-one-year-olds, including junior pilots Heathcote, Harden, Judd and Morton, who in some cases were just months out of training:

Now late in the afternoon of Thursday 27 May, Hector Heathcote sat alone at the controls of Yankee Charlie. The Wessex was parked facing north, rotors running, on a concrete hardstanding next to the newly converted field hospital, the red and green life machine. Behind the hospital and up the side of the hill at Ajax Bay was the Brigade Maintenance Area, destination for much of the vast amount of equipment and ammunition offloaded from the ships in San Carlos Water. Surrounding the helicopter were eight-foot-high piles of 105mm gun ammunition. In the cabin of the Wessex, Heathcote's Royal Marine aircrewman Kev Gleeson was poised to unload the pile of eighty empty fuel jerrycans they had just brought down from the Rapier sites on top of the hill. They were waiting for groundcrew to show them which full replacements they should be taking.

Days of Argentine air raids had made them less fearful of the warnings. They were still very much alert but blasé. Hearing the transmission 'Air raid warning red, SCRAM!', they thought it best to stay where they were.

Over his right shoulder, Heathcote saw the first pair of Skyhawks swoop low out of the Sussex Mountains and into the bay area. But instead of heading for the ships, this time their target was the headquarters area at San Carlos on the far side. He watched at least two explosions bloom amongst the settlement houses. 'I think we'd better get out of here,' he said to Gleeson, both of them suddenly and acutely aware that they were sitting amidst piles of live ammunition.

Gleeson called 'clear' and they lifted off, dropping the aircraft nose steeply in order to accelerate away. Heathcote immediately rolled the Wessex round to the left, staying just twenty feet above the hillside and heading back down to the south. Pulling the nose of the Wessex back into a high flare to kill his speed, he brought the big helicopter gently down onto a flat area of grass. They were now 400 yards from the Brigade Maintenance Area facing downhill into the bay.

As they landed, a second pair of Skyhawks sped past from right to left in front of them. Heathcote had a clear view of the bombs dropping below the jets and slamming into exactly the piece of hardstanding they had been on thirty seconds earlier. A massive explosion filled the air as one of the bombs set off a pile of the artillery shells. Two other bombs dropped into the field hospital, mercifully without exploding, where they were to remain for the duration of the war.

For Heathcote and Gleeson, it was their third miraculous escape. Together with Mike Crabtree, they had survived the streams of tracer fire on the night of the landings and then the following day being strafed by a Mirage down both sides of the aircraft. Now, one week later, they were just seconds away from being bombed by Skyhawks. Had the Skyhawk pairs attacked in different order, Heathcote and Gleeson would have been killed.

The Skyhawk attack on the ground forces at San Carlos blue beach and Ajax Bay red beach proved to be the only Argentine air strike of Thursday 27 May. One of the four Skyhawks was sufficiently crippled by gunfire from the assault ships *Fearless* and *Intrepid* that the pilot ejected soon after crossing Falkland Sound. Uninjured, he spent four days on the run in West Falkland before finding Argentine forces. Seven British soldiers were killed in the Skyhawk attack, one Royal Engineer on the San Carlos side of the bay and six Royal Marines at Ajax Bay. The explosions continued on through into the night as the pallets of shells destined for 2 Para burned.

Pete Manley and his crew, who had been based at Ajax Bay for the previous few days, were fortunate not to have been caught up in the attack. Shortly before the strike, they had been despatched with their Wessex, Yankee Sierra, to insert a MAOT radio team into Camilla Creek House. On the return journey, they collected the captured Argentine reconnaissance prisoners and returned them to brigade headquarters back in San Carlos. Crossing over the Sussex Mountains and to within four miles of the Argentine positions meant flying 'nap of the earth', staying as close to the ground as they dared, making use of valleys, folds and gulleys, and slowing to sixty knots or less.

In the end their mission was uneventful. But being sent up to the front line gave Manley hope that Yankee Sierra would at last be used in her role as a gunship. Armed with two-inch rockets, the Wessex could lay down a fearsome barrage of twenty-eight rockets. Even if the rockets were famously inaccurate, the high explosive would fill an area the size of a football field. At worst, it would keep heads down and frighten the living daylights out of any enemy troops in the firing line. At best, it would do serious damage.

But even if the Paras had asked for a gunship, the Wessex was soon taken out of the action altogether. As darkness fell, Yankee Sierra was shut down on the deck of *Fearless* as she sailed out of San Carlos. The Wessex had been earmarked to collect the incoming land forces commander, Major General Jeremy Moore RM, from HMS *Antrim*. It seemed odd to Manley that a key airborne weapon system, ideal for supporting the attack on Goose Green, was now no longer available. It was a curious use of resources and a potentially expensive oversight for the Paras.

It was not the only misallocation of helicopters. Oily Knight, Noddy Morton and Arthur Balls spent a very uncomfortable evening on a 'special mission' flying up and down Falkland Sound in pitch darkness, with their Wessex fitted with a thermal-image camera in the cabin doorway. The plan was to try and identify Argentine observation posts that might have been reporting the position of the British ships to the incoming Argentine jets. Just as Crabtree and Heathcote had noted on the night of the landings, the imager failed to distinguish between the heat of a sheep and the heat of a man. Morton had only a rifle night sight that could resolve little more than occasional blobs. The crew listened nervously as the camera operator reported lots of sightings. It seemed a fruitless task.

Having satisfied the operator, the crew still had to find their way back into San Carlos in complete darkness. With the aircraft lights switched off, they expected to be shot down at any minute. Morton could barely make out the outline of Fanning Head and the various ships with his rifle sight. It was just enough to pass instructions on to Knight, who could see nothing at all. As they slowed their approach towards HMS *Fearless*, it was touch and go whether they would have to use their bright landing lights, ruining the blackout that concealed the position of the ships in the bay from Argentine observers. Flying blind in the darkness, it was only in the final few yards that Knight could pick out the outline of the ship.

During the night, the Paras moved into their final positions ready to attack the narrow isthmus of land containing the settlements of Darwin and Goose Green. The night-flying Sea Kings lifted three 105mm howitzer guns and ammunition into position. No other *junglie* support was allocated for the forthcoming battle. To Brigadier Thompson, the amphibious force commander, Goose Green was a sideshow, a politically induced diversion from the main task of moving east towards Port Stanley. Other than offering naval gunfire support from HMS *Arrow*, 2 Para would have to do it alone.

The first few phases of the six-phase attack went according to plan, with the four ninety-man paratroop companies moving forward one by one, leapfrogging one another. It was only in the last few hours of darkness that the Paras hit trouble, closing in on well dug-in enemy positions on Darwin Hill. Fog out at sea prevented any assistance from ground-attack Harriers. Worse, *Arrow's* gun jammed, removing the ability to illuminate the battle-field for the 81mm mortars.

The Paras were now completely on their own. They were also pinned down by machine-gun fire as first light dawned on the morning of Friday 28 May. A failed attempt to break the deadlock led to the loss of several men, including the Para adjutant and a company second-in-command.

Impatient at the loss of momentum, Lieutenant Colonel 'H' Jones stood up and charged the enemy trench, with his bodyguard following behind him, but was cut down by machine-gun fire. A radio message was shouted to battalion headquarters 'Sunray is down'. There was disbelief among 2 Para that their commanding officer had been shot.

In the Argentine trenches, ammunition and morale were running low as the morning wore on. Their machine-gun posts on Darwin Hill were now overrun with help from well-aimed 66mm rockets fired from the shoulder. Within hours, the Paras had taken the high ground. Three Argentine Pucaras now swept over the scene, having taken off earlier from the airport at Port Stanley. Their first target was the gun position just to the north of Goose Green. The British gunners managed to drive off this attack, firing more shoulder-launched rockets, this time Blowpipe.

Two of the small Scout helicopters had been ferrying ammunition to the guns from San Carlos. They were now told to go further towards the battlefield and pick up the body of Jones and other wounded Paras.

As the Scouts approached their pick-up point, two more Pucaras swept past them, quickly turning for a second pass. The Argentine turboprops now lined up for a head-on attack on the two helicopters. It was the worst nightmare for the British pilots. The slow-speed Pucaras would keep coming at them until they had finished off their target. There was simply nowhere to run.

The Pucaras singled out one of the Scouts, Delta Romeo,

firing a deadly blast of machine-gun fire. The pilot, Lieutenant Richard Nunn RM, was killed immediately. Delta Romeo, now out of control, crashed and bounced across the grassy terrain, throwing clear the crewman Sergeant Belcher who had been badly hit by the machine-gun fire.

Watching this appalling scene unfold next to him, Captain Jeff Niblett had no choice in the other Scout, Delta Tango, than to land immediately. If he stayed in the air the Pucaras would chase him down. But the Pucaras broke off their attack and peeled away to the north. They had seen the second Scout on the ground and assumed they had shot it down as well. It was little consolation that the lead Pucara crashed into a mountain on return to Stanley. The wreckage was found four years later. The other Pucara returned safely.

The injured Belcher was loaded into Delta Tango and taken back to the field hospital at Ajax Bay. Niblett then returned to Camilla Creek House, leading two gunship Scouts armed with anti-tank missiles. The weapons were not fired. For his 'dashing leadership and courage throughout the battle', Lieutenant Colonel Jones was awarded a posthumous Victoria Cross. Lieutenant Nunn, posthumously, and Captain Niblett were both awarded the Distinguished Flying Cross.

By mid-afternoon, 2 Para were closing in on Goose Green airfield and the settlement. The soldiers were still fighting from trench to trench. To the south of the airfield came the disparaging sound of Argentine helicopters, a Puma and Hueys landing troop reinforcements, suggesting the battle had a way to run. Two Aeromacchi jets appeared out of nowhere. The Para soldiers watched the aircraft make their low-level runs towards them. The cannon shells and rockets streaked past, exploding harmlessly in the soft

Falkland peat. A quick-thinking Royal Marine from the attached air defence unit turned and fired a Blowpipe missile at one of the retreating jets. The high-speed missile roared away from him, quickly catching up with the slower jet as it retreated into the distance. The Aeromacchi dived towards the ground and exploded.

Two more airplanes followed up the attack minutes later. This time it was propeller-driven Pucaras crossing the battlefield at low level. A bomb fell from one aircraft, exploding in a ball of fire as it hit the ground. It was napalm. The other aircraft released its stream of rockets at the troops on the ground. Once again, all of the weapons missed their target. But a hail of rifle- and machine-gun fire was directed against the Pucaras. It was inevitable that some of the bullets would connect, damaging both aircraft. As one of the Pucaras tumbled from the sky, the pilot ejected. He was captured soon afterwards.

Almost immediately, a ground-attack Harrier shot through the low cloud that was just beginning to break up. Rockets spewed from the British jet, silencing the two Argentine air defence guns on the edge of the Goose Green airstrip.

Mark Evans had already been flying on and off all day. Summoned on board the assault ship HMS *Intrepid* well before dawn for another 'special mission', a Royal Marine major had briefed him to take some night sights and spot for Argentine soldiers lying in wait ahead of the British advance on the northern flank. Flying over land in the darkness can only be done at high level in order to avoid flying into a hillside. Attempting to fly blind beneath the cloud and pouring rain would have been a suicide mission. Turning the job down was not what the major expected to hear. It had been a tense start to the day.

Now, late in the afternoon on 28 May, Evans was heading south towards Goose Green in Yankee Whiskey. Although the cloud still hung low over the hills, there was only just enough of a gap to cross the high ground of the Sussex Mountains. Beneath the Wessex hung a pallet load of ammunition for the guns at Camilla Creek House. Leading Aircrewman Smiler Smiles was leaning out of the doorway keeping an eye on the net swinging below them, as they began their descent towards Camilla Creek.

Evans didn't see the Argentine aircraft at first. All he knew was that another helicopter in the distance had suddenly changed direction. Then he heard a shout over the radio: 'Fixed wing with propellers.'

The surviving Pucara suddenly appeared right in front of him. The two aircraft were lined up head to head, closing fast on each other.

'Shit, Pucara,' shouted Evans.

It was far too late to go to ground and run. The only option was to try and escape up into the clouds. Evans pulled back hard on the cyclic stick, completely forgetting that nearly a ton of ammunition dangled beneath him. The aircraft nose came up but the weight of the load dragged the aircraft down. It took only a second or so but it seemed an eternity before the sluggish Wessex gradually began to respond and gain height. Evans watched the needle on the vertical speed indicator point upwards, showing that they were now climbing. He willed the load to get lighter and to be engulfed by the clouds. It was a race against time before the Pucara got them.

Just as he expected to get a windscreen full of lead, the screen went white. They had beaten the Pucara to safety. It was a close call.

Although not hit as badly as his colleague, the second Pucara had also been damaged by the small-arms fire as it flew low over the British troops at Goose Green. The Argentine pilot was focused on the warning lights in his cockpit and whether he might have to eject. The British helicopter that loomed briefly in front of him was an opportunity target. But the opportunity didn't last, as the helicopter disappeared into the cloud. Despite his fears of ejection and the prospect of bumping into a Sea Harrier, the pilot managed to get the Pucara back to Stanley airport.

Flying in cloud is never much of a problem. All helicopter pilots are trained to fly on instruments. But for *junglies* who spend the vast majority of their time flying tactically, at low level, mostly looking out of the cockpit and only occasionally glancing inside for a quick check that all is well, switching from visual to instrument flying always comes as a bit of a shock. Evans switched his attention down onto the instruments inside his cockpit. After a couple of seconds to take in what he was seeing, his eyes began to settle into a regular search pattern that told him what the helicopter was doing.

Now safely in cloud, his next problem was going to be how to get back down without hitting a mountain. North and east were out because of the hills extending from the San Carlos area. South was out because, although the land was low lying and flat, it meant going back over Goose Green. The only option was to head out west. Between them, Evans and Smiles decided that ten minutes would put them safely out over the middle of Falkland Sound. They could then turn north and descend cautiously until they could see the sea.

It would have been a peculiar sight to the Argentine forces on the high ridgeline of West Falkland overlooking Falkland Sound. They would have heard the helicopter well before they saw anything. Their first sight would have been a pallet of ammunition dragging underneath the cloud in front of them, followed shortly afterwards by a large green helicopter attached above. It was a case of out of the frying pan and into the fire as Evans saw the stream of red tracer bullets hurtling across in front of him. Raising the nose and pulling power once again, he brought the Wessex back up into the cloud before descending again a little further out across the Sound.

Although forced to make such a dramatic detour, Evans and Smiles now flew back to Camilla Creek to complete their original mission and drop off the valuable load of ammunition. It was dusk as they returned to the relative safety of San Carlos. Unencumbered by the weight of the load, the Wessex was now far more responsive to fly. They sped back at low level, meandering through the grassy valleys.

'Right, that's enough for today. Back for tea and medals, Smiler?' remarked Evans drily.

On the ground, the end of the battle was tantalisingly close. During the late afternoon the advancing British troops reported seeing a white flag waving from one of the Argentine trenches. A Para officer stood up to take their surrender. He fell to the ground, shot from another trench. The Paras held off, shivering in captured trenches and shell holes, this time sending forward two Argentine prisoners with terms for surrender.

As night fell, a firepower demonstration of naval gunfire support and ground-attack Harriers was arranged for early morning. It wasn't needed. The Argentines surrendered on the morning of Saturday 29 May. It had been an ignominious day for the Argentine army.

When 2 Para's stand-in commanding officer Major Chris Keeble took the surrender, he was astonished to see an initial parade of 150 Argentine airmen followed by over a thousand Argentine soldiers. Conventional military wisdom suggested a three-to-one ratio in favour of the attacker in order to overrun a defended position. The British had defeated a force with a two-to-one ratio against them. It was a famous and dramatic victory. But with the deaths of eighteen British and forty-five Argentine soldiers and airmen, it had also been a costly political diversion.

With the break-out from San Carlos by 3 Brigade, there was no longer much question of the Argentines disrupting the beachhead. Air attacks now shifted to the British supply line, whether trying to sink further ships at sea or inhibit progress across East Falkland toward Stanley. On the ground, Argentine troops were well dug into the hills around Stanley. Extraordinarily, they had so far failed to mount any kind of counterattack against the British landings or even any fighting patrols. And now substantial reinforcements of British troops and helicopters were well on their way.

The question was, how much attrition the British could take before the Falklands winter worsened? The weather may have been unpredictable for the ships at sea, ranging from days of thick fog to boiling seas to flat calm. But for the land forces, it had been tolerable with mostly crisp clear days interspersed with days of low cloud, rain and drizzle. It couldn't last. Snow showers and strong winds would soon be on their way.

Chapter 11

Advance
30–31 May 1982

Running through the middle of East Falkland is a line of inhospitable hills. To the south of these hills at Goose Green were the men of 2 Para, having concluded their remarkable victory on the morning of 29 May. To the north were 3 Para and 45 Commando, moving forward on foot across the rough open terrain.

At the end of the line of hills lies Mount Kent. At 1,500 feet, it is not a huge mountain. But it dominates the approach to the capital Port Stanley from the west. For the British, the capture of Mount Kent was the lynchpin that would draw together the two-pronged advance on northern and southern flanks. It would also provide a focal point for the final assault on Port Stanley.

In the run up to the battle for Goose Green, an important development was taking place far out to the east in the mountains overlooking Stanley.

On the night of Monday 24 May, a four-man patrol of D Squadron SAS was exploring the slopes of Mount Kent.

206

Finding little enemy activity to trouble them, the patrol signalled back to San Carlos that the mountain was there for the taking. A plan was hatched to fly in the Royal Marines of 42 Commando and secure the position the following night. Unfortunately that afternoon all available helicopters at San Carlos, including the night-flyers, had been diverted away to the north of Pebble Island to help in the rescue of survivors from HMS *Coventry*.

On the evening of 26 May, four Sea Kings attempted to carry in the remainder of D Squadron, now released from their diversionary work at Goose Green. Flying the lead Sea King as usual was Lieutenant Nigel North, leader of the Pebble Island raid. His crew kept up their continuous chatter throughout the flight, double-checking their positions and keeping North informed of how far they had to run.

Worsening weather conditions of low cloud and hill fog soon forced him to slow the formation down. It also made navigation even more difficult and less certain. Navigating accurately over the featureless Falklands terrain at extreme low level, mostly by reference to contours, is difficult enough in the best of daylight conditions. But even though flying in appalling visibility using monochrome night vision goggles, North still expected his co-pilot and aircrew to get it spot on.

As the formation approached their intended target, the co-pilot misidentified the entrance valley and run-in point. To make matters worse, Bill Pollock's aircraft, flying as number two, called that they could see the reception team on the ground behind the leader. North landed the formation, thinking that they were in the wrong place but close. The SAS teams quickly unloaded their weapons and heavy equipment and the Sea Kings departed. It wasn't long after the helicopters had gone that the SAS teams realised they were completely lost. The team leader radioed through to HMS *Intrepid* that they needed extracting. They had no idea where they were. It was a rare error that could easily have proved costly for troops and helicopter crews alike.

By this time, the Sea Kings were all back at San Carlos and their crews asleep. North was woken and told to sort out the mess. He ordered the aircraft to be refuelled and the crews to be briefed again. But before they could get them to the right place, first they had to find them. Just two Sea Kings set off this time, North and Paul Humphreys followed by Pete Rainey and Peter Spens-Black. Retracing their headings, they soon ran into low cloud that forced them to climb and continue above it. It seemed an impossible task to get back to the unknown drop-off point. But the SAS team on the ground heard the helicopters coming and switched on as many torches as they could find. It wasn't much, but the burst of dull light gave the Sea King crews just enough of a reference to make their approach. As they came in to land, the troops materialised like magic through the cloud. They were a mile and a half from their planned destination.

With the men now back on board, the two helicopters lifted off towards Mount Kent. Flying conditions were already marginal. The low cloud meant that light levels for the night goggles were poor. As the formation slowed to hover-taxi up the rising ground, the low cloud turned to fog. Further progress was impossible. North landed and waited for fifteen minutes in hope that the cloud might clear. It didn't. The mission was aborted and the Sea Kings returned frustrated to San Carlos.

The following night, a single Sea King inserted some of the troops on Mount Kent while the other three Sea Kings lifted guns to Camilla Creek for the attack on Goose Green. The rest of D Squadron were brought in by two

Sea Kings the next day, on Friday 28 May, much to everyone's relief. However, on the return journey, North's Sea King diverted towards Darwin to pick up a casualty. Talk of white flags and surrender had reached the crew. They were under the impression that the battle for Goose Green had ended. It had not. As the helicopter came in to land, tracer streaked towards the aircraft on all sides. A bullet passed within a whisper of the main rotor gearbox. The tracer came from the enthusiastic troops of 2 Para, convinced that the helicopter was an Argentine Chinook.

Late the following day, the SAS found their position compromised by the arrival of five helicopters at the base of Mount Kent carrying Argentine commandos. A series of firefights and skirmishes continued throughout the night and into the next day. An attempt by the Sea Kings to insert 42 Commando by night was again thwarted by bad weather, this time heavy snow showers. The formation of Sea Kings made it to within five miles of their intended target before abandoning the attempt.

Improved weather on Sunday 30 May gave an opportunity to try to secure Mount Kent with a big lift of troops. With one Sea King out of action, the remaining three Sea Kings flew their 42 Commando troops straight onto the mountain. The bold move to within a few miles of Stanley had taken six days. As Colonel Mike Rose, the commanding officer of the SAS, was reported to have said nonchalantly to the reporter Max Hastings as he flew in the back of a Sea King, 'Who dares wins'.

Following behind the Sea Kings was the Chinook, Bravo November, carrying a huge load of three light guns and ammunition. Two of the guns and twenty-eight troops were carried inside the huge helicopter. A third gun was slung underneath. Although the Chinook had been in action since its arrival four days earlier, this was its first really significant contribution to the war. In a single lift it had delivered the equivalent of four Sea King loads or three Sea Kings and two Wessex loads. Its success underscored what an immense blow losing the other three Chinooks had been. Bravo November's mission was all the more remarkable for being flown in the dark using night vision goggles. Chinook pilot Dick Langworthy and his co-pilot Flight Lieutenant Andy Lawless had made great play of their previous experience, persuading Simon Thornewill to lend them his own goggles.

Freed from the constraints of their ten-ton load, the Chinook became far more manoeuvrable at a mere eleven tons weight. Their mission complete, Langworthy and Lawless pointed the vast helicopter down the side of the mountain and set course for San Carlos, using the goggles to fly at extreme low level. Flying so low to the ground left very little room for error or misjudgement. Just after heading down the hillside, a sudden snow shower made it almost impossible to see out as they passed over the stretch of tidal water at Estancia Creek. One of the Chinook wheels clipped the surface causing the aircraft to rock violently. It threatened to somersault. A huge plume of spray flew up into the engines making them lose power. One of the cockpit doors dropped away as Lawless pulled the jettison handle. His maps and code sheets flew out into the wind. Both pilots hauled upwards on their collective levers to try to gain height. As the engines surged back into life, somehow the Chinook remained airborne. The two pilots recovered the situation but were now worried that they had lost part of their undercarriage altogether. The only way to get back and land safely was to find a slope on which to set down.

Back at FOB Whale, Jack Lomas heard of the incident on the radio. The Chinook was coming in with a major undercarriage problem. He immediately radioed back that they had better land well clear of the other helicopters. A Chinook thrashing itself to death would wipe out any other aircraft unlucky enough to be parked nearby.

Normally the distinctive beating of the helicopter announced its arrival long before it could be seen. This time – the pilots having dispensed with their night vision goggles – the unmistakeable *waka waka* sound was accompanied by a full set of landing lights. Coming to the hover, the worried ground engineers had a good look at the supposed damage from underneath. All seemed well, other than the missing cockpit door. The wheels were intact: the helicopter landed gingerly but safely, declining the invitation to continue with a second mission.

To the amusement of other aircrew, the Chinook crew had survived the experience of 'waterskiing' in a helicopter. They deserved to keep their goggles.

Out at sea, Argentine warplanes remained intent on stopping the British fleet in its tracks. Flush with success from sinking *Sheffield* and *Atlantic Conveyor* with their first two pairs of Exocet missiles, the Argentine navy was determined to use the final missile to sink one of the British aircraft carriers. The plan this time was to launch two Super Etendards, one of which carried the remaining Exocet, and then follow up the chaos and confusion with a sustained bombing run from four Skyhawks.

The attack began as planned. Early in the afternoon of Sunday 30 May, the first of the Super Etendards spotted two targets on their radar during a low-level pop up. Assessing one of them to be the carrier HMS *Invincible*, the Exocet was released and sped away. What happened to the Exocet missile is not clear; it may have been splashed by a British missile, cannon fire or technical fault. Either way, it failed to hit any target and was lost.

The four Skyhawks followed in low behind the missile, spotting the first British ship from ten miles out. In fact, neither target was *Invincible*. The two ships were the Type-42 destroyer HMS *Exeter* and the Type-21 frigate HMS *Avenger*. Two of the Skyhawks overflew *Avenger*, releasing their bombs as they sped past. Huge plumes of water next to the ship signalled that their bombs had missed altogether. One of the remaining Skyhawks was shot down by Sea Dart from HMS *Exeter*. The other sped onwards.

Ian Bryant and Dave Ockleton were two of the frustrated Wessex pilots of 848 Squadron. Having observed the war at close quarters from the deck of a ship, at last they had an aircraft to fly. They had taken delivery of Yankee Delta – sole surviving Wessex from *Atlantic Conveyor* – from the carrier *Hermes*. With aircrewman Ginge Burns, they were now being used as a general taxi and load-lifting service. It wasn't the most exciting job in the world, but it meant getting airborne and it meant getting involved in the role they were trained for.

En route to HMS *Exeter* to drop off stores and messages, they were struggling to get any kind of response on the radio. As they approached the ship, there was a loud whooshing noise as a chaff rocket shot past the aircraft nose. At last the ship came on the radio, abruptly telling them to hold off to the stern. At first the jets looked like flying ants darting about on the horizon. One broke away and arced around to the left of Yankee Delta and to the south of the ship. As it got closer, the distinctive shape of a Skyhawk became more apparent. There was no time for any kind of fighter evasion. Without warning, the jet exploded in a ball of fire right in front of them. The raid was over as quickly as it had started.

Bryant and Ockleton flew over to the explosion site where the water was now tinged turquoise. Bits of debris were slowly descending through the water. A grappling hook thrown down from the back of the Wessex by aircrewman Burns caught on a one-man dinghy. It was peppered with little black holes.

For the British, the enemy mission was a total failure. For the Argentines, it was an amazing success. The Super Etendard pilots had fired their Exocet. Soon afterwards, they claimed to have glimpsed smoke coming from a very large ship that was clearly badly damaged. They returned to base victorious in the mistaken belief that they had successfully sunk HMS *Invincible*. Nor could this have been the remains of *Conveyor*. The burning hulk had sunk two days earlier, when the fire reached the store of cluster bombs. What they actually saw, if anything, remains a mystery.

As well as the SAS patrol on Mount Kent, other special forces patrols were operating out to the east ahead of 3 Commando Brigade's advance. Late in the evening of Sunday 30 May, a Royal Marine specialist Mountain and Arctic Warfare patrol spotted a group of Argentine commandos taking shelter from the worsening weather at Top Malo House, an abandoned house situated just north of the spine of mountains running across East Falkland. Three Para and 45 Commando were currently passing a little further to the north, through Teal Inlet and on to Estancia House, on a monumental thirty-mile trek. The Argentine troops posed an immediate threat to the rear of both units. It was too dark and the weather too poor for a Harrier air strike to be called in by the patrol. The best option was for a surprise assault.

Early the next morning, a Sea King crammed with

nineteen more specialist Royal Marines and their weapons flew in at extreme low level, landing almost a mile short of the house. By staying low in the small river valleys and landing out of sight in a dip in the ground, the assault team hoped that their approach would be unseen. However, the noise was unavoidable and the sentry briefly caught sight of the helicopter from an upstairs window of the house. The Argentine troops had been alerted.

Snow showers had given the tussock grass a white dusting. In other circumstances, the remote scene with barren mountains rising up on both sides of the valley would have looked stunningly beautiful. However, against the white background the Royal Marines now stood out in their green camouflage. They crawled silently to their assault positions. One group was to provide covering fire, the other to run in and finish the job.

Soon after dawn, a green flare signalled the beginning of the assault. The house was hit immediately by anti-tank rockets from the fire group. An Argentine sentry appeared briefly in the upstairs window and was shot by sniper fire. A second volley of rockets slammed into Top Malo. As the house started to burn, the Argentine troops ran out and took up defensive positions on the ground. The assault team charged towards them, firing and throwing grenades.

The firefight continued for fifteen minutes. Two Argentines were killed and six others wounded before the troops reluctantly surrendered. Despite three Royal Marines being injured, the assault on Top Malo House was a resounding success.

Back at San Carlos, Peter Manley was immediately ordered to casevac the wounded and dead of both sides back to Rick Jolly's field hospital at Ajax Bay. Manley and Dave Greet were quickly airborne in Yankee Sierra, heading directly towards Top Malo House. The destination was obvious from the plume of smoke rising in the distance. Manley brought the Wessex in to land close to the still burning house. Greet helped two of the badly wounded fellow Royal Marines into the Wessex cabin for their return journey to Ajax Bay. Manley and Greet then set off immediately to bring back three of the wounded Argentine commandos, two of whom were seriously injured. En route, one of the soldiers died.

There was to be a great deal of casevac work for the Wessex crews that day, Monday 31 May. It is especially true for the Wessex that the burden of looking after the wounded is entirely borne by the aircrewman in the cabin. The pilot up front can see the casualties coming into the aircraft behind and below him. But thereafter it is the aircrewman who must handle the bloody aftermath of battle at first hand. *Junglie* aircrew deal with these encounters in their own way. Black humour plays an important role. It is never a sign of personal disrespect, merely a way of coping with terrible situations that human beings should never have to face.

On the same day, two days after the surrender of the Argentine forces at Goose Green, Jack Lomas and Arthur Balls were sent over to the Ajax Bay field hospital. Assigned to Rick Jolly and his medical team, much of the day's tasking was spent shuttling wounded servicemen of both sides from the field hospital to the hospital ship SS *Uganda* where over 130 medical staff awaited.

The converted cruise liner, white with big red crosses painted on its sides, upper deck and funnel, sat exposed in the open water halfway across Falkland Sound. Landing across *Uganda*'s deck was a sheer pleasure for the aircrew. Helicopters were not allowed to shut down on deck, but while waiting for the stretchers to be removed from the aircraft, a nurse or deckhand would invariably bring out a cup of fresh coffee or a bag containing sausage or bacon sandwiches for the crew. After a prolonged diet of curried mush and Mars bars, it seemed like nectar.

But this day's pleasure was not to last long. Lomas and Balls were told to take Yankee Charlie over to Goose Green to collect bodies. It was the first time they had seen the area. The landscape around the isthmus was bleak and grassy with water on both sides. To the south were the neat settlement houses of Goose Green. A little further to the north, the smaller settlement of Darwin. With its stunning flat light it should have been so peaceful. Yet Lomas could see that Goose Green had very obviously been the scene of a brutal battle.

Approaching from the north, lines of gorse were still smoking from the ferocious firefight of the previous days. Separating the two settlements was the airfield. Several of the fearsome light green Pucara aircraft lay abandoned or damaged near the grass runway. One aircraft was almost unrecognisably burnt out and destroyed in a blackened circle. Lomas felt a jolt as he noticed the pieces of wrecked Sea Harrier near the edge of the field. But it was the slew of abandoned equipment that dominated the scene. Hundreds and hundreds of helmets and rifles and bits of webbing lay in long lines, guarded by the occasional British soldier. Around the outskirts of the field, Paras were walking around clearing the battlefield site.

Lomas landed nearby and sent Balls to find out where to go. Shouting to make himself heard above the noise of the helicopter, Balls told a Para soldier: 'We've come for the bodies.'

'There's loads of bodies here mate. Help yourself.'

Balls turned and moved his hand across his throat, signalling to Lomas to shut down the rotors.

Together with the Para soldier, Balls, and four Royal

Marines who had flown out with them, loaded half a dozen bodies into the back of the cabin. It was done silently and perfunctorily, without emotion, almost as if they were loading logs. The only noise was the whine of the port engine that Lomas had left running. There was nothing disrespectful about the way the bodies were loaded, but both of the crew were surprised at the lack of formality. Lomas started up the starboard engine and rotors and took off to return to Ajax Bay. A formal reception party was waiting for them when they landed. 'This is a bit more like it,' said Lomas.

After shutting down, Rick Jolly walked over to the Wessex and looked at the scene in the back of the aircraft. He turned to look up at Lomas in the cockpit: 'These are the wrong bodies.'

They were Argentine dead.

'We were told to get bodies. Would you like us to take them back?'

Jolly said he'd look after them.

Lomas and Balls set off again, this time flying to a very formal welcome almost into the middle of Goose Green settlement. They were met by Chris Keeble of 2 Para. With the Wessex shut down once again, two lines of soldiers prepared to say goodbye to their mates. Unlike the Argentines they had just taken, the British dead were not in body bags. Instead the hoods of their camouflaged jacket smocks were zipped up over their heads. The soldiers carried each body one by one out to the aircraft on a stretcher and rolled them carefully into the cabin. Each body was a friend. 'Right, that's . . . This next one is . . .'.

Lomas and Balls started the helicopter up for the return journey with the solemn faces of undertakers. They returned to Ajax Bay with the right bodies.

*   *   *

More trips to Goose Green followed, with more bodies loaded into the Wessex. All were treated with reverence. Just as the last body was being loaded, Lomas was approached by 2 Para's chaplain David Cooper: 'I've got to get back. I'm supposed to do the service.'

'You're welcome to come back with us.'

'But there aren't any seats.'

It seemed appropriate that one of his Para comrades should turn to the chaplain: 'Just sit on top of them. They won't mind.'

Seventeen British dead were buried later that day in a moving ceremony on the hillside above San Carlos. Paras lined the sides of the grave in the evening sunshine. Cooper's voice rung out crisply over the scene, listing the names of the dead. Six bearers carried each soldier on a portable stretcher into the grave and laid him carefully next to the previous one. Each body was covered with a union flag. The six stretcher bearers were the only ones to wear their red berets. After laying down each body, they saluted and turned to collect their next colleague. Throughout the service, the buzz and drone of helicopter activity across San Carlos Water formed a continuous backdrop. The war went on.

Before leaving Ajax Bay, Arthur Balls turned to Jack Lomas and asked: 'Do you think they have a brush, boss?'

'What do you need a brush for?'

'I need to brush out body parts.' He didn't want to leave the mess for the maintainers.

As pilots, we definitely had the easy job.

Back at the camp after dark, Jack Lomas grabbed a bottle of whisky and wandered over to the aircrew's tent. 'Drink and talk?' he said, handing over the bottle. It was the other main way of coping, when black humour just wasn't enough.

* * *

The flight out to the British hospital ship *Uganda* was to become a regular trip for the Wessex and Sea King crews throughout the war. But in a strange turn of events, Steve Judd, Ric Fox and Arthur Balls found themselves heading towards a very different hospital ship on the morning of Monday 31 May.

This time it was *Bahia Paraiso*, one of three hospital ships operated by the Argentines. Since the sinking of the *Belgrano*, they were the only Argentine ships anywhere near the Falklands. The British were keen to ensure that they were not breaching the neutrality given to them under the Geneva Convention and being used to bring in arms. During the war there were at least two unarmed inspections of Argentine hospital ships using British Lynx and Wasp helicopters, while the Argentines insisted on a reciprocal (though armed) inspection of *Uganda*.

Judd, Fox and Balls began the trip by taking Yankee Tango over to the assault ship HMS *Fearless* to collect an inspection team comprising a Royal Navy commander and six Royal Marines. The brief was to fly at low level down to the far south of East Falkland, across Goose Green and over the flat boggy land known as Lafonia, board the Argentine ship and conduct the inspection. It was a fifty-mile transit over land still occupied by the Argentine forces who had been helicoptered in to the south of Goose Green towards the end of the battle.

There was a very real risk of bumping into a Pucara. It was only three days since Pucaras had shot down the Royal Marine Scout. The British were still uncertain whether Pucara were operating or not from other airfields. In fact they were now only operating from Stanley. But the risk and the fear remained real. Pucaras dominated conversations in the aircrew camps each evening. Mark Evans had already escaped one head-on encounter. An encounter over the open terrain of Lafonia would be unlikely to turn out so well.

My 845 Squadron colleagues – Arthur Balls (left), Ric Fox (middle) and Steve Judd (right) – look rather more relaxed than they felt after taking an inspection team on board the Argentine hospital ship *Bahia Paraiso*. They had no choice but to shut down because their Wessex was chained to the deck as soon as they landed.

White with a large red cross painted on it, the *Bahia Paraiso* was easy enough to spot from a long way off in the sea beyond the flat Lafonia landscape. The ship appeared to be a converted icebreaker, capable of carrying two Puma helicopters on its large flight deck. Judd hovered alongside the ship until a flight-deck director came out to wave him across. As soon as Yankee Tango landed, the Argentine flight-deck crew rushed out to lash the helicopter to the deck with chains. It was a completely normal procedure, but it gave Judd no choice but to shut down. Uncertain what to do next, Judd, Fox and Balls got down from the aircraft and asked a flight-deck crew member to take a photo of the unusual scene. They were then ushered into a crew room.

For over an hour, they sat on one side of the room face to face with their Argentine hosts, waiting for the inspection team to complete their tour. The young Argentine junior officers were dressed in smart naval whites; the *junglies* were in their well-worn and well-flavoured green combats, armed with loaded 9mm Browning pistols. The welcome they received was civil and the coffee was good. The only interruption was the need to wave to a passing Sea King sent to check they were alright.

As soon as the inspection team returned, the crew climbed back into their Wessex and flashed up. It was exactly as if they were starting up on a British ship: once the rotors were going, the flight-deck crew ran in to remove the lashings; Judd signalled that he wanted to take off; the flight-deck officer waved his arms upwards and the Wessex lifted away.

On the way back, the risk of attack by a Pucara remained the same. Yet somehow the crew felt immune. They had landed on an Argentine ship and it was completely normal. The whole episode had felt surreal. The team leader plugged in to chat to them on the intercom. He had found some large boxes in the ship's hold that his team hadn't been able to shift. Otherwise they had found nothing that shouldn't be there. He didn't say as much, but it was clear they had been looking for Exocet.

Chapter 12

Reinforcements
1–7 June 1982

The battle for Goose Green may have been instigated by politicians in Britain worried by losses and impatient for success, but the victory by 2 Para against such a weight of Argentine opposition was good for morale. What it also showed was that Argentine forces would be no pushover. Even if they had failed to counterattack against the British landings at San Carlos, they had defended their own positions with courage and vigour. The same could be expected of their defences, dug into the hills to the west of Stanley.

For the British forces, the overwhelming problem was how to advance sufficient troops and equipment over fifty miles of inhospitable Falkland terrain between San Carlos and Stanley without a significant proportion of the anticipated helicopter support. The sixteen helicopters currently available were never going to prove adequate. A further thirty helicopters were due to arrive imminently in Atlantic Causeway, *along with the additional troops of 5 Brigade brought south on the QE2. Reinforcements were on their way. The question was whether the Argentines could do to* Causeway *what they had just done to her sister ship,* Conveyor.

For the week after the landings, the commando helicopters had been used almost exclusively for two main roles: building up supplies at San Carlos by day, and inserting special forces teams around the islands by night. There was little or no spare capacity to move any of the 3 Brigade units or their heavy equipment forward, let alone build up the supplies of ammunition and food they would need for the final attack. The loss of *Atlantic Conveyor* had forced the decision to send 3 Para and 45 Commando off eastwards towards Stanley and to send 2 Para off southwards to fight at Goose Green – all of which had to be done on foot.

The relatively benign weather of the first week had proved a double-edged sword. For the troops in San Carlos, conditions were cold and wet, much like Dartmoor in February, but manageable. The flip side was that frequent clear skies exposed the landings to fearsome attacks from the air. Keeping most of the supply ships out of harm's way during the day meant shuttling them in and out of the anchorage at night, thus slowing the process of unloading.

For Jack Lomas, now in charge of the Wessex FOB Whale at Old Creek House, the way his helicopters were being directed was causing him to lose sleep. His aircrew were becoming deeply frustrated watching the Royal Marines and other troops below them marching across the rough Falklands terrain with heavily laden bergens, yet unable to give them a lift. The troops in turn were similarly frustrated hearing the sounds of helicopters all around and yet getting little or no support. Surely some of the air assets could be released from unloading ships.

The Exocet attack on *Atlantic Conveyor* had cast a long shadow over the land campaign.

Still 2,000 miles north of the Falklands, my own journey south on RFA *Engadine* with the rest of 847 Squadron remained painfully slow. At least my deck-landing skills had improved dramatically. I no longer bounced from wheel to wheel in ground resonance on landing. And my personal fitness was ensured by days of flight-deck hockey, hundreds of press-ups and sickening star jumps, and miles of running around the outside deck of the ship. I had even given up smoking.

Being a merchant ship, we had no fixed-weapon systems on board. However, we had a load of machine guns, rifles and rocket launchers. Air raid warning drill meant spreading our most valuable cargo – the twenty-eight pilots and aircrew – around the ship while the rest of the crew and engineers pointed as many weapons as possible outwards at any incoming threat. It still seemed more of an irritant than anything else when the alarm was sounded during lunch. They hadn't even waited until we finished our apple crumble.

The siren went off, followed by the dramatic announcement 'Hands to action stations. Hands to action stations. Assume NBCD State One Condition Zulu'. NBCD stood for Nuclear Biological Chemical and Damage Control. My adrenalin flowed as we all rushed down corridors, bolting watertight doors behind us to get to our assigned stations. I waited for the call 'This is for exercise'. It never came. This time it was for real.

My action station was in a briefing room with Lieutenant Ray Colborne, a lovely man and experienced Wessex pilot who had done everything and been everywhere. If there was anything a junior officer like me ever needed to know about matters Wessex or matters Navy, the first person to ask was 'Uncle Ray'. Despite being immensely professional and skilled in the air, he had a very relaxed view of naval life on the ground. Amongst the least physically fit of all *junglie* pilots, and a heavy smoker, passing his annual medical check was always touch and go. 'You see Doc,' he'd say, 'we only have a limited number of heartbeats in our life. I just don't want to use mine up too quickly.' Humour, popularity and experience usually saved the day. A bottle of whisky left on the table undoubtedly helped.

A dozen other senior and junior ratings were stationed with us. As Colborne and I sat in the corner, I became increasingly scared. My worries escalated and I told him what I was thinking: 'This is bloody great. We are stuck in a tin can. Bombs or missiles will just come straight through the sides. We can't see anything. We can't fire back. We've got no chance.'

Very surreptitiously and quietly, Colborne leaned over to me and spoke through gritted teeth: 'You listen to me. Everybody in here is shitting themselves. There are sailors younger than you – eighteen, nineteen – who are looking at you. You're an officer. So get a grip. Be a man. Live with the fear and show some gumption.'

Colborne's wise words would ring in my ears for the whole of the war. It was a powerful lesson that I have never forgotten.

Mike Booth's action station, as squadron boss, was on the upper deck. He got outside just in time to see an Argentine air force Boeing 707 pulling away at low level, having overflown and identified *Engadine* at less than 500 feet. Booth could clearly see the light blue Argentine air force markings down the side. It was an astonishing sight in the middle of nowhere. The Boeing jet then peeled away and disappeared over the horizon.

One of our Royal Marines was on duty manning a machine gun, mounted on the upper-deck railings. Booth was annoyed. Nobody had thought to fire at the big airliner, yet they could have been rolling bombs out of the back. 'Why didn't you shoot at it?' he berated the gunner unfairly. Although it would have been nice to have bagged a 707, the rules of engagement were less than clear. London never answered Booth's subsequent request for clarification.

Recovering from the surprise and shock, Booth went straight to the bridge of *Engadine*. 'Look,' he asked Captain Freeman, the master, 'could I suggest as an initial reaction we do about a twenty-degree detour on our way down to the TEZ just to open our range from the Argentine coastline?'

'Yes,' Freeman replied, 'that's sensible.'

Two hours later, *Engadine* received a flash signal suggesting that the ship alter course by twenty degrees. 'Not bad for a little aviator,' thought Booth.

While the Paras were fighting it out at Goose Green on 27 May, the Scots and Welsh Guards had been in the relative calm of Grytviken harbour in South Georgia, transferring from the luxury of the *QE2* to the merely comfortable *Canberra* and *Norland*. Along with the 1/7th Gurkha Rifles, these were the reinforcements of 5 Brigade. Their arrival in the Falklands was now only days away.

On the same day, other reinforcements were arriving in the Total Exclusion Zone, much closer to the Falklands. Following their misadventures on Fortuna Glacier and as prison guards, Mike Tidd's flight had taken two replacement Wessex from Ascension and sailed south once again on RFA *Tidespring*. Having got within sight of the Falklands, it seemed extraordinary to Tidd that their badly needed commando helicopters weren't being sent into San Carlos straight away. Although much of the tasking was undoubtedly vital – such as transferring weapons from the RFA supply ships to HMS *Hermes* and other warships – anti-submarine Sea King helicopters were available, even if they too were operating around the clock. The fact was that managing limited British air assets was a tricky balancing act.

The reinforcements of 5 Brigade sailed south on board the luxurious *QE2* as far as South Georgia, thus staying well out of range of the Argentine Super Etendard jets and their Exocet missiles. These two Sea Kings of 825 Squadron then helped transfer them to the only slightly less luxurious *Canberra* and *Norland*, arriving in the danger zone of San Carlos a few days later.

Two days later, on Saturday 29 May, the container ship *Atlantic Causeway* joined the fleet. On board were the majority of 847 Squadron's Wessex and four of our crews, led by Lieutenant Commander Peter Hails. *Causeway* also carried 825 Squadron's anti-submarine Sea Kings, their sonar gear stripped out to convert them for their commando role. Just as a new front-line squadron of aircraft and crews had been formed from the Wessex training squadron at RNAS Yeovilton in Somerset, another new squadron was formed from the Sea King training squadron at RNAS Culdrose in Cornwall. Almost every Fleet Air Arm unit was now involved in the Falklands War one way or another.

Having lost *Conveyor* on the way into San Carlos four days previously, it was not surprising that the Royal Navy command were nervous at the prospect of sending *Atlantic Causeway* in on a similar mission. All of the aircrew on board *Causeway* knew perfectly well they were at serious risk of attack from Exocet. But they also wanted to get on with it. Hanging around at sea seemed pointless.

The armed forces are awash with various inter-service and inter-unit rivalries. The vast majority of it is healthy, good natured and tongue-in-cheek. There can sometimes be a hard edge that reflects competition between units that do similar things, such as between Paras and Marines, or between Fleet Air Arm and Royal Air Force. This is generally a good thing because it encourages excellence.

Within the Fleet Air Arm there is a long tradition of friendly banter between the anti-submarine squadron *pingers* and commando squadron *junglies*. Any potentially hard edges are much softened by a network of long-standing friendships, mostly because all aircrew start their training together and many serve together on the carriers and larger ships. So it is usually with good humour that *pingers* generally view *junglies* as little more than house-trained orang-utans, operating in the field; dirty, smelly and barely civilised. *Junglies* generally view *pingers* as fancy typewriter operators. Push a few buttons in the cockpit and the helicopter moves automatically from one hover over the sea to the next. It doesn't sound very taxing or exciting. Neither can see the appeal of the other.

The difference this time was that *Atlantic Causeway*'s *pingers* were about to infringe on *junglie* territory. Could they cope with life in the field? Could they read a map?

Aside from the constant banter, the journey south on board *Causeway* had been largely uneventful. The Wessex flight, led by Lieutenant Commander Peter Hails, comprised four pilots, two aircrew, various maintainers and twenty Wessex 5s. The small number of aircrew gave the feel of an embarked flight but the large number of aircraft meant there was work for a squadron. All of the usual jobs needed filling but there were only six aircrew to fill them.

One of the jobs was ship's met officer. Although all aircrew are trained to forecast weather, most will admit that the subject remains a bit of a mystery. Proper met officers claim to predict the day's weather by reading the weather chart, interpreting the assorted isobars, air masses, temperatures and fronts. Aviators usually start with this method but soon resort to a quick look out of the window, a few radio calls to other ships, and a wise hedging of bets.

Peter Hails and aircrewman Chief Petty Officer Bill Tuttey had served together for two years on an RFA. 'We haven't got a met man,' said Hails, 'and you did it for two years.'

'I lied,' replied Tuttey.

'Well lie on this one,' said Hails.

When Tuttey's subsequent briefings of a cloud base at 10,000 feet were questioned by *pingers*, he would ask whether it was normal practice to doubt met briefings in this way.

Another of the essential jobs was ship's vicar. Hails called Tuttey in again: 'We haven't got a vicar.'

Tuttey was duly seconded. Only a few people turned

up for his first Sunday service. The second took place a few days after the sinking of *Atlantic Conveyor* and attracted a hundred converts.

On 29 May, the same day that Goose Green fell, *Causeway* was within flying range of the task force. With the loss of *Conveyor* still fresh in everyone's mind, it was vital to start offloading helicopters from the ship as soon as possible.

The first four of the radar-equipped Sea Kings launched straight away for San Carlos, stopping en route on the carriers *Hermes* and *Invincible* for fuel. The four-hour-long transit over the sea was a task for which the *pingers* were especially well equipped. Their arrival at the beachhead added significantly to the available helicopter resources on land.

Remaining on board *Causeway*, Lieutenant Tim 'Flipper' Hughes was one of the four Wessex pilots. He had been dragged away from his 'best job in the world', flying a smartly painted Wessex, callsign Romeo November, around schools and agricultural shows for the Director of Naval Recruiting. The choppy and freezing South Atlantic water was far removed from the glamour of posing in blue overalls on an English summer's day.

Having finally arrived in the Total Exclusion Zone, he and all the other embarked *junglies* were raring to go. Having watched the first four *pingers* disembark, it seemed inexplicable that the rest of them were being made to spend a thoroughly tense and frustrating three days hanging around.

Causeway finally headed towards San Carlos exactly one week after the ill-fated attempt by *Conveyor*. *Junglies* and *pingers* alike couldn't know it then, but they were about to be thrown together into the same maelstrom.

*   *   *

The end of May marked a turning point for Wessex operations on the Falkland Islands. Operating together from a single base at FOB Whale had already allowed Jack Lomas to mix up his crews, making them more like a small squadron and less like a collection of separate flights. Lomas also knew from his time in Germany that any idiot can be uncomfortable under canvas. A more substantial operating base was needed, especially given the imminent arrival of the rest of 845 Squadron and the whole of 847.

The departure of 3 Brigade troops from Port San Carlos offered the possibility of regrouping the growing number of aircraft in one place and housing most of the air and groundcrews under a solid roof rather than flimsy canvas. A quick chat with Tim Stanning on board HMS *Fearless* for approval was followed by a visit to the Port San Carlos settlement manager, Alan Miller, who was generous and welcoming. Lomas invited the Chinook crews to join him in the move. So, on Sunday 30 May, the tents came down and the joint FOB moved around the corner of the bay to Port San Carlos.

Argentine air attacks on the British landing area at San Carlos had now dwindled almost to zero. The deteriorating South Atlantic weather and heavy attrition amongst the Argentine air force and navy jets both played important roles in this. By the end of the battle for Goose Green, the Argentine forces had lost forty aircraft. By comparison the British had lost seven aircraft comprising five Sea Harriers and two ground-attack Harriers.

Subsequent Argentine attacks would be focused on disrupting supply lines, whether the ships at sea or the troops on the ground. In any case, after the attack on Ajax Bay and San Carlos that had so nearly wiped out Hector Heathcote and Kev Gleeson, only two further daylight air raids were to reach San Carlos during the entire war.

That said, life in San Carlos Bay still had the potential to be extremely alarming. Argentine Canberra bombers, their crews trained by the British, launched two high-altitude bombing strikes at night. In the first raid in the early hours of Saturday 29 May, four bombs were dropped without success. The second raid two nights later put four bombs into Fern Valley Creek, the commando Sea King base, wiping out one tent and causing serious injury to the squadron's air engineering officer, Richard Harden.

Most of the other occupants were fortunate to miss the raid. They had transferred overnight back to *Fearless* after the assault ship had returned to San Carlos with land forces commander Major General Jeremy Moore. One day earlier and the bombing raid would have produced many more casualties and fatalities.

In the cold darkness of the morning of Tuesday 1 June, the container ship *Atlantic Causeway* sailed into San Carlos Water. The liner *Norland* was also arriving that morning from South Georgia, followed by SS *Canberra* a day later, to disembark the Scots and Welsh Guards of 5 Brigade. It was a critical moment in the war.

If *Conveyor* had been vulnerable to Exocet out at sea, *Causeway* was even more exposed to air strikes in San Carlos Water. Losing nine British helicopters on *Conveyor* had been a disaster; losing another twenty-four helicopters on *Causeway* could prove catastrophic. It was therefore vital to get aircraft off the ship as quickly as possible before daylight and the arrival of Argentine jets. On the improvised and crowded flight deck, there was initially only room to spread the rotor blades of one Wessex at a time. Manoeuvring the aircraft into place ready for launch involved a complicated game of flight-deck chess.

The day started badly. Flipper Hughes had just run

through his pre-flight checks in the dimly lit cockpit of X-Ray Echo. Time was now crucial. He pressed the starter button for the port engine. To the collective dismay of aircrew and engineers waiting to prepare the next aircraft, the engine spun up but was not followed by the usual cracking of the igniters and *whoosh* of flame through the jet pipe. The igniters had failed. Hughes decided to get the starboard engine going and fly off unconventionally on a single engine. As an experienced pilot, he knew the Wessex could handle this. Alas the starboard igniters also failed to fire.

A sense of panic now began to grow. Twenty Wessex and four Sea King helicopters sat immobilised on the deck of the most obvious target in San Carlos Water. Thoughts of *Atlantic Conveyor* edged closer. History threatened to repeat itself. Precious minutes were lost as the frantic senior maintenance engineer decided which other aircraft to rob for spare parts. X-Ray Echo was minutes from being unlashed and pushed into the sea. The hastily fitted replacement igniters worked and the disembarkation process could begin.

Lieutenant Paul McIntosh had recently qualified as an instructor at the grand age of twenty-three with several Wessex tours in Northern Ireland already under his belt. While Hughes struggled to get X-Ray Echo started, he had been waiting anxiously alongside the second aircraft X-Ray Golf with its blades still folded. He could just make out the first glimmer of dawn as his cab was wheeled out onto the landing spot where the blades could be spread.

Hughes held in the hover alongside the ship, waiting for McIntosh to launch so that they could approach Port San Carlos together in the early morning light. Lieutenant Willie Harrower followed in the third aircraft to ferry the pilots back to *Causeway* for their next delivery. Not knowing the number of other Wessex already ashore, the plan was to disembark the first twelve aircraft and leave eight aircraft on board *Causeway* in reserve.

For the newcomers getting airborne for the first time, the scene in San Carlos Water was incredible. Warships, newly arrived passenger liners and supply ships jammed the bay. As the two Wessex approached the settlement of Port San Carlos, the unmistakeable shapes of the other Wessex became apparent in the bottom of a small valley. There was not going to be space for a dozen more aircraft. Worse, to McIntosh, the aircraft were not well dispersed and looked highly vulnerable to air attack themselves. Lieutenant Commander Peter Hails made the same observation when he arrived soon afterwards and told McIntosh to sort out a new landing site immediately.

From the air at dusk, these dozen Wessex at Port San Carlos look like a juicy target. There was an ongoing discussion about whether it was better to keep the aircraft close together like this at night – easier to defend – or spread them out – harder to bomb. I suspect we simply parked them closer so we wouldn't have to walk so far!

After all the nerves and fears about what might have been, the day turned out well. The new arrivals were able to get most of the Wessex and the four Sea Kings safely off the ship without incident. *Causeway* sailed back out to sea with eight Wessex left on board as a reserve. A very relieved Lieutenant Ralph Miles and Sub-Lieutenant Jerry Thomas and Leading Aircrewman Martin Moreby also joined the influx of crews that day. Originally sent down on MV *Norland* as passengers, it was their third visit to the Falklands. At last they now had aircraft to fly.

With thirty helicopters operating out of Port San Carlos, overcrowding was going to be a real problem. The Sea King new arrivals sensibly moved around the corner of the bay the next day to base themselves at San Carlos, leaving the Wessex and Chinook.

Jack Lomas found himself in charge of what amounted to an entire Wessex squadron of nineteen helicopters and twenty-five aircrew. For the first time since the landings, groups of Wessex could be allocated to units on the ground or even to lift an entire battalion into action.

The only Argentine air activity that day involved an unfortunate C-130 Hercules, intercepted and shot down north of Pebble Island by a Sea Harrier flown by 801 Squadron's Sharkey Ward. Apart from a couple of ineffective bombing runs by Argentine Canberras on the Mount Kent area, there were no other daytime air raids on San Carlos that day, or indeed for the next few days.

Setting up camp required a great deal of ingenuity and making-do. Some of the aircrew found spaces to sleep in the settlement buildings. The engineers found an outbuilding in which to keep their books and tools organised and dry. The Royal Marine cook improvised using rocket boxes for his field kitchen. Other aircrew and most of the engineers stayed in tents. With so much flying to sort out, an operations and briefing tent was also set up.

Some new arrivals used more ingenuity than others. Bill Tuttey and his fellow aircrewman Petty Officer Jed Clamp didn't fancy setting up their own tent. A glance at a nearby tent spattered with chicken supreme confirmed it would be best to find somebody who knew what they were doing. They headed instead for a smart-looking tent nearby. The two Royal Marine stores sergeants inside were quick to invite them in. Tuttey and Clamp merely wanted to know where they could store thirty bottles of assorted spirits landed from *Atlantic Causeway*.

Aircrew were quick to take advantage of their ability to transport goods to keep the squadron fed. Pilots Sparky Harden and Ric Fox simply helped themselves to a pallet full of ration packs from the Brigade Maintenance Area at Ajax Bay one afternoon. Aircrew were masters at persuading stores managers to part with other goods. There were also other ways when persuasion didn't work.

On the way south, Bill Tuttey had noticed a large cage deep in the bowels of *Atlantic Causeway*'s vast interior that was full to the brim with boxes of Mars bars. The stores chief on *Causeway* was adamant that the chocolate 'nutty' was to remain locked away. It would return to Plymouth in the absence of any documented destination. The Mars bars were most likely a gift from a corporate well-wisher. It seemed ungrateful to send them back home.

Just before *Causeway* sailed back out to sea, Peter Hails and Bill Tuttey shut their Wessex down on the big foredeck and wandered casually down below. They felt it best not to draw attention to the large bolt croppers they had signed out from the aircraft maintainers, after promising to return them with interest. Several trips up and down the stairs later, the helicopter returned to Port San Carlos loaded with 15,000 Mars bars.

As well as treating themselves to the occasional Mars bar, Wessex crews were able to make themselves very popular with troops on the ground. The freezing and remote Rapier air defence missile sites surrounding San Carlos were especially grateful for their box gifts. There was no shortage of food or 'nutty'.

Nor did their sister squadrons miss out. One of the *junglie* Sea Kings had been lifting a pallet-load of Mars bars, this time donated by NAAFI, from one of the stores ships in the bay. The load started swinging from side to side underneath the helicopter. Eventually the swing got so bad that the load had to be jettisoned. Fortunately they were now over land. The pallet plummeted out of the air and landed on an otherwise unremarkable patch of Falklands grass. With resources stretched so thin, there seemed little point in flying out a new pallet and repacking the load. The 'nutty mountain' was left where it had fallen. However, Bill Pollock made sure all his Sea King crews were given the grid reference so that they could stop for refreshments. The labels on the boxes showed that the 'donated' Mars bars were out of date. But they tasted just fine.

Not all of the new arrivals were happy campers. Although the decision to keep the Wessex close in together at night turned out to be a deliberate one, it was clear that some operating practices had definitely slipped. With no flying possible during the long nights, aircrew were happy to drink and play spirited games in the great *junglie* peacetime tradition. However, this was war.

Of far greater concern was the routine use of too much power in the air. In their understandable enthusiasm to get desperately needed ammunition to the guns as quickly as possible, aircrew had noticed that they could physically lift an extra layer of shells in an underslung pallet load if they were prepared to pull more power than was usually allowed. One of the great strengths of the Wessex was that it could fly a medium payload on only one engine. With both engines running, the power limitation was usually the torque that could be applied to the transmission. Too much torque meant overstressing the helicopter drive shafts and gearbox. And nobody knew how much of this punishment the Wessex would take before it all broke and a helicopter simply dropped out of the sky.

Junglie aircrew were living in tolerable, if spartan, conditions. However, it was a completely different story for the troops advancing across the northern flank of East Falkland.

Most of the work for the newly enlarged fleet of support helicopters in the early days of June was necessarily focused on supporting 45 Commando and 3 Para. Both units had endured appalling conditions to march in long lines across miles of streams and bogs carrying enormous 80-pound bergens on their backs and weapons in their hands. As well as the physical endurance, they had to cope with the mental strain of when and where they would encounter enemy troops or enemy aircraft. In fact they encountered neither. The epic yomp, or tab, was an extraordinary feat. But it also took its toll, injuring Royal Marines and Paras alike. Every soldier fought their own private battles with wet and blistered feet, aching and strained shoulders, and the icy cold and wind of the Falklands winter.

Three days after leaving Port San Carlos, the Royal Marines arrived at Teal Inlet as the Paras were setting off. On the following night, 42 Commando were flown onto

Mount Kent by the 846 Squadron Sea Kings. So, by Friday 4 June, three major units of 3 Brigade were in position on the hills around Mount Kent waiting to make their final push on the Argentine defences surrounding the capital Port Stanley.

Although the Argentines were not threatening the British advance on the ground, their vigorous defence of Goose Green had dispelled any hope that their defences might crumble. Major General Jeremy Moore wanted to add the 5 Brigade units of Welsh and Scots Guards and Gurkhas and form a second advance on the southern flank. The problem was how to get them there with most of the support helicopters focused on keeping the supply line open along the northern flank. They would have to do it on foot, joining up with 2 Para at Goose Green along the way.

Five Brigade troops dig in at San Carlos. Freezing muddy trenches are quite a contrast to the comfort of the *QE2* and *Canberra* luxury cruise liners. But as we used to say in the military, 'If you can't take a joke, you shouldn't have joined.'

Five Brigade and their commander Brigadier Tony Wilson were concerned they might miss out on the action, presuming that 3 Brigade on the northern flank could finish off the job while 5 Brigade were still muddling around San Carlos and Goose Green.

Meanwhile, 2 Para were less than impressed at the prospect of waiting for the Guards units to arrive, and still having to walk all the way east towards Fitzroy. So, on Wednesday 2 June, they hatched a unilateral plan for a *coup de main* to achieve a giant leap forward. Five Scout helicopters armed with anti-tank SS-11 missiles and a small group of Paras conducted an air assault on a group of outbuildings at Swan Inlet. Finding the buildings empty, they then made a telephone call to the settlement manager at Fitzroy. Confirming that it was safe to talk and that there were no 'Argies' in the area, the Paras told the surprised Falkland islanders to expect to see them soon.

Back at Goose Green, Brigadier Wilson commandeered Bravo November, cramming the helicopter far above capacity with eighty-one heavily armed Paras. The Chinook set off at low level across the open terrain to land the troops at Fitzroy, following up with a further load of seventy-four Paras.

It so nearly ended in disaster. Royal Marine Mountain and Arctic Warfare observation posts in the hills overlooking Fitzroy heard the Chinook and spotted large numbers of troops on the ground through breaks in the low cloud cover. They hadn't been told to expect any British operations in the area, so had to assume the helicopter troops were Argentine reinforcements. By radio, they set up a fire mission with their headquarters to the north at Teal. Communication limitations between San Carlos, Teal and Goose Green meant that nobody outside 2 Para had any idea of the surprise move to Fitzroy. The fire mission was accepted. Guns were prepared and ready to bring down the first burst of three targeting rounds 'for effect'. It was only a break in the clouds that revealed a British Scout helicopter. The observation team realised what was going on and cancelled the fire mission with seconds to spare.

The Royal Marines and Army Air Corps operated these Scout helicopters that were used extensively for casualty evacuation and missile firing. These Army Scouts are taking off from Darwin, just yards from where a Pucara shot down their Royal Marine colleague during the battle for Goose Green.

The first Major General Jeremy Moore knew of this *coup de main* was when the RAF Chinook pilots, Flight Lieutenant Nick Grose and Flying Officer Colin Miller, marched into headquarters back at San Carlos declaring: 'You'll never guess what we just did . . .'. With their giant leap forward, 5 Brigade had catapulted themselves into the action. Moore was now forced to switch his attention towards strengthening the southern flank and supporting the isolated units at Fitzroy.

It was now essential to reinforce the position at Fitzroy with more troops and equipment. Although the Gurkhas made light work of their march to Goose Green, the Welsh Guards found the going more difficult. Progress was slow. Vehicles became bogged down, lacking the cross-country manoeuvrability of the Royal Marines' snowmobiles. After just twelve hours marching, the Welsh Guards were recalled to San Carlos, inevitably attracting derision and disbelief once news had filtered through to the 3 Brigade units on Mount Kent.

The only way to get 5 Brigade to Fitzroy was now by sea, exposing a landing ship to attack from the air. A further danger was the risk from land-based Exocet missiles fired from Stanley. Days earlier, a missile had been fired at the Type-21 frigate, HMS *Avenger*, causing the Royal Navy to establish a twenty-five-mile no-go zone around the Falklands capital.

Even with the arrival of the new Sea Kings and Wessex, most support helicopters were still busy ferrying equipment between the new Brigade Maintenance Area at Teal and the growing number of troops in the hills around Mount Kent. Bad weather restricted flying availability and flying into the front line meant frequently coming under fire. Simon Thornewill's Sea Kings had arrived in the middle of a firefight while landing the first batch of 42 Commando Royal Marines on Mount Kent. During a troop move in the same area, newly arrived Flipper Hughes found his Wessex rocked by a mortar blast. As the net closed in around the Argentine ground forces, almost all aircrew came into contact with the blast from mortar and artillery shells at some stage.

It wasn't the only unnerving experience for aircrew.

On Thursday 3 June, Sparky Harden was carrying an

underslung load of munitions beneath his Wessex to the gunnery positions now establishing themselves in the hills around Stanley. At the exact same time that he pressed the red button on his cyclic stick to release the net from the load hook, an almighty blast shook the hovering helicopter. He thought his load had gone up, only to realise it was the guns firing. Even above the thundering noise of the Wessex, the blast from a 105mm howitzer makes a spectacular heart-stopping bang. Later that day, Harden fondly recalled the close encounter: *'I nearly shat myself.'*

A consequence of the constant exposure to extreme danger was that pilots risked becoming blasé and even reckless. After two weeks of surviving air raids and conducting daring rescues from burning ships, Hector Heathcote wondered if he really was invincible. It was late afternoon the same day. Heathcote and his crewman, Kev Gleeson, had one final task to complete in Yankee Charlie, dropping off an urgent load of jerrycans full of fuel for the gun battery on Mount Kent.

'Why don't we see if we can see Stanley,' said Heathcote as he pulled in power to lift away.

Gleeson was not quite so keen on seeing the capital: 'I really don't think this is a good idea, Hector.'

In the dwindling light, Heathcote headed east at very low level towards the skyline, ignoring Gleeson's objections. It soon became obvious that there was little to see in the poor visibility and he turned back. The incident was harmless, but Heathcote knew that he'd upset his crewman.

Though only two years older than Heathcote and Harden, new arrival Paul McIntosh was something of a Wessex veteran. Despite the poor weather and visibility, one of his first missions was to lead a six-aircraft detachment to set up a new forward operating base at Teal Inlet on Friday 4 June. Flying X-Ray Bravo, McIntosh slowed the formation into a low-level hover-taxi across the high ground, one helicopter following behind another. He had then found the 45 Commando headquarters in the murk, got out and talked to the staff to establish their needs and those of the special forces. It was a good example of how close cooperation between the Royal Marines and the commando squadrons worked really well.

However, McIntosh's particularly unnerving experience wasn't due to overconfidence or bad weather or dangerous tasking. Approaching a landing site downwind to pick up troops meant that he needed to reverse track to land into wind. As he passed the troops, he flared the nose of the Wessex up sharply and tipped the aircraft on its side. At the same time, he dumped all power by lowering the collective lever as far as it would go, allowing the aircraft to slow down. The manoeuvre was technically called a 'downwind fast stop' but to the rest of us it was known as a 'steely commando landing'. As he levelled the aircraft in front of the troops, he tried to pull in power to cushion the landing. The lever jammed solidly down. He almost pulled his arm out of its socket as he wrenched desperately upwards on the lever. It still wouldn't move. He shouted 'Brace, brace!' through the intercom. Through skill, he had judged the landing perfectly without the need to use any power at all. But it was only through luck that the grassy terrain was level.

After settling heavily but without breaking anything, he shut the aircraft down to one engine to try and work out what had caused the jam. He never found out what it was. The geometric lock on the controls, or whatever the actual cause was, mysteriously cleared itself. His skill, and a little luck, helped him avoid a nasty crash which would inevitably have been blamed on pilot error.

* * *

At this time, I was still plodding south at a painfully slow twelve knots on board *Engadine*. I and the thirteen other Wessex pilots and fourteen aircrew were all beginning to doubt that we would get to the war in time. We had already been delayed by the detour following our visit by the Argentine 707 jet. The converted airliner paid us a further visit a few days later just before we reached the rest of the fleet. To the frustration of my colleagues on the upper deck, armed with machine guns and rifles, willing the airliner to come in closer, the jet had a quick look at us from five miles away before turning and heading for home.

All the little delays were mounting up. We'd spent a day fixing *Engadine*'s engine in Gibraltar; we'd detoured away from the 707; we'd stopped in the middle of the South Atlantic to recover a supply of anti-submarine torpedoes airdropped into the sea from a Hercules; and we'd stopped again to recover a team of SAS soldiers airdropped into the sea from another Hercules.

Nor was our mood helped when the boss, Mike Booth, switched off the beer taps so that we would be ready for battle. We had no idea that our colleagues at Port San Carlos felt no such need for restraint.

So it was with barely constrained excitement and relief, on a hazy Monday, 7 June, that *Engadine* finally joined the other ships of the task force in the choppy South Atlantic waters. All four Wessex were used to move the huge volume of weapons and stores we had brought for the other ships. It was our first chance to put into action the procedures, codes and flying techniques we had practised on the way south.

It was my first operational encounter with Royal Navy warships. I flew as left-hand seat co-pilot to Adrian Short, a major on exchange with us from the Army Air Corps.

A charming and gung-ho ex-Royal Artillery officer, Short also had a reputation for being a bit deaf. This reputation was wonderfully enhanced by the story of a recent incident in Northern Ireland where his co-pilot pointed out the town of 'Portadown' passing beneath them.

'*Put her down*?' shouted Short, dumping the aircraft into an emergency autorotation. 'Where? Where?'

My role as co-pilot was to find out ships' callsigns and positions and help with fuel management. With a hundred ships changing codes every day, we had a huge list. For example, taking a load from 'Kilo Uniform Eight Echo' to 'Golf Tango One Juliet' meant running down the list of names to find out that this meant a journey from our own ship RFA *Engadine* to the stores ship RFA *Fort Grange*.

Because we were always trying to take the maximum possible mix of fuel and stores, we had to stop for fuel every half hour or so. As we ferried stores from *Engadine* to the other ships, our focus was on flight flexibility and on trying to find ships that were not in the sector to which they were assigned. Often we would be queuing up behind other helicopters to drop a load. *Pingers* in their anti-submarine Sea Kings seemed to test our patience especially and gave us an easy target on which to vent our frustrations. We needed to get on with it.

Trying to land on the flagship aircraft carrier HMS *Hermes* ('Charlie November Two Eight') to drop off senior pilot Rob Flexman for an operations brief was almost impossible. We were not the first Wessex crew to be put in our place at the bottom of *Hermes*'s list of priorities. While we were relegated to hover behind and to the right of the ship in the 'starboard wait' or 'spot 10 starboard', we had plenty of time to reflect on how all of the warships looked the worse for wear. From our bird's-eye view,

One of the iconic shots of the Falklands war. Pete Manley and Ric Fox fly Wessex Yankee Sierra over the broken back of HMS *Antelope* in San Carlos water.

This was the astonishing sight confronting Oily Knight and Arthur Balls in their Wessex on the afternoon of 25 May. The helicopters hovering over the upturned HMS *Coventry* are all 846 Squadron junglie Sea Kings.

My 847 Squadron colleagues Tim Hughes and Bill Tuttey were first on the scene after the dreadful attack on RFA *Sir Galahad* and *Sir Tristram* at Port Pleasant. The identity of the SAS soldier kneeling in the doorway remains a mystery. After helping them throughout the rescue, he simply vanished.

Another of the iconic shots of the Falklands war. Hugh Clark's 825 Squadron Sea King hovering in and out of the smoke from *Sir Galahad* while trying to blow the life rafts away from the ship.

(*Facing page*)
(*Above*) Former Wessex boss Tim Stanning was in the back of Hugh Clark's Sea King that was hovering in and out of the smoke from the burning Sir Galahad. This was his view from the aircraft cabin.

(*Below*) On 8 June, HMS *Plymouth* took the brunt of an attack by five Mirage jets in Falkland Sound. Amazingly none of the bombs went off. This is Paul McIntosh winching Rick Jolly and a stretcher onboard to help with the wounded.

The Forward Operating Base at Port San Carlos got a bit crowded after the reinforcement helicopters disembarked from Atlantic Causeway on 1 June. So the dozen Pinger Sea Kings moved around the corner to a new base at San Carlos the next day, leaving behind nineteen Wessex and the Chinook.

I may have been a highly trained and highly capable young pilot. But I nearly blew it the time I pushed down on the tail of a Pucara with a collapsed nose wheel at Goose Green just after the war. When I moved sideways to release, the Pucara's tail flipped violently back up, narrowly missing the explosive flotation canister on the Wessex wheel.

(*Above*) Every squadron likes its formation fly pasts. These are some of our 847 Squadron Wessex celebrating the move from Port San Carlos to snow-covered Navy Point, opposite Port Stanley, a few days after the war. Stanley airfield is in the distance behind the helicopters.

(*Left*) As the war ended, the weather became our new enemy. Al Doughty and I were half way across San Carlos water with an underslung load. We had just enough time to turn back and land before being hit by a sudden massive snowstorm. Seconds later, one of the engines flamed out under the sudden deluge of snow.

Having arrived late for the war, 847 Squadron was probably the last active service unit to leave the Falkland Islands. We flew back in dribs and drabs first to Ascension by Hercules and then on to Brize Norton by VC10. I was very relieved to be back after four and a half months away. There was no official welcome for us. But my mum was happy.

Two years after the Falklands war, I'm in warmer climes as Lieutenant Benson RN, Wasp pilot and flight commander of HMS *Apollo*.

looking down on the seven Sea Harriers parked out on her deck, *Hermes*'s sides looked almost more brown than grey, dripping with streaks of rust and weather damage.

It felt good to be airborne for the first time in a week and to have arrived with the fleet at last. Next stop was San Carlos. We really needed to get in before dawn to get the aircraft safely off the ship and disembark our accompanying SAS passengers. It was already taking longer than we had planned to get rid of all our stores. The final straw was when one of the supply ships, for reasons best known to themselves, would only accept a delivery when ordered to do so by the Admiral. It added yet another hour.

Engadine turned to the west and headed into the Falklands. Our final delay was to prove crucial.

Chapter 13

Disaster at Port Pleasant
8 June 1982

The leap forward to Fitzroy by 2 Para on Wednesday 2 June had paid off so far. Opportunistic, it put tremendous pressure on land forces commander Major General Jeremy Moore to prevent the Paras from being isolated. Four major units of 3 Brigade – over 2,000 men of 2 and 3 Para, 42 and 45 Commando – now lay exposed thirty-five miles to the east of the beachhead at San Carlos. The successful arrival of Atlantic Causeway *had more than doubled the number of Wessex and Sea King helicopters. Every one of them was needed to keep these troops supplied.*

The newly arrived troops of 5 Brigade's Scots and Welsh Guards were keen to get involved in the action. But with the helicopters fully occupied supporting 3 Brigade, the men of 5 Brigade would have to walk from San Carlos.

Throughout the land campaign, the Argentines had yet to show an appetite for counterattack. They had reinforced Goose Green. They had defended their own positions fiercely. They had attacked vigorously from the air.

Nonetheless the threat of counterattack had to be taken seriously.

Two Para's great leap forward at Fitzroy had been precipitated by the arrival of 5 Brigade in San Carlos from the liners *Canberra* and *Norland*. Their commanders simply hadn't fancied sitting around at Goose Green watching the new arrivals wander past and take the next bit of glory. Having seized land at Fitzroy and opened up the southern flank, they were now in urgent need of support and reinforcements.

But the three units on the northern flank still needed supplies. An overnight run by HMS *Fearless* and two of its landing craft helped to move 3 Brigade's stores area forward to Teal Inlet. Many of the troops on the front line were still without their bergens, having been forced to dump them during their long march from Port San Carlos. The early days of June were the coldest of the war so far, with temperatures dipping well below freezing. The constant need to build up forward supplies and the demand for ammunition and water meant restricting other requirements.

On the morning of Thursday 3 June, the remainder of 2 Para were helicoptered into Fitzroy by Chinook and 825 Squadron's Sea Kings. The remaining 1/7 Gurkhas Rifles, the first of the 5 Brigade new arrivals, were also helicoptered across the Sussex Mountains to Goose Green. The Gurkhas were to conduct patrols into Lafonia, where the Argentine reinforcements had fled towards the end of the battle for Goose Green.

Getting 5 Brigade to Fitzroy as well was proving difficult. Equipment shortages, the lack of independent helicopter and marine support, the sheer confusion of linking equipment with people, and a general lack of communication were all contributing factors. After the aborted attempt by the Welsh Guard to cross the Sussex Mountains, it became clear that the only serious option for reinforcing Fitzroy was by sea.

The Royal Navy, however, were acutely aware of the potential threat to assault ships or landing ships in the exposed water south of Port Stanley, whether from land-based Exocet or air attack. Their ships at sea had already taken a beating from the South Atlantic weather. If the Navy lost another major warship, the political pressure at home for a ceasefire might prove irresistible. Commanders at Task Force HQ Northwood in the UK, and HMS *Hermes* at sea, signalled conflicting intentions to the amphibious warfare commanders on *Fearless* in San Carlos.

On the evening of Saturday 5 June, the assault ship *Intrepid* sailed out of San Carlos Water, through Falkland Sound, and around the coast to the south of East Falkland. Both assault ships *Intrepid* and *Fearless* had huge open tank decks underneath their flight decks that could carry LCUs (Landing Craft Utilities). Opening the rear doors flooded the deck and allowed the landing craft to float out of the stern. The plan was to offload *Intrepid*'s four LCUs, under the command of Major Ewen Southby-Tailyour RM, near to Elephant Island for the relatively short transit to Bluff Cove. Although Fitzroy was the preferred landing site, with buildings in which to shelter, the retreating Argentines had blown up a small but vital bridge linking the two settlements. Landing the troops directly at Bluff Cove would save them a long detour around the coast.

With the sea swell rising as the weather worsened, *Intrepid* flooded her stern and despatched her landing craft, each crammed with 150 soldiers from the Scots Guards. However, in an attempt to keep clear of the Exocet threat, *Intrepid* chose to do this off the coast of Lively Island, to the south of Choiseul Sound. They were supposed to be to the north. It meant that the landing craft now had an extra twenty miles of open water to cover, on top of the original ten-mile journey they expected to make along the coast and inland.

Off the coast of East Falkland, the destroyer HMS *Cardiff* and frigate HMS *Yarmouth* had not been informed of British movements in the area. As part of the bid to improve communications between units on the southern flank, a radio re-broadcast station had been set up on Pleasant Peak between Goose Green and Fitzroy. Shortly before midnight, an Army Gazelle helicopter carrying two signallers and replacement equipment approached Pleasant Peak to land. HMS *Cardiff* picked up the radar contact, thinking it to be an Argentine Hercules, and fired a Sea Dart missile. The Gazelle exploded in a ball of fire in front of the horrified radio operators on the ground.

Soon afterwards, *Cardiff* began firing her 4.5-inch guns at the unknown surface contacts near Choiseul Sound. Crashing explosions near the landing craft threw huge plumes of water into the air. Illuminated by starshell bursts above their heads, and unable to outrun the pursuing warships, the coxswains stopped their landing craft in the water. A hurried exchange of light signals in Morse code prevented further shelling and complete disaster.

Crammed into each flat-bottomed landing craft, the Scots Guards were now soaked and frozen from the sea spray, as well as traumatised by the near-misses. Food, hot drinks and rest were out of the question. The journey should have taken four hours at most. Instead the long night transit in the rolling seas became an agonising nightmare of human endurance. It was eight hours before the LCUs finally limped up to the jetty at Bluff Cove, to be met by the astonished soldiers of 2 Para. Dazed and exhausted, many Guardsmen were unable to move by themselves because of prolonged exposure, stiffness and cramp. The Paras had to lift them physically off the craft and onto land.

The whole episode was a monumental cock-up. Through a series of miscommunications, the British had lost a Gazelle helicopter and four men. Far worse, they were a whisker away from losing an entire battalion of 600 Scots Guards to naval gunfire, exposure and drowning – almost twice the number of lives lost in the sinking of the *Belgrano*. The pressure from so many grieving families back home might have made it impossible for the British government to continue the campaign.

The following evening, 6 June, it was HMS *Fearless*'s turn for the night-time run around the coast, carrying the battalion of Welsh Guards and various other specialist units. Only two landing craft were available to go with them inside the tank deck. The plan was for the four LCUs that had dropped off the Scots Guards at Bluff Cove earlier that morning to come out to *Fearless* and offload the Welsh Guards.

The good news was that *Fearless* had chosen to make the rendezvous at Elephant Island. It meant a mere four-hour journey in the landing craft in the rain and cold, and hopefully no naval gunfire. The bad news was that the four LCUs they expected to meet failed to show up. Poor weather and further miscommunication meant that the landing craft crews never got the message to come out. With *Fearless* desperate to get back to the cover of San Carlos before dawn, the Welsh Guards were forced to load half of their number, as well as the sappers sent to repair the Fitzroy bridge, into the two LCUs on board. *Fearless* returned with the other half of the Welsh Guards and no landing craft.

At the same time that half of the Welsh Guards were landing at Bluff Cove in the two landing craft, the landing ship RFA *Sir Tristram* was also on its way to Port Pleasant, the inlet just around the corner from them. When *Tristram* arrived in the early morning, loaded with her cargo of ammunition, stores and bridge repair equipment destined for Fitzroy, the missing LCUs were there to help the ship unload. The flatness of the landscape around the inlet of Port Pleasant meant that *Tristram* stood out starkly. With the weather beginning to improve, it was clear that all of the LCUs would need to work at full tilt to complete the offload by the following night.

Early that morning, 7 June, four Argentine photo-reconnaissance Learjets overflew Falkland Sound at high altitude, believing themselves to be safe from missile attack. Two Sea Darts sped upwards from HMS *Exeter*. Aircrew in San Carlos had watched the missile trail hanging like a piece of string from the sky. One missile fell short. The other, at extreme range, blew the tail off one of the Learjets. It was *Exeter*'s third success and Sea Dart's fifth. The three other Learjets returned safely to the mainland with photos of the British activity in San Carlos and around East Falkland. It included a landing ship offloading in the distance at Port Pleasant.

Former Wessex boss Tim Stanning had been at the heart of command and control of the land war. He had helped plan helicopter operations on board HMS *Fearless* before the landings. He had sat in the 3 Brigade headquarter tent at San Carlos after the landings as the commanders wrangled over who could have what aircraft in between diving into trenches during the air raids.

His role had now switched to recceing forward bases

for helicopter operations. At Teal Inlet on the northern flank a few days earlier, he had flown up to watch the unloading of the RFA *Sir Percivale*. It was an incongruous sight seeing the dark shapes of its largely Chinese crew dotted around the Falkland landscape in their blue raincoats. They had disembarked from the ship during unloading for their own safety and had no camouflage kit. Even though they stood out like sore thumbs, Stanning still thought they were far better off on land than on the ship.

It was now early morning on Tuesday 8 June. Stanning was sitting in the back of one of the 825 Squadron Sea Kings recently disembarked from *Atlantic Causeway*. He was on his way to explore possible locations for a forward refuelling site in the Fitzroy area.

The last thing anybody needed at Port Pleasant was more work for the LCUs. So it was a surprise when the landing ship *Sir Galahad* sailed into the calm waters to join her sister ship *Sir Tristram* under the clear blue skies. Now there were two landing ships in the inlet, both of them vulnerable and defenceless. It made sense to keep as many people off the ships as possible until they had finished unloading.

Ewen Southby-Tailyour immediately motored over to *Sir Galahad* in one of the LCUs, only to find the remaining 300 Welsh Guards on board. His encouragement that they disembark urgently quickly turned to agitated protest, even giving a direct order at one stage. The senior Welsh Guards officer initially refused to offload his men, insisting he had been ordered to wait until the LCUs were free to take them around the corner to Bluff Cove.

Opposite Tim Stanning in the back of the Sea King sat Commander Mike Cudmore, a senior air engineer officer tasked to investigate the crash of the Gazelle helicopter three nights earlier. Cudmore looked deeply worried as the Sea King came in to land on the side of Pleasant Peak. He was to be abandoned on a bleak and remote hillside miles from anywhere. A pile of ash marked the remains of the Gazelle. Before disconnecting from the intercom, he turned to Stanning and insisted: 'You have to promise you'll come back and get me.' His plea invited a mischievous reply. But Stanning decided it wouldn't be a good joke. He looked him in the eye and promised to return. The Sea King lifted off to continue its journey east towards Fitzroy.

As they came in to land at the little settlement of Fitzroy, the two landing ships at Port Pleasant stood out clearly through the door windows in the clear morning light. 'Sitting ducks', thought Stanning. Having seen the surplus crew offloaded at Teal, it never occurred to him that there would be many people on board. It would be madness. After a quick discussion with the pilot, Lieutenant Commander Hugh Clark, commanding officer of 825 Squadron, the Sea King landed and shut down just on the edge of Fitzroy settlement. Stanning got out to have a good look around.

It was another classic Falklands day.

Tim Hughes and Bill Tuttey's job that morning was to deliver urgent stores and mail to the two landing ships and then return to San Carlos. As they flew up towards the ships, still a few miles short of Fitzroy, they spotted a lone soldier wandering across the bleak terrain. It seemed a little odd that somebody should be out completely on their own. It wasn't even obvious whether he was British or Argentine. But they decided to land their Wessex, X-Ray Quebec, and offer him a lift.

'Where are you going?' shouted Tuttey.

'Just drop me off when you get there,' the man replied vaguely and jumped in the back.

Hughes and Tuttey presumed he was SAS. The M16 assault rifle was the biggest clue, aided by the droopy moustache and the small rucksack. But he seemed happy to get a lift and stayed in the helicopter while Hughes landed on the deck of *Sir Galahad* for refuel.

As the Chinese flight-deck crew connected the hose up to the Wessex, Hughes watched the *junglie* Sea King Victor Zulu lifting loads off *Sir Tristram*. Lieutenant John Miller and Petty Officer Aircrewman 'Splash' Ashdown had spent the night on board *Sir Galahad* as she sailed around the coast from San Carlos with the Welsh Guards. Having got airborne at first light, both the Sea King crew were surprised that stores and ammunition were being unloaded by pontoon, yet the Guardsmen had been left on board ship. It didn't seem sensible considering how much the ships stood out in the morning light. Victor Zulu was now busy offloading the Rapier air defence missile systems from ship to shore. Some of the missiles and their control boxes had been set up but were not yet ready to fire. It was a vital task. Rapier had already been credited with shooting down one Argentine Mirage jet at San Carlos, and probably a Skyhawk as well. Once the system was up and running at Fitzroy, the two landing ships would no longer be quite so exposed.

The newly arrived 825 Squadron Sea Kings had dramatically boosted the available lift to the land forces. Each Sea King could carry roughly double the load of their Wessex counterparts. Lieutenants John Boughton and Phil Sheldon were both experienced pilots but well aware of *junglie* suspicions about the ability of *pingers* to cope in a commando environment of featureless Falkland terrain and poor visibility. They hadn't helped their cause when, soon after disembarking from *Atlantic Causeway* a week earlier, they were briefed to move artillery and other equipment forward to Mount Kent as underslung loads. Standing on the slopes of Mount Kent, Brigadier Julian Thompson had watched a Sea King approach, with a jeep underslung. Major Peter Cameron, boss of 3 Brigade Air Squadron 'teeny-weeny' helicopters, came running up: 'Do you see that helicopter there? It's got my rebro vehicle hanging underneath and it's flying straight towards the enemy.'

The Sea King overflew the commanders into no-man's land before dropping the jeep and three Royal Marine signallers onto a hilltop in full view of the enemy. There was just time for a shout of 'fuck me that's Stanley' before the stranded Marines came under sustained artillery fire from the Argentines.

Thompson was worried code books may have been left in the vehicle. As well as despatching a patrol from 45 Commando, Cameron himself took one of the Marines back up to the site on foot just to make sure. The unfortunate, and thankfully rare, navigational error cost a jeep and a serious shrapnel wound to one of the signallers.

Now, on the morning of Tuesday 8 June, both John Boughton in Sea King 504 and Phil Sheldon in Sea King 501 had been told to help move equipment off the two landing ships at Fitzroy. But with Miller's *jungle* Sea King Victor Zulu already on the job when they got there, they returned to Goose Green to shuttle men and equipment back to Fitzroy.

Bad weather and attrition had prevented the Argentines from launching any meaningful air strikes so far in June. But this was to be a big one. Soon after midday local time, fourteen Argentine air force jets powered into Falklands airspace in three waves intent on sinking British ships. It was HMS *Exeter* again that raised the alarm 'Air raid warning red'.

The first Argentine jets were decoys. Four Mirage 3s ran in at low level across the northern half of West Falkland. They broke off their attack after the Sea Harrier Combat Air Patrol started to intercept. Within minutes, the main attacking force of five Skyhawks was crossing the southern end of Falkland Sound and winding its way across Lafonia through the occasional rain shower. The arrowhead formation sped onwards towards Fitzroy, ignoring two British helicopters. One of the helicopters was Boughton's Sea King. He immediately radioed a warning of the contact before taking cover in a fold in the land, talked down by his Leading Aircrewman Roy Egglestone. To the Argentine pilots, the only other sign of British activity appeared to be a lot of troops on the ground at Fitzroy who opened up on them with small-arms fire. But as the Skyhawks climbed and banked steeply on their starboard wings, the two ships came into view. Circling round to the south of Bluff Cove, the Skyhawks continued their turn to run in from the east. The first three jets aimed at *Sir Galahad*, the nearest target. The second two went for *Sir Tristram*.

On the ground at Fitzroy, some of the Rapier batteries had been deployed but were not yet properly calibrated. To the frustration of the operators, their missiles failed to respond at all when fired, sitting uselessly on their rails as the Skyhawks streaked past. In the air, the Combat Air Patrol was nowhere to be seen. The brand new airstrip at Port San Carlos had been put out of action earlier that morning after an RAF ground-attack Harrier crash-landed, while *Hermes* had withdrawn further to the east for repairs, shortening the available time on task for the Sea Harriers anyway. *Galahad* and *Tristram* were defenceless.

Meanwhile a third wave of Daggers crossed Falkland Sound, intending to follow the Skyhawks to Port Pleasant. However, the frigate HMS *Plymouth* appeared unexpectedly in the open water, providing an opportunity that was too good to miss. The Daggers swept past the ship and turned in to attack from the north. One by one they ran in, dropping their bombs and spitting cannon fire. *Plymouth* returned fire with cannon and a Seacat missile that missed. One of the Dagger's bombs went straight through *Plymouth*'s funnel. Two bombs ricocheted off the ship. A fourth lodged in a rear compartment, causing a depth charge to go off. Miraculously, none of the bombs exploded. Yet the smoke billowing from *Plymouth*'s fire caused the Argentine pilots to leave the scene convinced that they had sunk another British ship.

Paul McIntosh was at the controls of X-Ray Tango, assigned to the field hospital at Ajax Bay for the day. He had fled to a small gulley overlooking Falkland Sound on hearing the warning from *Fearless*, 'Air raid warning red, SCRAM!'

Leading Aircrewman Martin Moreby managed to spot two of the five Mirages as they sped through. The scene was lit up with an array of weaponry fired from the ships. As the attack cleared, smoke could be seen pouring from *Plymouth*'s funnel and flight-deck area. A radio call summoned the Wessex to stop by to pick up the senior surgeon from *Fearless*. McIntosh lifted from the gulley and headed down across the water. As soon as their wheels touched the deck of *Fearless*, Rick Jolly ran across the flight deck. They now flew straight out into Falkland

Sound where *Plymouth* had already turned to limp back in towards San Carlos, escorted by a Type-21 frigate.

With smoke pouring from the ship, Jolly was winched down onto the foc'sle. It was a scene reminiscent of his rescue of the sailors from the burning HMS *Ardent*. A few minutes later, the Wessex was called to approach the flight deck, now smoking less vigorously, to collect one of the wounded sailors on a stretcher. The flight deck of *Plymouth* was designed for the much smaller Wasp helicopter and in any case was now cluttered with damage control and firefighting equipment. McIntosh improvised by edging his starboard wheel onto the deck, leaving his port and rear wheels suspended over the sea. One wheel of the Wessex had landed. Martin Moreby helped medics slide the stretcher into the hovering helicopter. Jolly jumped in afterwards and X-Ray Tango headed straight for Ajax Bay.

Hearing the air raid warning red call on the long-range HF radio, *junglie* helicopters Sea King Victor Zulu and Wessex X-Ray Quebec immediately left the landing ships for the relative safety of land. Hughes called down to Tuttey: 'If you don't mind, I think we'll go and hide behind those rocks.' He lifted off the deck of *Sir Galahad* and set the Wessex down on a spit of land a few hundred yards away to the south-west. Even though their refuel had been interrupted, X-Ray Quebec had taken on just enough to get back to San Carlos. As soon as the all-clear sounded, they could head back. The landing ships were not to be so lucky.

From the cabin door, Tuttey and his unknown SAS passenger had a clear view of the RFAs out to their right in Port Pleasant. Hughes picked up his camera from the dashboard to take some photos of the ships. Boughton's voice over the radio soon made it clear the raid was heading their way. 'All stations, four enemy contacts west of Fitzroy.'

It was the soldier who spotted them first, pointing out the swooping black shapes that were now heading directly towards them. The Skyhawks sped past the ships, behind the Wessex, and away. It was just too far away to see the bombs falling from each jet. But their effect was soon apparent. To the helicopter crew with their helmets on and the Wessex whirling away noisily, the explosions appeared strangely silent. Numbed and in shock, Hughes could only think that his photos would be a scoop.

Sea King Victor Zulu was on the beach pointing west as the raid approached. From his cabin doorway, aircrewman Splash Ashdown was watching soldiers lying on the ground, test-firing their rifles to align the sights. He couldn't see the Skyhawks as they sped down the other side of the helicopter. So when John Miller shouted 'We're under attack!' Ashdown calmly replied: 'No we're not. They're just zeroing their weapons.' The noise of the explosions shortly afterwards made it clear that he was very wrong.

The first Skyhawk scored direct hits with three of its four bombs. Two bombs detonated towards the rear of *Sir Galahad*. The second and third aircraft either failed to release their bombs or missed altogether. But the damage was done. Almost immediately afterwards the second pair of Skyhawks swept past *Sir Tristram* leaving unexploded bombs that killed two Chinese crewmen and started fires. Black smoke started to billow out of the rear end of *Galahad*, although *Tristram* appeared relatively unscathed.

Inside *Sir Galahad* was a scene from hell. The exploding bomb had ignited a cache of fuel. The resulting fireball gathered pace and rolled through the tank deck. The intense heat set fire to clothes, flesh and hair of the exposed Guardsmen and crew. Ammunition cooked off causing new explosions. The subsequent evacuation from the tank deck and up onto the foc'sle was a model of exceptional order and individual courage. Stories abound of badly wounded and burnt men helping others worse off than themselves.

Hughes and Tuttey had no idea whether the Skyhawks would come back for a second strike. Had *Plymouth* not taken the hit out to the west, the Daggers would also have added to the horror at Fitzroy. X-Ray Quebec lifted off almost immediately. *Sir Galahad* now began to spew black smoke and flames from the stern. As the Wessex approached the ship, they could see crew members escape the blaze by jumping over the side into the freezing water. At the front of the ship, smoke and men were beginning to emerge up through the hold onto the forward deck.

Hughes hover-taxied the Wessex sideways across to the stern. Several Chinese crewmen were thrashing around in the water with suitcases floating next to them. Tuttey lowered the orange strop; one crew member managed to put his arms through it. As he was raised out of the water, two other crew clung onto him, their suitcases blowing across the surface. Somehow Tuttey managed to haul the three men into the cabin without any of them falling back into the sea. The two others were lifted up one by one. Hughes eased the aircraft's nose forward and pulled in power to transition away towards the shore.

Immediately after the attack, Miller and Ashdown had fled from the beach to the nearest cover and shut down. Within just two minutes they were starting up again. It was all too obvious that the Welsh Guardsmen would need urgent help. Over the short-range UHF radio an officer from *Sir Galahad* called: 'Please hold off the front until we've launched the dinghies and lifeboats'. By now, the first two Sea Kings, Victor Zulu and 504, were approaching *Galahad*. Hughes repeated the request: 'Approaching helos, hold off while they launch their boats.'

Both aircraft flared sharply to slow down, but the huge downdraft upturned several of the empty dinghies. 'Wankers!' Tuttey said to Hughes. His frustration reflected the horror of the situation more than anything else.

One behind the other, the two Sea Kings began winching shocked and bedraggled survivors from the foc'sle of *Sir Galahad*. Having dropped off the shivering crew, Wessex X-Ray Quebec returned to the stricken ship to join in. Thick layers of paint were now peeling from *Galahad*'s overheating funnel.

To the north of the ships, Stanning and Clark had watched the appalling event from a different angle. They and their crew, Sub-Lieutenant Brian Evans and Chief Aircrewman David Jackson, ran for their Sea King 507 in a desperate rush to get airborne and help. Within minutes a third 825 Squadron Sea King was on the scene as Sheldon and his crewman Petty Officer Tug Wilson arrived from Goose Green in 501. They were followed soon afterwards by a fourth, Steve Isacke in 509.

Sheldon was already low on fuel and directed 501 towards the apparently unscathed *Sir Tristram*. Her lifeboats had been launched to assist *Galahad*. As the helicopter approached the flight deck, the only indication that *Tristram* had been hit was a bomb hole below the flight deck. The big Sea King was cleared to land. Sheldon had no idea that the stern of the ship was on fire directly underneath him. Shortly afterwards, X-Ray Quebec took its place on the flight deck. Like Sheldon and Wilson before them, Hughes and Tuttey landed on *Tristram* completely unaware that they were on top of a raging fire. The Chinese flight-deck crew, like so many in Port Pleasant that day, displayed exceptional bravery.

It was a cruel twist that *Galahad* took the brunt of the day's bombing. After the initial blast and fireball that caused so many appalling burns, the worst of the fire and smoke was confined to the stern. Bodies scrambled over the side from the central deck into liferafts and other small craft. All of the helicopters were now either winching people from the front of the ship or directly from the rafts. The enthusiastic arrival of the first helicopters had given an idea about how to get the evacuees to shore faster. Now aircraft started using their downwash to blow the rafts towards shore, where shocked soldiers and medics from 2 Para acted as reception and first-aid parties.

Some of the liferafts began drifting towards the blazing stern of *Sir Galahad* and into extreme danger. Clark manoeuvred his Sea King in and out of the billowing black smoke, behind the mangled ruins of *Galahad*'s flight deck, to blow the liferafts away from the exploding ship. Behind Clark, in the cabin of the Sea King, Stanning assisted Jackson with the wounded as the thick smoke and acrid stench of burning metal and flesh filled the cabin of the helicopter. The fires on *Tristram* had now taken hold and she was also being abandoned.

All six helicopters took turns in winching wounded men from both ship and liferafts, dropping the blackened and bloodied bodies onto the immediate shoreline and later on into Fitzroy settlement. Hovering over the front of *Sir Galahad*, all crews felt the random blasts and heat of the exploding munitions eating away at the tank deck. Sheldon closed his window after one particular blast, somehow hoping it would add protection. Winching soldiers up from a nearby dinghy, Tuttey could hear the *bumphs* going off next to Sheldon's Sea King, even with his helmet on and above the sound of the Wessex. 'They're doing a good job,' he said to Hughes.

As Boughton winched the last few men off, the task shifted towards moving the badly wounded back to the field hospital at Ajax Bay and on to the hospital ship *Uganda*.

In the back of each aircraft, crewmen including Tuttey, Ashdown, Wilson, Jackson and Egglestone, all came face to face with the full horror of terrible burns and wounds: the blackened hairless faces and the stink of burning flesh. At the beach first-aid post, Tuttey loaded several wounded soldiers on stretchers to take them back to Ajax Bay. At first he thought one of the Guardsman was Indian; his head was like a big black football. It was the very badly burned Simon Weston. Tuttey lit a cigarette and stuck it in Weston's mouth. The burns gave off a terrible heat as well as smell. A medic at Ajax Bay later told Tuttey that it was the worst burns he'd ever seen.

In the cabin of the Wessex, the unknown passenger seemed remarkably unfazed. A wounded Guardsman was bleeding badly from a severed hand that was hanging by a few tendons. The SAS man simply pulled out his knife and cut off the useless hand, despatching it out of the cabin door without ceremony, whilst shoving a shell dressing onto the wounded stump. But it had clearly affected him. At the end of the day, Tuttey asked where he wanted to get off. 'Anywhere,' he replied, 'except where we have just come from.'

War viewed through the windscreen of an aircraft can seem remote. It is largely a visual experience, without the noise, smell or even temperature of the battlefield. The acrid smoke and terrible smell of burning flesh had made it very real indeed. Even if it was a dreadful day for the crewmen, it was almost worse on this occasion for the pilots, unable to see their passengers but often over-come by waves of appalling stench. Hughes was not the only pilot to tell his crewman during the rescue that he was not feeling very well.

Back at San Carlos, McIntosh and Moreby had been one of several crews to hear the 'All stations: all available aircraft required for casevac' radio call from a clearly very agitated Gazelle pilot.

McIntosh had answered immediately as the assigned casualty aircraft: 'Request location.'

The reply from the Gazelle was ominous: 'Head towards Fitzroy and it will be obvious.'

In the distance, they could soon see the smoke rising, still not knowing what awaited. It didn't take long to find out. *Sir Galahad* was ablaze from end to end. Casualties were being ferried ashore and there were floats everywhere in the water. Shutting X-Ray Tango down to load casual-ties, McIntosh was struck by the calmness of the situation. A Royal Marine officer seemed to be taking efficient charge. The two of them were left to conduct a sort of field triage, prioritising which casualties should go back to Ajax Bay first and, worse, who would be left behind. A journalist insisted on taking a space in the Wessex. McIntosh left him behind.

As X-Ray Tango returned to San Carlos, a second wave of Skyhawks sped past them. It was one of two further Argentines raids on that day. Three hours after the attack on Fitzroy, four Skyhawks sent as a follow-up attack were driven away from Port Pleasant by sheer weight of small-arms fire. As they fled to the south, they sighted the landing craft at the mouth of Choiseul Sound. The craft was returning from Goose Green with 5 Brigade headquarters vehicles and vital radio equipment. Having previously been shot up near Elephant Island by the naval gunfire of HMS *Cardiff*, the coxswain of the landing craft unwisely thought it safer to travel in daylight. For the Skyhawks, it was an undefended target. Two of the jets swooped in for the attack. The first overshot but the second sunk the landing craft with a direct hit, killing six men.

High above their heads, two Sea Harriers spotted them. Diving in for the attack, Flight Lieutenant Dave Morgan and Lieutenant Dave Smith destroyed three of the Skyhawks, including both attackers. Two were shot down by Morgan's Sidewinders. The third eventually crashed into a sand dune, after attracting cannon fire from Morgan and a Sidewinder from Smith. The fourth Skyhawk escaped without help from the four accompanying Mirage escorts that failed to provide their top cover.

Forty-five minutes later, a further attempt by a flight of three more Skyhawks was also driven off by small-arms fire in the Fitzroy and Mount Kent areas. All three aircraft were damaged and fortunate to return safely to the mainland.

Amidst the drama of the situation, pilots still needed to make a stream of complex practical judgments and decisions about how to manage their mission. Aviators call this 'captaincy'. Captaincy includes managing aircraft capabilities, mission priorities, route planning, fuel and payload. Hughes, Boughton, Miller, Sheldon, Clark and the other aircraft captains involved with the *Galahad* rescue showed exceptional captaincy on this day.

In the extreme situation of war, there is often a fine line between great captaincy and cock-up. For example, most *junglie* pilots bent the rules by squeezing one or more wheels of a large helicopter onto a small flight deck for which they were not *officially* cleared. You looked great if you got away with it. You looked a prat if you left your rotor tips behind, or worse. Managing fuel was where pilots most frequently came close to the fine line. McIntosh was already concerned about fuel before he set off from San Carlos for his second run. He reckoned he should have just about enough for the return journey. After starting his rotors again at Fitzroy with more terribly wounded soldiers in the cabin, he asked other helos if there was a 'bollock' – a massive fuel container – anywhere, as there was at Teal. No luck. The journey back was going to be very tight indeed.

McIntosh knew the Wessex manual said the aircraft uses less fuel with one engine shut down. Bill Pollock had already applied the theory years before in a Wessex and now in a Sea King on the way back from the Argentine fishing trawler *Narwhal*. On both occasions, it had kept him airborne long enough to avoid ditching into the sea.

Unsure whether he would make it back to San Carlos, McIntosh bravely tested the theory for himself on the Wessex. But, as a single pilot, there was nobody to double-check his move. He would have to do it on his own. He very carefully pulled back the speed select lever for the port engine and closed the fuel cock. As the port engine stopped, the starboard engine took the strain. His fuel flow gauges confirmed that he was using less fuel. It might give him the valuable few more minutes in the air that he needed. He flew low over the ridge of the Sussex Mountains and down towards the heavily armed warships below in San Carlos Water. These were nervous moments at the best of times, wondering whether he would be shot down or caught in crossfire. Seeing that *Fearless* was a mile nearer than the facilities at Ajax Bay, he requested an urgent refuel. That extra mile could be one too many.

Sod's law intervened at exactly the wrong moment with

the final 'Air raid warning red' of the day. As McIntosh approached the big assault ship, the flight-deck officer waved him off, refusing permission to land. No way! He gingerly brought X-Ray Tango into a hover alongside the flyco control room and insisted on landing 'Now'. Meanwhile, Moreby frantically pointed out the bandages and wounded soldiers inside the cabin. The flight-deck officer immediately waved the aircraft across, ignoring the apoplectic senior officer in flyco. Safely on deck and very relieved to be taking on fuel, flyco asked for the pilot's name. McIntosh replied that he would get back to them later.

The rescue and casualty evacuation from *Sir Galahad* continued on after dark with other aircraft. Both Sea King squadron commanding officers were involved, each flying back to San Carlos from Fitzroy at low level at dusk.

Eight-four-six Squadron boss Simon Thornewill's day had started with a surreal early morning assault operation to land troops near a suspected Argentine stronghold at Cape Dolphin, the remote tip of East Falkland fifteen miles to the north of Fanning Head. Intelligence had warned that it was a possible site for land-based Exocet missile launchers, a deadly threat to the ships entering Falkland Sound. As his formation of three Sea Kings drew closer to the obvious activity ahead of them on the beach, the situation turned to one of hilarity. The activity was neither Argentines nor Exocets, but penguins.

Now loaded with badly burned men in Victor Alpha, Thornewill looked up from the valley and thought to himself: 'I'm glad we're down here and not up on that high ground.' He had no idea that he was looking at exactly the area where the Gazelle had been shot down two days earlier.

269

It was where his opposite number, 825 Squadron boss Hugh Clark was now heading in Sea King 507. Tim Stanning reminded him to stop and pick up Mike Cudmore, the engineer abandoned there earlier in the day. Clambering into the back of the Sea King, Cudmore was taken aback by the gruesome scene that confronted him; it was like something out of *M*A*S*H*. There was blood everywhere and crewmen holding drips to wounded men. Stanning wrote a quick note and held it up: '*GALAHAD* hit, on fire. Other LSL being abandoned.'

Imagine being an air engineering officer dropped off on a remote hillside to investigate the scene of a crash. When your helicopter returns to pick you up later in the day, the scene that confronts you inside the cabin is straight out of *M*A*S*H*, full of horribly burnt and wounded men. This is the note Tim Stanning wrote to try to explain what was going on.

Altogether it had been a disastrous day for both sides. Fifty-one British lives were lost at Port Pleasant and a further six at Choiseul Sound. Forty-six wounded soldiers and crew had been evacuated to Ajax Bay. The British had also lost two landing ships, one landing craft and suffered damage to HMS *Plymouth*. The great leap forward by 5 Brigade had turned into a nightmare.

Had the Argentines left it at that, it would have been

their day. Instead they lost three pilots and aircraft in ill-advised follow-up missions to Port Pleasant, with several more aircraft badly damaged. It turned out to be the last attack on British shipping by Argentine jets from the mainland.

Images of the dramatic *Sir Galahad* rescue reached British TV news screens several days later. To the public, the helicopter crews were heroic. Medals were later awarded to some pilots and crewmen, yet not to others doing an identical job. None were begrudged.

Chapter 14

Dash and panache
9–11 June 1982

Although the bombing of Galahad *and* Tristram *on 8 June had appalling consequences in terms of human suffering, its strategic effect was only to delay the final build-up of troops by a day.*

The arrival of RFA Engadine *boosted the Wessex contingent to twenty-five helicopters, adding to the twenty Sea Kings and one Chinook. This modest helicopter force would have to support the thousands of troops preparing for the assault on the hills surrounding Port Stanley. Front-line helicopter operations now moved up to Fitzroy on the southern flank and Teal Inlet to the north, from where a daring attack on the Argentine high command was about to be launched.*

At 3 a.m. local time, I was woken and told to get to the briefing room with my kit. All the aircrew were gathering there. The boss, Mike Booth, briefed us that the last few hours' delay meant we would not arrive in San Carlos until well after dawn. So *Engadine* had now turned around rather than risk being exposed as we entered San Carlos past Fanning Head. Intelligence had predicted a major Argentine air strike. But the need for pilots and aircrew on the islands remained urgent. Some of our own aircraft were sitting idle on board *Atlantic Causeway*. Ray Colborne, Chris Eke and I were told to get airborne and winch all aircrew onto our escort ship HMS *Penelope*, which was now steaming in as we were steaming out.

The prospect of a night winch to a frigate was exciting, even if I was going to miss out on a day's action. But the plan was abandoned almost immediately. It quickly became obvious that the sheer logistics of transferring twenty aircrew over an ever-increasing distance between the ships was impossible. *Penelope* wasn't stopping for anyone. Several of the aircrew went up on deck to watch the eerie glow of naval gunfire exploding in the Port Stanley area forty miles away.

Turning back was the right decision. We would have been an easy target, sailing through Falkland Sound at about the same time *Plymouth* was attacked. We spent the following day frustrated but comfortable, checking our kit and thinking about what was to come, while the Welsh Guards were dealing with their hell of Port Pleasant. *Engadine* never even made it as far as the battle group. Late afternoon, we simply turned around and headed back in towards San Carlos.

The following morning, Wednesday 9 June, we were all up well before dawn. I took good advantage of the last home comforts I expected to see for a while: breakfast, warm shower, comfortable loo. As the sun rose, *Engadine* finally slid quietly into San Carlos Water and the relative protection of other warships. I went up on deck to have my first view of the grassy Falkland hills rolling past in the early morning sunshine. Deep rumbling noises from the flight deck announced that the first aircraft were off, disembarking the squadron around the headland to our forward operating base at Port San Carlos. As I was due to fly on the second wave, I hung around with my bergen packed and my gas mask around my belt.

Within a few hours, Lieutenant 'Spiny' Norman Lees and I were standing inside the hangar watching X-Ray Juliett land for our planned crew change. It's always a slightly unnerving experience approaching seven tons of noisy machinery: the whirling blades above one's head, the low growl of the gearboxes, the high-pitch whine of the engines, the hot blast of the exhausts. There is a real knack to climbing up a Wessex, dodging the explosive flotation can on the wheel, getting your feet into the right footholds, ducking under the exhaust without getting burnt, swinging your leg into the cockpit without knocking the flying controls.

I strapped in for my first flight. As aircraft captain, Lees took the controls and lifted the Wessex clear of the deck. The Falklands were mostly what I had expected: a cross between the barrenness of Dartmoor and the beauty of northern Scotland. My excitement quickly dissipated as we concentrated on the job. After a straightforward few loads lifted from ship to shore, I decided to jump out back on *Engadine* in order to reduce the payload and wait my turn to replace Lees as solo pilot.

Almost as soon as I reached the hangar, I was already regretting not waiting on land at Port San Carlos. The welcome sound of helicopters buzzing low around all the ships in the bay was interrupted by the repeated blasts of sirens and the dreaded words 'Hands to action stations'. I was now stuck on deck without my anti-flash gear for some reason worrying that I was the only person not carrying a gas mask. Once again I felt horribly exposed, sitting in a tin can, waiting to be attacked. But with Ray Colborne's stern warning ringing in my ears, I kept my cool. As the all-clear sounded, I put on my helmet, life-jacket and bergen and ran out to the next Wessex that landed.

It was a case of out of the frying pan and into the fire. I sat in the back with some of our maintainers and loads of squadron kit as we lifted off and headed round the coast. The next thing I knew was that we were rolling into a tight turn and darting into a valley on the headland. Leading Aircrewman Smudge Smyth mouthed the words 'Air raid warning red' to me. As we landed, all of us jumped out and ran. This was good stuff. I ran up a hill just above the Wessex and lay down with my pistol cocked and ready to fire. I shouted at some of the lads nearby: 'If a jet comes over, fire well in front of it.'

After lying in the wet grass for a few seconds, I looked down at my Browning. I was horrified to see that there was no magazine. The release catch must have caught on something as I jumped out of the helicopter. Back in Northern Ireland we'd been warned that losing a single bullet would result in an £80 fine. Here in the Falklands I'd just lost an entire magazine and thirteen bullets. 'Bloody hell,' I thought. I immediately reloaded my second magazine and wondered what on earth to do. Smyth waved at us to go. I ran back and shouted that I needed to find my magazine. The Wessex rose into the air leaving me alone on my own little piece of the Falklands. I searched fruitlessly for fifteen minutes until X-Ray Juliett returned. Smyth calmly got out, bent down and picked up the lost magazine from the grass. My relief was huge and I patted him gratefully on the shoulder.

Lees dropped us all off at Port San Carlos near a pile of bergens and other equipment. I tried in vain to find my own bergen that had been dumped there while I was still wandering around the opposite hillside. No luck. Almost immediately, X-Ray Juliett was back again and Lees waved me in for a crew change.

For the next two hours, I was on my own, King of San Carlos, darting at low level, flying between *Engadine* and the FOB with people, equipment and loads. The flying was straightforward enough. Even deck landings were easy with the flight decks not moving around. It felt brilliant, an extraordinary responsibility given to a twenty-one-year-old fresh out of training. The temptation to sing out loud Wagner's *Ride of the Valkyries* was too much to resist. Smyth had to put up with it.

Job done, we were told to shut down in a valley just behind the farm buildings and come in for a brief. Port San Carlos is a remote settlement of a few farmhouses and trees amidst the bleak grasslands and hills of East Falkland. Not far away from the settlement was a temporary short runway made of steel mesh for use by the Sea Harriers. Bobbing in the sea a few yards down the hillside was a long black tube containing aviation fuel.

Smyth and I wandered back through the settlement, glad to be wearing wellies in the oozing mud. The ops tent was hidden amongst some trees and gorse in the garden of one of the farms. Jack Lomas had just begun to give us all a warm welcome when the makeshift alarm system announced yet another air raid warning. I ran for the nearest trench and leapt into the muddy pit under a piece of corrugated iron. Thankfully, it was another false alarm. As I returned to the briefing tent a few minutes later, I spotted a loose bergen in a hedge. It was mine.

Somehow, Jack Lomas managed to find floor space

around the settlement for all the 847 Squadron new arrivals. Nine of us were crammed onto an upstairs attic floor. It was far better than I had expected. Frankly, anywhere dry would have been brilliant. Just before heading upstairs, Mike Booth called me over and told me to get a shave. My feeble contribution to the squadron beard-growing competition thus came to an undistinguished end.

Each of us kept our bergens fully packed for a quick getaway. The only items taken out were sleeping bags and rollmats. Jerry Spence managed to find a pile of blankets that meant he wouldn't need to take anything out at all. It was a decision that would come back to haunt him later when he acquired a nasty dose of the lice. Norman Lees had brought an inflatable mattress with him and inevitably found himself on the receiving end of a torrent of abuse. The first night ashore would have been peaceful but for Ray Colborne's periodic snoring interspersed with pleas of 'Shut him up somebody, will you?' It made sleep all but impossible.

I was well primed for the early morning call to breakfast, two mess-tins worth. We then walked over to the ops tent in the freezing darkness, two hours before dawn, for our briefing.

With Mike Tidd's flight, who joined the fray later that morning after sailing in overnight on the supply ship *Fort Grange*, there were now thirty-two Wessex pilots and twenty-three Wessex aircrew to fly the twenty-five Wessex helicopters.

Briefing was a complete melee with about forty of us crammed into the small ops tent. It was great to catch up with old friends, such as Sparky Harden and Jerry Thomas. I couldn't see my closest friend Hector Heathcote, who I learnt was at FOB Teal. As one of three baby pilots fresh out of training – along with George Wallace and Dave Kelly – there were several faces I didn't recognise. But there was a tremendous feeling of comradeship, of being in it together. This was what we'd trained for. It was both warm and intimidating at the same time.

Jack Lomas once again welcomed us newcomers and then ran through the flying programme, including a brief on threats. In particular he warned us to watch out for a possible SAM (surface-to-air-missile) site on the south side of Mount Kent. A Gazelle had been shot down. He suspected it was most likely a 'blue on blue' – friendly fire – but to watch out anyway. He also mentioned the dreaded Pucaras.

Everybody worried about Pucaras. All of us had trained to evade fighters. We reckoned we could handle an attack from a high-speed fighter jet. We had practised evasion techniques back in the UK. But that was with fast jets. Helicopters would never be more than an opportunity target. The slow-speed Argentine Pucaras, with their cannon and rocket pods, were something else. A Pucara would not overshoot. It would simply sit on our tail and ripple off a salvo. Pucara was a common topic of conversation amongst all helicopter pilots.

Mark Evans had already had a head-to-head. Oily Knight thought he'd seen a pair of Pucaras a few miles away. The solution was not to get spotted. If you did, land, jump out and run. Or head for the clouds.

I was down to fly with Evans, my future flight commander when I returned later to the UK. 'Jayfer' was wonderful to fly with. He inspired confidence because of his laid-back manner that concealed a consummate professionalism. He seemed to think I'd enjoy today's aircraft, Yankee Tango. I was about to find out why. We both signed for the aircraft because after a quick introductory flight he was going to get out and let me get on with it on my own.

Yankee Tango was at the far end of a whole hillside full of Wessex helicopters. We walked out with our aircrewman Chris Eke and one of the maintainers. It was still dark as we finally found the right helicopter 200 yards from the maintenance tent. Evans and I had a good look around the aircraft. Great, I thought. The front left windscreen was cracked and covered in fablon from Oily Knight's bullet hole. We couldn't open the top platform to check the gearbox oil because it had been wire-locked shut. The engineer with us said he *thought* it had been filled. Evans and I looked at each other.

As I strapped myself into the left seat, I found my vision further obscured to the side. Yankee Tango was one of the few aircraft fitted with armour plating in the cockpit seats and side windows. I strained hard to pull up the heavy window plate and lock it beside me. For a moment I thought I couldn't lift it and would have to deal with the embarrassment of asking for help. The seat armour under my bottom was definitely a good idea. But I would have preferred to do without the window armour for the extra visibility and lighter weight. After all, it hadn't stopped Oily's bullet.

Our maintainer plugged a battery into the ground supply socket and we pressed the start button on the port engine. Provided you could get the engines started, the Wessex would usually keep going all day. Their incredible reliability was down to two factors. First, our maintainers were superb, both pragmatic and creative. All of their field maintenance had to be done in the pitch dark and numbing cold of the Falklands night. If the pilot could accept certain faults and limitations, the aircraft would be signed off as flyable. If the fault was too serious, the aircraft became a source of spare parts to be robbed – a 'Christmas tree'.

The additional faults we had to accept on Yankee Tango

were a dud oil pressure gauge and a dud fuel gauge. At least the other fuel gauge was working. Provided we kept the fuel flows to each engine the same, we could reasonably assume that both tanks held roughly the same amount of fuel. The list of assumptions was beginning to build up. My first mission of the war was to be in an aircraft with limited visibility, a main gearbox that might grind to a violent halt at any moment, and a fuel system that might run out without warning. Apart from that, Yankee Tango was great.

We wound up the rotors, completed our final checks and, with Chris Eke in the back armed with his machine gun, we launched into the South Atlantic dawn. Flying over the Falklands terrain in the early morning light was beautiful. Glorious blue skies, stunning rugged scenery, no wind. It was hard to believe there was a war on.

Our task was to head straight to Goose Green and help move the remaining Gurkhas forward to Fitzroy. We departed due south at low level from Port San Carlos climbing up over the Sussex Mountains. We spent as little time as possible on the skyline as we rolled downhill into a narrow valley that offered some concealment. The flying was exciting and fabulous. Rarely did we climb much more than twenty or thirty feet above the ground. Whilst keeping his eyes on the scenery around us, Evans managed to pull out a packet of cigarettes and a lighter from the side pocket of his combat trousers. 'Light one for me, would you Harry? And help yourself.' Most aircrew smoked. I'd given up on the way down south to get fit. 'What the hell,' I thought. 'This is war' – although we were not supposed to smoke in the aircraft.

It felt good having Evans show me the ropes. But I couldn't wait to boot him out and have the controls to myself. As we approached the grassy airstrip next to the settlement, I could see two damaged Argentine Pucara and the remains of Lieutenant Nick Taylor's shot-down Sea Harrier. It was a sobering sight.

This was my first view of a dreaded Pucara, thankfully with its wings clipped. The combination of slow speed and a couple of rocket pods made the Pucara the biggest threat to our helicopters. These two at Goose Green airstrip were put out of action by the very first Sea Harrier raid on 1 May.

Our cabin was filled up with the first load of stores and equipment. We headed east towards the front line, flying close to the ground and steering a couple of miles south of the suspected SAM site. Well before we reached the inlet at Port Pleasant, the two landing ships *Sir Galahad* and *Sir Tristram* stood out starkly against the flat grasslands and sea. They were both still smoking and horribly charred. The reality of war was shocking. Our normal in-flight running commentary and jokey banter turned to silence. There was nothing to say. As we flew past the ships in the now dull morning sunshine, I slid my window open and took a photo. With the image scarred in my mind, we flew on to the grid reference we had been given to deposit our load.

The burning hulks became an all too familiar landmark that day. I flew past them many times. Fortunately, there was little opportunity to linger over such thoughts. Completing our tasking took our full attention, not just in working out how to get from A to B, but how to manage our fuel and load. We were constantly calculating the minimum and maximum fuel needed to complete the next few trips. Too little and we ran out. Too much and we couldn't do the job. Although FOB Fitzroy was established that day, Tim Stanning's forward refuelling station had not yet been set up. Our only sources of fuel were the dozen or so flight decks and the airstrip thirty miles away in San Carlos Water. Even with fifty helicopters airborne, competition was never fierce. However we would occasionally have to wait on a hillside for a few minutes until cleared to come in. All pilots, including me, had their own scare stories of getting perilously low on fuel. Amazingly, nobody ever actually ran out.

After an hour and a half of lifting and shifting equipment between the ships at San Carlos, Goose Green and the southern end of the front line, Evans said he was happy for me to do the rest of the tasking on my own. It felt good. We landed in an open area next to Goose Green airfield so that he could get out. He would catch a ride back to Port San Carlos and get another aircraft for himself.

The usual routine for swapping seats, since I needed to be in the right seat, would be to shut down. However, with an old helicopter in a cold wet climate there was always the chance that the Wessex wouldn't start again. So as we kept the rotors turning, I got out and Chris Eke got in. While Eke held on to the stick for dear life, Evans climbed gingerly out making sure not to knock any of the flying controls. I then climbed very quickly into the empty right seat, hauling up the heavy armour plate in my window. My non-pilot crewman seemed strangely reluctant to relinquish his temporary and highly unofficial command of a large Royal Navy commando helicopter. 'Sorry Chris, my turn now,' I grinned. 'I have control.' I couldn't wait.

Our first task was to ferry Gurkhas. As the first group of men approached Yankee Tango, all I could see were these enormous bergens with boots sticking out of the bottom of each, an array of weaponry on the side, and a huge set of gleaming teeth near the top. Having walked over the Sussex Mountains, the Gurkha troops were clearly thrilled to be given a lift for the next stage.

Although we were supposed to take a maximum of twelve troops, Eke kept on waving them in. I'm sure I counted sixteen men disappear into the cabin behind me. Take-off with such a heavy load was hard work. At full power, I could just about make a low hover. By gradually drifting forwards across the grassy airstrip, I eventually achieved the fifteen knots or so needed to escape from the recirculating air and into the clean air that gave us translational lift. We were away.

Every few miles we passed another Wessex or Sea King coming back from the front line, flying just a few feet above the barren grassland. It was a good game to radio a hello to the other aircraft without using names and see if we could guess whose voice it was.

In our introductory brief on arrival, Jack Lomas had explained the various warning codes to us. 'Air raid warning red' meant an incoming attack. 'SCRAM, SCRAM!' meant hit the ground fast. My adrenalin levels shot up the first time I heard that radio call and the final crackled words on the HF radio that may or may not have been 'SCRAM!' All I knew was that I didn't want to be in the air. I reacted accordingly.

From hurtling downwind some fifteen feet above the ground at over 100 miles per hour, I executed a perfect downwind fast stop of which I was extremely proud. Rolling the aircraft into a sharp turn and flaring the nose up to reduce speed, I brought the heavily laden Wessex gently down to a peach of a landing with the aircraft partly hidden in a small depression. That was definitely a steely commando landing.

The Gurkhas leapt out and took cover, spread around the aircraft. The whole manoeuvre felt thoroughly impressive, right up to the point when a Wessex flew past me and a familiar voice came over the radio: 'Yankee Tango, are you OK?'

I recognised my boss Mike Booth.

'Just waiting for the air raid to clear,' I replied.

He told me not to worry and to get on my way. So that was that. Thanks boss, I thought. The Gurkhas piled back in and, with my tail between my legs, we continued on our way.

The incident brought home to me two things. The first was how incredibly competent we were at handling the aircraft. Here I was as a baby pilot thrust straight from training into a war. I may have felt out of my depth on the ground, but I felt completely at home with a helicopter strapped to my back. And it really was a case of strapping it to me rather than strapping me into it. Coming in to land for example, I could sense exactly when the tail wheel fifty feet behind me was about to touch the ground. I could feel the Wessex as if it were a part of me. The training really had been brilliant.

The second was how uncertain war is. Our morning brief may have given us a reasonable idea where the good guys and the bad guys were located. But once airborne, we just had to focus on our task, ignoring distractions like air raid warnings, and hoping like mad that whoever was giving us instructions knew what they were doing. Most of the time, they did. But in the midst of the unknown, we just had to get on with the job calmly and professionally. We were good at it.

After a day of lifts between Goose Green and Bluff Cove settlement beyond Port Pleasant, I brought Yankee Tango back to Port San Carlos having completed our tasking. As I was approaching almost the exact spot from which we had lifted off seven hours earlier, a shout in my ear from Eke warned that we were about to land on a telegraph wire. A quick burst of power and we moved up and over. I was greatly relieved to get back safely.

With a little daylight still left, Eke and I decided we would wander the half-mile or so across the hill from the briefing tent to the temporary runway. An RAF Harrier had overshot the end of the runway and collapsed its wheels in the soggy turf. A green tarpaulin had been thrown over the cockpit to protect it from rainwater. We steered clear of the two-inch rocket pod nestling in the wet grass. Eke posed manfully for a photograph in front of the Harrier with his rifle. The light was fading as we trudged back into the settlement area and remembered we had been up since well before dawn. Food and sleep were now our priorities.

Because our squadron had been cobbled together from a variety of sources, our arrival brought in an incredible amount of flying experience. Mike Booth had spent a tour as a 'trapper' with Naval Flying Standards Flight, carrying out annual squadron inspections. Although outstanding pilots, trappers were also social pariahs, revered and feared in equal measure. As squadron boss, he had rejoined the ranks of the ordinary. His relief at finally getting to the action was tempered by the nagging thought that we could easily have lifted the Welsh and Scots Guards, as well as the Gurkhas, if only we'd got to the Falklands a few days earlier. All those little delays had probably cost lives.

Booth's number two, Rob Flexman, had just returned from a two-year exchange with the French navy. His appointment fell hardest on Neil Anstis, the most experienced pilot on our squadron. Their occasional tiffs were well camouflaged from us Junior Joes. The charming Mike Spencer, the test pilot from Farnborough responsible for getting hold of the night vision goggles for the Sea Kings, had also joined us. Our combined Wessex squadron at Port San Carlos now had eight officers of lieutenant commander rank or equivalent. Six of them were pilots. All of this experience meant that there was a hierarchy to keep an eye on the junior pilots like me. Nine of us were sub-lieutenants in our early twenties. Some of the lieutenants were only a year or two older.

Now Flexman and Spencer took responsibility for running operations, matching up crews, and allocating roles and jobs. It took the pressure off Jack Lomas.

Sparky Harden was one of the sub-lieutenants, a feisty and popular junior pilot who had joined the Navy six weeks before me. For our first day in the Falklands we, the new arrivals, were paired with pilots who were older hands. Harden was paired with my colleague Jerry Spence. Despite Spence having completed nearly a full front-line tour as the more experienced pilot, Harden had already been in the Falklands for over two weeks. Like me, Spence's first mission was the Gurkha battalion lift from Goose Green to Bluff Cove. Altogether some six Wessex spent the day crossing to and fro between the two settlements.

Sparky Harden's Wessex was unmistakable. I thought my own flying had been pretty low and exciting at fifteen feet above the ground, but Harden was almost beneath me as he flew past at five feet. Whilst I was impressed at his skill and accuracy at flying so low, I was also thinking 'Bloody idiot'. There was no scope for error. One tiny lapse in concentration, one misjudgement, and it would be curtains for him, his fellow pilot and aircrewman, his passengers, his payload and a vital helicopter resource. Even a hardened Royal Marine SBS captain riding in the back signalled to the aircrewman that he thought it might be a good idea to fly a fraction higher. After two trips, his co-pilot Jerry Spence could stand it no longer: 'Sparky, take me back to Port San Carlos, will you mate. You don't need me.'

Three years later, Harden flew a *junglie* Sea King through some wires in Norway, cutting off the tail of the aircraft as he crash-landed into a snowy field. His reputation as a hooligan had followed him. His new boss warned that he would be court-martialled if he stepped out of line. Ironically, Jerry Spence had been appointed Provost Marshal.

'Look at this Sparky.' Spence showed him the official letter. 'I've got to take you by the ear and drag you in!'

Harden was thrown out of the Navy. Later that evening back at Port San Carlos, I asked Harden why he flew so low. 'You remember during training Crabbers used to tell us what being a *junglie* was all about. "Dash and panache, Sparky," he'd say. "You've got to have a bit of dash and panache."'

On the morning that we were disembarking to Port San Carlos, Jack Lomas called Pete Manley over for a chat. He'd been asked by Colonel Mike Rose if a Wessex could park an AS12 air-to-surface missile on General Menendez's desk in Port Stanley. Intelligence suggested that his orders group met every morning around 8 a.m. in the Town Hall. 'Can you do it, Pete?' asked Lomas.

'Tell me more,' Manley replied.

Within an hour they were shutting down Yankee Hotel on the deck of special forces headquarters, *Sir Lancelot*. Descending deep into the interior of the landing ship, Lomas and Manley entered a darkened operations room. Six men stood leaning over a large map table. Rose welcomed the two pilots and introduced the outline mission and the latest intelligence. A roll of photographic paper displayed a panoramic view of Stanley, taken covertly from one of the hills to the west. Some of the houses, such as 'Town Hall' or 'Mr & Mrs . . . , ex-Navy', were marked with arrows. Manley immediately proposed that the best approach route for a missile attack would be from the north. Rose agreed, advising that there was nobody up there apart from 'our guys'.

Manley then asked about the Argentine assets that would be brought to bear against them. The SAS artillery specialist described two main threats. The first was a couple of anti-aircraft Oerliken guns on the quayside near Government House. He wasn't sure which type they were. The absence of a dish suggested they weren't radar guided. Their effective range would be about 4,000 yards, although the shells would fly twice that distance. The second and more serious threat was the radar-guided 105mm howitzer guns currently pointing out to the east towards Mounts Longdon and Two Sisters. 'If they're good,' he said, 'they'll turn them round and get their first rounds down in about four minutes.'

Manley said he'd give it a go with his best missile aimer, Arthur Balls, who was particularly good at dusk and low-light conditions. He'd need to check everything was working beforehand by firing a test missile at a rock somewhere out near Teal. 'Absolutely,' said Rose. 'Fire as many as you like.' He'd also need to check that Balls was happy to do it in case he thought it was all too gung-ho.

The following morning Balls was instructed to return to Port San Carlos for a briefing. He and Manley went for a quiet chat. Within an hour, they were sitting on the deck of *Fearless*, loading two live AS12 missiles onto the wing pylons, ready to head off to Teal. In the cabin were a weapons electrician and two more missiles.

Having unloaded at FOB Teal, Manley headed across the meandering inlet of Port Salvador until they came to a small island of grass and rock some seven miles to the north. Bob's Island was remote and uninhabited: perfect for a practice firing. Both missile firings went well and they returned to Teal to reload the replacements. To the three other Wessex crews operating out of Teal, including Oily Knight, Flipper Hughes and Pete Skinner, it was obvious something was afoot. Yankee Hotel had left the FOB with two missiles fitted and returned with none. 'We're just practising,' Manley told them. It was not a very convincing explanation.

Even though rumours quickly circulated among the other Wessex crews back at Port San Carlos, all of us knew better than to probe. Manley and Balls, though very different characters, were equally well liked amongst the wider *junglie* community. In the war so far, Wessex had crashed and been sunk and attacked with missiles and mortars. We'd lost two Wessex engineers, but not a single pilot or aircrewman yet. Whatever they were up to, we just hoped like mad they'd come back alive.

That evening, in one of the Teal farm buildings that had become an operations room, Manley handed a piece of paper to Lomas. It was a letter to his wife in case of the worst. 'Don't worry,' said Lomas. 'When you come back, I'll give it back to you.' They had been given the go-ahead for an early morning strike.

Visibility was poor at first light on Friday 11 June. Yankee Hotel launched anyway into the mist, the noise attracting a great deal of attention around the settlement. Jack Lomas and Jerry Thomas found that their back-up Wessex – intended as search-and-rescue helicopter in case anything went wrong – wouldn't start. Lomas ran back to the ops room, quickly briefing Hughes and Skinner to take over the role in X-Ray Tango.

Yankee Hotel was by now heading due east at low level, along the coastline of Berkeley Sound and on towards Stanley through a gap in the hills. Visibility was still gloomy though improving a little. Balls lowered the M260 sight from the cockpit roof, like a periscope, and started to get it ready. The early morning mist had fogged up the lens. Because they were still well clear of any known troop movements, Manley put Yankee Hotel down on the ground so that Balls could climb halfway out of the cockpit and give the windscreen a wipe. It was hardly a high-tech solution and not especially good for the optics, but it sorted out the immediate problem.

As they lifted off again, Manley called up the SAS observers hidden somewhere on the hillside of Beagle Ridge and Mount Low, five miles to the north of Stanley. 'This is Yankee Hotel approaching IP [Initial Point], any movements your location?'

'It looks quiet, although a Huey has been operating in the area,' came the reply. 'Do you have means to counter?' asked Manley.

'Yup.'

The special forces man's reply confirmed that he had

a Stinger missile available just in case. It sounded good to Manley. Stinger had already knocked down a Pucara on the first day of the landings.

'Keep an eye on us?' asked Manley.

'Yup. I can't see you but I can hear you,' came the reply.

By now Manley and Balls were approaching what seemed a good range to fire at their target. Manley eased the big Wessex helicopter up into a high hover 200 feet above the grassland, using the ridgeline behind them as a camouflage and a backdrop. He could see the lights of Stanley twinkling in the gloom just beyond Wireless Ridge as they edged slowly forward.

'Any good yet?'

'No, no,' replied Balls.

'We'll keep going.'

Seconds later, Balls reported that he could now make out the target. 'Is it good enough?' asked Manley.

'Yes.'

'OK, in your own time, select missile one and let's go for it.'

Immune to the sounds of the Wessex, it seemed to Manley that they were suspended in a bleak soupy bowl, quiet as a grave. Not for long. The AS12 missile made one hell of a racket as it flew off the port launcher, trailing sparks behind it like a firecracker. There was nothing for Manley to do but hold his hover and count off the seconds. With very small movements on the controller, Balls adjusted the flight path of the missile along the thin wire now dangling invisibly between launcher and AS12. At fifteen seconds, Balls switched to ten-times magnification on the sight slightly earlier than expected. Switching too soon risked losing sight of the orange dot altogether.

'. . . 20, 21, 22, 23 . . .' Manley called out.

'Impact,' said Balls calmly.

'Christ, we're too far in,' said Manley.

To stay out of range of the Oerlikons, he had planned that they fire at 7,000 yards, which would take thirty-two seconds. The early impact suggested they were nearer 4,000 yards. 'OK, cut the wires, select second missile and go for the alternative target.'

Balls found the second target, an Argentine Chinook, on a field in front of Government House.

'Got it,' he said. 'Fire the missile.'

There was another blazing racket as the starboard AS12 shot off its rail and out into the gloom.

Suddenly Manley could see flashes of gunfire and tracer coming at them from quite a bit nearer than the lights of Stanley. At first it looked as if the Argentine gunners were firing from Wireless Ridge across the harbour. But he soon realised it was an illusion caused by the low visibility, the same illusion that had led them in closer than they had intended. Tracers were now shooting past the helicopter from the Oerlikons. The Argentines could hear them but not see them, although they might have spotted the initial sparks from each missile launch.

'. . . 16, 17, 18, 19, 20 . . . I've lost control,' said Balls. 'It's gone down and right.'

'Cut the wires, let's get the fuck out of here,' said Manley as he kicked the helicopter around to the left, away from the wire, and pushed the nose down to gain speed. As the Wessex accelerated away to 120 knots, the first few artillery rounds from the 105mm howitzers began to crash down into the peat just out to their right. For Balls, moving his head away from the tunnel view through the missile sight, it was like emerging into the middle of some Second World War movie, but with the sound turned off. Brown puffs of smoke exploded in the air all around them but there was nothing to hear above the noise of the helicopter. 'How the hell did he keep such a steady hover?' Balls wondered.

Acting as search-and-rescue cover in X-Ray Tango, Flipper Hughes and Pete Skinner had to work out their own mission plan on the hoof. Given little more than a grid reference and an outline of the mission by Jack Lomas, they were now following on at low level about ten minutes behind Yankee Hotel. Navigating from the left seat, Skinner could see that the grid reference was on virgin map. There were no markings at all because the firing point was so far inside enemy territory. They flew much the same route that Manley had taken, hitting the coastline of Berkeley Sound and then heading south.

As they came through a gap in the hills, a thin column of smoke billowed from the ground at about the missile-firing point. Hughes and Skinner could clearly see the lights of the Stanley seafront as they edged forward towards the smoke. They hadn't been able to contact Manley and Balls on the radio, nor were they having any joy talking to the SAS guys on the frequency given. Now it looked like the mission had been a disaster. As Hughes crept slowly forward assuming the worst, artillery shells began to rain down around them. The 105mm howitzer was trying to lock on to their position. Not fancying becoming a burning wreck themselves, Hughes turned tail and headed back through the hills.

It looked like we'd lost our first Wessex crew. Cockpit conversation on the return journey was limited to little more than grunts of 'bloody hell', 'fuck', 'shit'.

Landing back at FOB Teal, Hughes and Skinner were disconsolate as they trudged slowly across to the ops room.

They were also feeling the guilt of leaving their friends under fire. But to their amazement and delight, there in front of them sat Pete Manley and Arthur Balls sipping tea with Jack Lomas. 'You bastards,' Hughes cried with a huge smile, as relief swept over him.

It was one of the most daring raids of the war. Pete Manley and Arthur Balls fired two AS12 missiles into the capital Port Stanley from two miles away. The aim was to give Argentine General Menendez a breakfast he wouldn't forget. The first missile missed by just one yard, before flying down an alley and demolishing the roof of the police station. The second missile went rogue.

Yankee Hotel had cleared the area with only seconds to spare. 'Well done, it looks excellent to me,' reported the SAS observer to them over the radio. Manley and Balls then headed at very low level back up past Berkeley Sound and onward to FOB Teal, tea, whole-hearted congratulations from Jack Lomas, and half-hearted abuse from Flipper Hughes.

* * *

It was only after the Falklands War that the outcome of their daring raid emerged. It turned out that General Menendez had not held his officers' meeting there that morning after all. In any case, the first AS12 missile missed the Town Hall first-floor target by a matter of just three to four feet. As an anti-ship missile, a few feet either side was well within the AS12's normal margin of error. So Arthur Balls had done a brilliant job as aimer under extremely demanding conditions. Instead, the missile had flown on down an alleyway and exploded into the top half of Port Stanley police station, which had been requisitioned by the extremely unpopular Argentine political officer, Major Patricio Dowling – who had reportedly been unnecessarily unpleasant towards the captured Royal Marines of Naval Party 8901 and to the islanders. Although the major fled back to the mainland soon afterwards, news of the attack on the occupiers went down very well with the locals.

The second AS12 missile appeared to have snagged its wire, ironically on top of Wireless Ridge. Once the missile lost control inputs from the aimer, it was programmed to fall down and to the right. The missile had splashed short of Port Stanley seafront and into the harbour. In overexcited media reports, the Argentines accused the British of trying to sink their hospital ship *Bahia Paraiso*, anchored a short distance away.

The origin of the plume of smoke spotted by Hughes and Skinner remains unclear. It may have been caused by an artillery shell setting light to the peat surface. Years later, a former special forces soldier told Pete Manley that his hidden position on the ground was heavily shelled immediately after the Wessex hovered overhead. As far as Manley was concerned, there was nothing whatsoever on the ground below Yankee Hotel as they fired their missiles.

It is probable that the Wessex involved was X-Ray Tango, creeping slowly forward before being targeted by the radar-guided 105mm howitzer. As a result of the successful firing, one further AS12 attack was planned for a hardware depot on West Falkland, but was never carried out.

Chapter 15

'Follow me boys'
12 June 1982

The land war so far had involved the politically expedient battle for Goose Green, the assault on Top Malo House, and a handful of skirmishes with special forces.

The war was now about to reach its climax. Well dug-in Argentine positions on high ground awaited the British troops. Artillery and mortar fire threatened British helicopters foolish or daring enough to venture near the front line. In the early hours of Saturday 12 June, the final phased assault on the Argentine defences surrounding Port Stanley began.

The net was now closing in on the Argentines forces in and around the capital. To the east at sea was the British task group. Air superiority was dominated by the Sea Harriers. To the west were the troops of 3 Brigade and 5 Brigade, poised for the final push. No-one underestimated the difficulty of completing the task in hand. Thousands of Argentine soldiers remained between Stanley airfield to the east and the hills to the west. The main task now was to overpower the Argentine defences in the hills as quickly as possible. The prospect of urban warfare with hundreds of civilians in the middle was too horrible to contemplate. We hoped the Argentine commanders would reach the same conclusion.

While Pete Manley and Arthur Balls were leaving the forward base at Teal on the northern flank to attack Port Stanley, Lieutenant Willie Harrower and Leading Aircrewman Steve Larsen were in one of several Wessex on their way to Fitzroy, the new base on the southern flank. They were flying X-Ray Quebec, the same aircraft used by Hughes and Tuttey to lift survivors from the burning *Sir Galahad* three days earlier.

At Fitzroy, the first job they were given was to lift several pallet-loads of artillery shells up to the 105mm guns near the summit of Mount Kent. Artillery bombardment, together with naval gunfire support from sea, would play a crucial role in weakening and demoralising the Argentine defences.

Manoeuvring a ton of artillery shells beneath a Wessex meant flying slower and more carefully than our usual uninhibited style. The full power that was needed just to get off the ground left little scope for manoeuvrability or for dealing with sudden downdrafts. Fuel levels had to be kept deliberately low, meaning that pilots were always wondering where to get the next suck of fuel.

When load-lifting went well, it was a fairly mundane activity. When it went badly, it did so horribly quickly. A little bit of swinging on the load was normal. But once the momentum got to a certain point, the whole aircraft would start to swing with it. It was tempting to try to correct the uncomfortable sideways movement with the cyclic stick. This usually made things worse. The ultimate response would be to hit the red release button and 'pickle' off the load. Aside from the odd incident with Mars bars, few of us ever got that far. Smooth flying and gentle turns usually solved most problems.

Harrower and Larsen were therefore quietly relieved once they had finished lifting the external loads. Their next job was to move boxes of ammunition, stacked inside the Wessex's cabin, up to the Royal Marines who were waiting in the hills for the go ahead to attack.

Larsen sat in the cabin facing the huge piles of boxes. The cabin door was partly open, giving him a view of the Falklands scenery rushing past. The two crew kept up the usual chat about what was going on. As X-Ray Quebec flew low up a ridgeline to their planned drop-off point, Larsen edged back in his seat, aware that he would make a nice target sitting in the doorway. As Harrower flared off speed, Larsen could see a group of Royal Marines lying flat on the ground below them. A big moustachioed Marine was waving anxiously at the helicopter now hovering above his head. It didn't need a degree in lip-reading to tell him that there was something bad going on and that they were in big danger. 'We're being told to get out of here,' Larsen told Harrower hurriedly over the intercom. The Wessex nose dropped straightaway as X-Ray Quebec accelerated into a tight left-hand turn.

At first they weren't even aware of what was happening: there was nothing to hear above the usual grinding roar of the helicopter gearbox and whine of the Gnome engines. As the Wessex gathered speed and raced back down the valley they had just flown up, Larsen was amazed to see several large black circles appear in the ground alongside them, but he just didn't compute. The circles appeared as if by magic. And then daylight suddenly poured into the rear of the cabin in front of him.

'We've been hit, we've been hit,' shouted Larsen. The

sudden black circles in the ground were the result of mortar blasts peeling away the mossy green grass and instantly revealing the black peat underneath. Shrapnel from the explosions had punched several fist-sized holes in the aircraft fuselage. Amazingly, the aircraft was still handling fine. They decided their best option was to get back to Fitzroy to sort things out. The ammunition boxes appeared largely untouched, other than by bits of Wessex debris. Larsen leant over and picked up one of the culprits, a short fragment of metal from a mortar shell.

Two of the Wessex maintainers, Mould and Trims, met them as soon as they landed back at Fitzroy. As the ammunition boxes were cleared out of the way, Leading Mechanic Charlie Mould had a good look around. There didn't seem to be any damage at all other than to the skin of the aircraft. A bemused Larsen could only stand a few yards away and light up a cigarette to recover from the shock of it all.

Within a matter of minutes, Mould had covered the holes with aluminium tape. It made the side of the aircraft look unduly shiny. Grabbing a handful of Falklands mud, he smeared it over the tape. Harrower and Larsen looked at each other and laughed: 'Operational maintenance!'

Larsen finished his cigarette. Time for the next job.

Neil Cummins and I had spent most of our day within the confines of San Carlos Water, flying X-Ray Lima around the ships and shore bases for five hours. As Helicopter Delivery Service aircraft, we were general postmen and taxi drivers to whoever needed us.

After landing back at Port San Carlos, I wandered back to the briefing tent, bergen on my back, helmet in hand. I was met by Mike Spencer who told me not to bother getting too comfortable. I was to catch a ride up to FOB Teal for the night. Minutes later, I was sitting on the cabin floor in the back of another Wessex, grinning stupidly at the crewman opposite me.

Riding in the back was a whole different experience to sitting up front and driving the thing myself. With the cabin door wide open and the port window out to make way for a second machine gun, the noise and wind were tremendous. The helmeted crewman sat perched in the doorway facing backwards, attached to the aircraft with a harness around his waist. Map reading with only a view of what has just gone past is a challenging skill. Just outside the door on the right-hand side, the huge starboard wheel hung suspended in mid-air on the end of two metal oleos. At the front of the cabin was the amusing sight of the pilot's feet dangling down beneath his seat. I hadn't been paying attention when I got in and spent the journey wondering whether or not the feet belonged to my colleague Lieutenant George 'I'm sorry but you're wrong' Wallace. Meanwhile, the ground hurtled past at over a hundred miles an hour, the aircraft fuselage rolling from side to side as we followed the contours of the valleys.

Teal, our forward base on the northern side of the mountain range, was twenty-five miles east of the landing area at San Carlos. Just like Port San Carlos and most other Falkland settlements, Teal comprised a few scattered houses, farm buildings and windswept evergreen pine trees. Royal Navy Wessex and Sea Kings and Royal Marine Gazelle helicopters were constantly buzzing in and out to pick up, drop off or refuel. The distinctive *thump* of the RAF Chinook made its presence known before we could see it. Underslung below the huge double-headed helicopter were four black 4,000-pound fuel containers known by all as 'bollocks'.

I began to realise how fortunate it was that we had Bravo November. Whereas Sea Kings could and did bring fuel up to our forward bases at both Teal and Fitzroy, they could only carry one 'bollock' at a time. The Chinook could carry four. The importance of this cannot be underestimated. Without the need to flog the fifty-mile round trip to and from the San Carlos landing area, the commando squadron helicopters were far better able to support the front-line troops another twenty miles further east beyond the FOBs. This was especially important for the twenty-five Wessex that lacked the speed and capability of the larger Sea Kings. The fuel provided by the Chinook at a stroke more or less doubled our capacity to support the front-line troops.

As night fell, the Wessex aircrew gathered in one of the old sheep-shearing sheds to be briefed by our own Major Adrian Short. He had just returned from the main 3 Brigade briefing with a numbered copy of the ops order, classified 'Secret'. Tonight was the beginning of the final phase of the war. Troops from 3 Para, 42 Commando and 45 Commando were to attack the Argentine defences on Mount Longdon, Two Sisters and Harriet at midnight 'Zulu time' – 8 p.m. local time.

All of us were keen to get stuck into the action and get up to the front line. But Short was categorical that we should not expose our valuable helicopters to unnecessary risk. We had lost enough helicopters already and any more losses would significantly reduce our ability to get the job done. His tone became very dark. We were not to fly into any 'hot' landing zones. If we had wounded soldiers in the back and any died, we should be prepared to offload them as necessary to give us the extra power and manoeuvrability. The bottom line was that we were not to be overzealous. The prospect of front-line action was exciting but to be avoided. And now we were to get our heads down and get some sleep.

The air was clear and icy cold as we headed out of the

shed into the pitch darkness towards the hut we'd been assigned. About twenty miles away to the south-east, we could see the first flares light up the hills on the horizon. After ten days waiting for 5 Brigade to get into position on the southern flank, the Paras and Marines had finally been given the go-ahead. After our naïve and cocky demands to get involved in the action, it was a deeply sobering thought that the poor grunts on the ground were now in a full-scale firefight. We were suddenly very nervous about getting shot by our own sentries as we wandered around the camp.

Twenty miles to the east, British troops were advancing towards their respective start lines for the night assault on the line of hills surrounding Stanley. At long last, the final phase of the war to reclaim the Falklands was to commence. For the troops who had endured the long march from Port San Carlos, followed by days out in the open exposed to the freezing South Atlantic weather, now was their chance to shine. Over previous nights fighting patrols had tested the Argentine defences of Mounts Longdon, Harriet and Two Sisters. Several patrols left behind Argentine casualties following vicious firefights whilst, remarkably, suffering none of their own. But it confirmed what they had already learnt from Goose Green – that the enemy would defend their positions robustly.

For the British, the prospect of attacking well dug-in positions on high ground was daunting. Defenders would once again outnumber their attackers, the reverse of the conventional principle that attackers should have a three-to-one advantage. Before even reaching each hill, the British would need to cross a long stretch of open ground and minefields.

In order to get all attacking units as close to their objectives as possible before alerting the Argentine defenders, each attack was to start in silence. The occasional enemy artillery starshell pierced the blackness and illuminated the surrounding rocky hillside, causing the advancing troops to freeze and drop to the ground. Astonishingly, they appeared not to have been seen and were able to continue onwards as darkness resumed.

Their luck couldn't hold. The troops of 3 Para were first into action. The silence of their approach towards the northernmost hill, the imposing Mount Longdon, was shattered when an unfortunate Para corporal stepped on a mine. Over the next eleven long hours, through dawn and well into the morning, the battle raged. Artillery and mortar shells from both sides, and naval gunfire support from the British frigates, mixed with heavy machine-gun and small-arms fire. Clearing the Argentine defensive positions was a slow and lethal process. Snipers and 50-calibre machine guns wreaked havoc. Soldiers saw their friends and colleagues killed or wounded. Extraordinary acts of individual bravery were required to advance upwards and onwards through each trench, sangar or pile of rocks.

The initial assault on the western approach by B Company threatened to fizzle out after six hours of fighting. Sergeant Ian MacKay was posthumously awarded the Victoria Cross for his single-handed assault on a key Argentine bunker near the western summit. His action broke the stalemate and allowed A Company to advance through along the ridge. Sixty-six millimetre Light Antitank Weapons, my former nemesis, were used to great effect to destroy sangars and were unofficially renamed Light Anti-Personnel Rockets. Stretcher bearers brought ammunition in and wounded out. In amongst the hell of it all, soldiers found time to brew tea or smoke a cigarette. Many took advantage of Argentine stores or weapons left behind in trenches. Some soldiers even removed their sodden boots and replaced them with dry boots requisitioned from dead Argentines.

By the end of the battle for Mount Longdon, eighteen Paras lay dead and forty-seven wounded. Three more Paras and one REME craftsman were killed by Argentine shelling from Mount Tumbledown to the south during the subsequent thirty-six hours spent out on the mountain. Argentine losses included over thirty dead and 120 wounded. The eleven-hour battle for Mount Longdon proved the longest and fiercest of the final phase, even prompting the British commanders to consider withdrawal at one stage.

The battles for Mounts Harriet and Two Sisters were similarly fierce, though shorter in duration. British losses were lower. The southernmost hill, Mount Harriet, was expected to be the toughest objective of all. The Royal Marines of 42 Commando approached their start line silently through two minefields, dropping to the ground without being spotted as again, starshell flares illuminated overhead.

As the Argentine defenders faced a softening-up barrage of naval gunfire from HMS *Yarmouth*, the Marines watched in horror as a land-based Exocet missile flashed towards them out of Stanley. They fired in vain at the missile before it sped out towards the destroyer HMS *Glamorgan* far away to the south. *Glamorgan* had time only to turn away as the missile exploded into the ship's hangar, destroying the flight deck and Wessex 3 helicopter, and killing thirteen men.

Instead of attacking Mount Harriet from the west, the Royal Marines of K Company and L Company circled the hill to the south across open ground. The assault from the south-east took the defenders by surprise. K Company approached to within a hundred yards before engaging the enemy. As with the Paras, the Marines moved from bunker to bunker clearing out enemy positions and taking dozens of prisoners. Milan missiles were used as well as 66mm rockets. Remarkably just two Marines were killed during the approach and initial attack, but with many more wounded on both sides.

Four-five Commando's assault on the two peaks of Two Sisters began with yet another heart-stopping march across open ground. The first of the two peaks of Two Sisters was secured by X-Ray Company directly from the west with minimal difficulty, leaving the victorious Marines with a bird's-eye view of the battles raging on the adjacent hills. The second peak proved far more troublesome. The Argentine defenders were well dug in and determined. Shortly after crossing their start line to attack from the north-west, Yankee and Zulu Companies became engaged in a firefight. Fifty-calibre machine guns and other machine-gun positions pinned down the Marines for several hours. Artillery shells were beginning to fall amongst both companies, killing and wounding. Eventually, Zulu Company Commander, Lieutenant Clive Dytor, took the initiative and led an exceptionally courageous charge across the 400 yards of open ground. His men followed through, clearing heavily defended positions one by one. Dytor's charge, for which he was subsequently awarded the Military Cross, changed the course of the battle. A three-pronged attack by Yankee and Zulu Companies, with X-Ray following through along the connecting ridge, convinced the defenders to flee what should have been an impregnable position.

By mid-June the Falklands autumn was beginning to give way to winter. The land forces endured more frequent squalls of rain, bitter hail, sudden snow showers, fine drizzle, enveloping mists and dense fog. In comparison with the impossibly courageous acts of the Paras and

Marines, exposed to appalling weather conditions, our experience of war as aircrew might have seemed pathetically tame and benign. But it didn't feel like it.

In many ways, the South Atlantic weather proved our greatest challenge: it was volatile and could change in an instant. Some days brought brilliant sunshine with calm air and we could see for miles. The next might be atrocious with dangerously low levels of visibility. Sharp winds adversely affected helicopters transporting heavy slingloaded artillery ammunition pallets.

One day after the war, Al Doughty and I were crossing San Carlos Water with an underslung load. An hour earlier we had climbed up to 5,000 feet in beautiful blue sky just to admire the view. Halfway across the bay, the Sussex Hills turned white without warning. We had just enough time to turn back and land our load and ourselves on the hillside before the snowstorm struck. Within thirty seconds the port engine wound down, extinguished by a deluge of snow that had built up inside the nose intake. On another occasion I spent one unnerving flight trying to get some stores out to an island settlement. Low cloud and strong winds meant that I had to fly around the coast. I ended up flying lower and lower until I was hover-taxiing alongside the cliffs just above the crashing waves. Thankfully the cliffs gave way to flatter land and I was able to pull over and shut down in the fog.

To do our job in support of the troops, we needed to be fully alert. Back in the relative safety of FOB Teal, at least for those aircrew resting anywhere near the sheep shed, it was nigh on impossible to get our badly needed sleep. The HF radio loudspeaker bristled intermittently with 'Helquests' for helicopter casevac from their regimental aid posts (RAP). Behind the Mobile Air Ops Team (MAOT) manning the radio nets, Major Adrian Short was pacing up and down, wondering how best to respond to the mounting casualties from the ongoing battles. Flying a Wessex blind into pitch-black hills at night could easily be a one-way mission. It was still two hours before dawn. His crewman Al Doughty stood nearby, trying to gather as much tactical information as possible from overheard snippets of conversation. He was marking his map with details of RAP grid references, radio frequencies and callsigns.

Eventually Short asked Doughty to go and remove the covers from X-Ray Juliett. Doughty was surprised that they weren't going to take X-Ray Tango, Short's aircraft from the previous day. Then he remembered his colleague Petty Officer Sandy Saunders laughing that Short had landed on top of a telegraph wire after returning from the 3 Brigade brief. Somebody else would have to deal with that particular problem.

It was a spooky feeling wandering around the settlement alone in the darkness. Doughty could just make out the distant cracks and *whoomps* of battle. He took the covers off the rotor blades, engine intake and exhausts, and returned to the shed. MAOT was telling Short that there were now seriously injured soldiers that needed to be casevaced from the RAP on the north side of Mount Kent. Short turned to Doughty, 'Are you ready to go?'

'Yes, sir.' It felt better than addressing the Major as the more usual 'boss'.

Visibility was much better than either of them expected as they lifted off into the clear night and headed southeast. It was still half an hour before dawn, yet there was just enough contrast to be able to fly at a few hundred feet. Small pockets of low-lying radiation fog lay scattered across the landscape but were easily avoided. Passing Estancia House, the last easily recognisable feature that fixed their position, they picked up the track that wound through the valley and up towards the north side of Mount Kent. Without any obvious features on the ground, the only way to find the RAP in the darkness was through dead reckoning, flying an accurate course and speed for the right amount of time. The task was made easier this morning as there was no wind to take into account.

Doughty had hastily drawn one-minute markers onto his map. By now the first hints of dawn gave them just enough light to be able to drop down to fifty feet above the ground at exactly sixty knots. The RAP should be four minutes' flying time up the valley. Any further and they risked entering the battle area. 'If we haven't seen them at five minutes, we do a 180,' he instructed Short.

Just as Doughty was beginning to wonder if Short had heard him, he spotted a tiny green light out to his right. 'I've got the LS visual at 3 o'clock,' he shouted, to make sure.

'Don't shout and keep calm.'

Doughty smiled to himself as he talked Short around a tight left-hand circuit and into an uneventful landing near the medical tent. Doughty unhooked his despatcher safety harness and walked over to the medics. There were already some twenty wounded men. Numbers were mounting. The first group to go would be three stretcher cases and four walking wounded from both sides, British and Argentine. While he helped arrange the stretchers, he reconnected his harness and plugged back onto the intercom. 'Back on, sir. You're clear to go. We need another Wessex out here to help us.' As they lifted away, reversing up the valley and back towards the field hospital at Teal, Short radioed MAOT for a further aircraft to help out.

The second Wessex was quickly airborne. Given the ferocity of the battles raging just a mile or two away, the two aircraft completed the casevac from Mount Kent with remarkable ease. Yet throughout what turned out to be a fairly routine mission for both aircraft, the thoughts of pilots and aircrew alike were dominated by a single relentless nagging fear: Where were the Pucaras?

I have no idea how or why I managed to sleep so well. Apart from seeing the first flares way off in the distance, I missed the distant booms of the British 105mm howitzers on Mount Kent and a high-level attempt to bomb them by five Argentine Canberras during the night. But I was wide awake and packing away my sleeping bag by the time I heard X-Ray Juliett's port engine power into life.

I was tasked as co-pilot with RAF Flight Lieutenant Andy Pulford. Our crewman was Jan Lomas, survivor of the second Fortuna crash in Yankee Alpha (no relation to 845 detachment commander Jack Lomas). All three of us were new arrivals to the Falklands and looking forward to the action.

With the likelihood of a very long day ahead, it was important that we ate while we had the chance. My favourite item in the Arctic ration packs was rolled oats. Tear open the foil packet, pour the powder into a mess tin with a bit of hot water, and you have a delicious hot sweet porridge. Together with my green plastic mug of hot sweet tea and some 'AB' – tooth-breaking biscuits, nicknamed 'Ard Bastards' – it was an excellent breakfast with loads of calories.

After a short brief from MAOT in the shed, we gathered our bergens and crossed the hard ground towards our cab, X-Ray Tango, parked on the edge of a small valley and stream. Two telegraph poles leant in precariously toward the aircraft. So we were the unlucky crew who'd have to sort out Major Short's mess. It seemed extraordinary that neither wire nor helicopter had given way. We ducked under the telegraph wire to get the covers off the Wessex.

All the windows were frosted up from the cold night air and the green skin of the helicopter had a faint white tinge from the frost.

A second Wessex started up behind me as I climbed up the side of X-Ray Tango. I slid open the lightweight window and eased myself into the left seat of the cockpit, unsure whether to be relieved or not that there was no window armour. On the one hand, I wouldn't have to haul the heavy shield up into place and I would be able to see a lot better; on the other, this was the one day when I could definitely have done with a little more protection.

Once the engines were started and the rotors turning, I busied myself with adjusting the heating system to defrost the windscreen and rearranged my map for the first task of the day. We were to return to San Carlos to pick up passengers from HMS *Fearless*.

Take-off was very ginger. Pulford eased the aircraft slowly off the ground in order not to let the wire snap up behind our tail wheel and into the tail rotor. From the cabin, Lomas gave us a running commentary as the two telegraph poles established something close to their former upright position.

We headed west, back towards San Carlos, passing the distinctive marker of Bombilla Hill. It was a stunning morning. As first light dawned, thin wisps of fog hugged the ground like cotton wool. We raced just above the white carpet which we knew would clear as soon as the sun rose. Back on *Fearless*, we refuelled, picked up our passengers and headed back towards Teal. Like schoolboys eager for a thrill, we were hoping like mad to be given a task up near the front line. Flying onward from our drop-off at Teal, we headed at low level towards the forward operating base up near Estancia House. As we approached, we heard Adrian Short's voice over the radio inviting us to join him to pick up wounded soldiers from 3 Para's battle on Mount Longdon. A Royal Marine Gazelle would show us the way. It seemed like Short had forgotten his own brief and was as unable to resist the pull of action as the rest of us.

The two Wessex joined up. X-Ray Juliett led with X-Ray Tango following about thirty yards behind in loose tactical formation. The formation slowed to sixty knots and dropped down to ten feet above the ground. We climbed over a small ridge north of Mount Kent, both aircraft rolling quickly through the skyline and downhill into a valley. We then wove our way south towards Two Sisters which loomed in front of us. The two Wessex were now on the rear edge of the battle area and yet there was no sign of life anywhere.

The eerie feeling of impending doom suddenly shattered. As if in slow motion, I watched a small green Gazelle helicopter emerge out of nowhere to our right and fly straight into the path of X-Ray Juliett in front of us. There was no time for a warning as Pulford and I held our breath. We were about to witness an appalling mid-air collision. Amazingly, the Gazelle shot from right to left in front of the X-Ray Juliett. We breathed again as the Gazelle, flown by Navy pilot Lieutenant Commander Gervais Coryton, radioed instructions: 'Follow me boys!'

The three aircraft formation headed north to our left, slowing further and dropping even lower. Our wheels were now practically running across the grass. If it was possible to hide a twelve-foot-high Wessex helicopter in a five-foot deep valley, we managed it. By now, I had total confidence in Pulford's superb flying. I followed our progress across the featureless terrain as best I could on the map, occasionally glancing across the cockpit instruments to make sure the Wessex was doing what it was supposed to, and mostly scanning the skies for Pucara.

Scram!

As we rounded the corner of a small river bed, the Gazelle led us uphill onto Mount Longdon itself. There was still virtually no wind and so we had no worries about turbulence and downdraft from the lee of the hill. The yellow grass turned to grey rocks and scree as we climbed the slope. Occasional puffs of smoke from mortar fire exploded far out in front of us as we approached a line of sheer rocks overhanging a ridge at the top of the hill. Underneath this protective wall were several troops crouching amongst the scree. It was the 3 Para regimental aid post. The Gazelle cleared away to the left and X-Ray Juliett hovered up toward the troops. We dropped our front wheels on to the grass fifty yards back down the hill and watched as stretchers were lifted across into the other aircraft.

In the final days of the war, we flew our commando helicopters right up to the front line, often coming under artillery or mortar fire, taking ammunition in and casualties out. This is one of our Wessex on Two Sisters, which had just been captured by the Royal Marines of 45 Commando.

* * *

313

From the moment Coryton had radioed his request to Short, there was never any doubt that the rescue mission should go ahead. X-Ray Juliett had already changed course when Short asked Doughty: 'Are you happy to fly into the battle area?'

It was not really a question.

Now high up on the northern side of Mount Longdon, the two Wessex were hovering just below the skyline and a matter of yards from the battle over the hill. Doughty was talking to his pilots, Short and Ric Fox. The angle of the slope made it impossible to put three, or even two, wheels down. Short lowered the aircraft so that only the starboard wheel was in contact with the ground. The rest of X-Ray Juliett now hung suspended above the slope. Doughty jumped down from the cabin that was higher off the ground than normal. Two soldiers rushed in under the hovering helicopter with the first stretcher containing a wounded paratrooper. Doughty could hear the occasional shouted words picked up by Short's throat mike. 'No fucking stiffs,' he bellowed down. The situation was incredibly tense. They needed to get out of there as soon as possible.

Sitting next to Short in the cockpit of X-Ray Juliett, Fox was doing the same job of co-pilot as I was behind him in the cockpit of X-Ray Tango. His eyes frantically scanned the horizon on all sides for Pucaras. It barely occurred that the more immediate threat was from the Argentine artillery. Yet the roar of the two Wessex presented a very obvious target. Short and Fox watched the first round explode into the soil a few hundred yards out in front. As an artillery man, Short knew exactly what was coming at them. 'Look at that Foxy,' he said gleefully, 'that's a 155. It must be Argie as we don't have any of those.'

It was taking longer than usual to get the wounded on board because Doughty had to strain to lift the casualties an extra few feet above the ground. Two Paras were trying to lift up an injured Argentine soldier who was shaking with terror. He refused to board. There was no time for polite discussion. Doughty grabbed his lapels and gave him a full-blooded head butt, hard enough to crack his own helmet visor. The soldier was knocked out and bundled into the cabin.

The next round was far too close. The ground erupted with a puff of smoke just yards in front of X-Ray Juliett's cockpit window, sending clods of earth up through the rotor blades. 'Definitely a 155,' said Short excitedly.

'I think we need to go,' urged Fox.

'One more,' shouted Doughty as two Paras dragged another Argentine soldier down the hillside in a poncho. His legs flapped over the rocks; it looked as if his spine was broken. He was hauled unceremoniously on board. 'Go now,' shouted Doughty as he manned the machine gun. It seemed they had been on the hillside for an eternity. In reality, it was little over a minute.

The Wessex in front of us called 'Lifting' and sped away at low level to our left. We lifted off and edged forward to take our position next to the first-aid post. More puffs of smoke exploded directly in front of us, further away than the round that nearly took out X-Ray Juliett, but still much too close for comfort. The artillery fire seemed less of a concern than the possibility that we would be caught out in the open by a Pucara.

Our situation remained extremely precarious. X-Ray Tango was now balanced on one wheel on the front line of the battle, under artillery fire and with Argentine soldiers just a few hundred yards away behind the cliff face of Mount Longdon. I looked across the cockpit past Pulford at the few soldiers and medics sheltering from the violence of our downdraft. A medical officer dressed in combats accompanied a wounded Para on a stretcher into the back of our aircraft. One of the soldier's legs had been blown off, but he was smiling. With only one casualty on board, the doctor waved us off. We didn't need a second invitation. Pulford eased up on the collective lever and, as the helicopter rose from the ground, executed a classic over-the-shoulder take-off. I looked behind me out of my window and called 'Clear' as we pirouetted around our tail wheel. Adrenalin was flooding through us as X-Ray Tango sped away down the hill.

From the cabin beneath, Jan Lomas started to give graphic and gruesome details of the field dressings and bloodstains on our passenger who was still smiling and awake, though clearly in shock. In the cockpit we concentrated on the task in hand. We hugged the ground and stayed in whatever valleys we could find until we were completely clear from the battle area to the north of Mount Kent. The cockpit banter became overexcited and immodest as we headed back east toward Ajax Bay. Lomas and I both congratulated Pulford on a fabulous piece of flying. We all congratulated each other on our teamwork.

Our Wessex was still required for lifting and shifting in the forward area. So we deposited our wounded friend back at Teal Inlet for transfer to the field hospital at San Carlos.

After refuelling, we moved our aircraft into position to pick up an underslung load. Flying a little higher this time, we made our way up toward the artillery position on the top of Mount Kent and brought our load in to a flat area at the top of the peak – taking care to approach *behind* the array of 105mm artillery guns and shells. As we dropped off our load there was an almighty blast from one of the guns; it ripped through the huge noise of the Wessex and almost caused me to jump out of my seat.

A few lifts later and we were back at FOB Teal, shut down and waiting for new instructions. As we waited in the hall outside the ops room, a tall man dressed in combats wandered in smoking an enormous cigar. After the adrenalin rush of the morning, it was an incongruous sight that made me laugh for quite some time afterwards. I assumed he must be a special forces officer. In fact it was the journalist Max Hastings.

While we continued our assignments on the northern flank, a lot more helicopter activity was taking place on the southern flank. The last time I had seen my squadron boss was two days earlier, somewhere between Goose Green and Fitzroy, as he swept past and told me to get on with it. Mike Booth then stationed himself at the new FOB in Fitzroy in order to take charge of Wessex operations in support of 5 Brigade. At least four units were now closing in on the Argentines. The two thousand or so men of 2 Para, the Scots Guards, Gurkhas and Welsh Guards all needed helicopter support and constant resupply. With the final phase of the war approaching, Major General Jeremy Moore had also moved his headquarters forward, from San Carlos to Fitzroy.

There was an awful lot of flying to do. Wessex and Sea Kings flew almost continuously for two days. On Friday 11 June, the day of Pete Manley's AS12 attack, Hector Heathcote and Leading Aircrewman Jock McKie put in eight and a half hours. Over the Friday and Saturday, Mike Booth and Ian Georgeson flew almost continuously. On the Saturday, Jack Lomas, Oily Knight and Smudge Smyth put in a mammoth twelve-hour day, finishing in the dark. Peter Manley and Andy Berryman, back in his day job after a stint as South Georgia prison guard, were airborne for four hours.

Life and death decisions put huge pressure on the pilots. At FOB Teal, Adrian Short had succumbed twice to the desperate pleas for casevac from Mount Kent and then Mount Longdon. At Fitzroy, Mike Booth was trying to catch some sleep in a corner of a shed after an exhausting day. A head popped round the door saying there was an urgent need for casevac from the hills. Booth scrambled to his feet and went outside to be briefed further. 'Have they got a MAOT team out there? Any lights? Anyone to help us get in?' asked Booth. A Mobile Air Ops Team would know how to set up the torches for a night-time landing site.

The answer was no.

'You'll have to ask the Sea King guys. We just can't fly around the mountains in the pitch black.'

It was a terrible choice but the right one. Two hours after the original request, Booth was woken again in his shed and asked to do a casevac back to San Carlos. As if to make amends, he agreed. Two stretchers were loaded into the cabin of X-Ray X-Ray which lifted off into the darkness. The only way back was to stay just south of the ridgeline and then nip over the top into San Carlos.

In the darkness, Booth and Georgeson never even saw the snowstorm until the flakes started pelting the windscreen. 'Shit, we're going to die if we don't get this right,' thought Booth, switching his attention instantly to his illuminated instrument panel and hauling the Wessex into a tight left-hand turn. Because the storm had only just hit, he knew they could backtrack 180 degrees and descend without running into a mountain. Nevertheless, the thirty seconds or so before the Wessex was spat back out of the storm and heading back to Fitzroy was an alarming experience. The two wounded soldiers were taken back to Ajax Bay a few hours later at first light.

Turning down one casevac and turning back on the next

played on Booth's mind all of the next day. In two days, he and Georgeson spent over twenty hours airborne. He recorded the marathon in his logbook as his 'Fitzroy bender'.

After another trip back to Ajax Bay with wounded from Teal, we were frustrated to be told to land back at Teal and await further tasking. Our mission onto Longdon had given us a taste for adventure and we wanted more. Pulford and I spent much of our time in the ops room badgering our MAOT team to send us back up into the hills. Eventually, they relented and we were back in the air, off to shift the kit left behind by 42 Commando Royal Marines as they moved forward to attack Mount Harriet. As we flew on up to Mount Wall, we made contact with a Royal Marine Gazelle that radioed grid references and descriptions of the pick-up and drop-off points to us.

An army Gazelle approaches Goat Ridge, between Two Sisters and Mount Harrier, the day after their capture by the Royal Marines of 42 and 45 Commando. The Wessex is Yankee Hotel, the gunship that fired two AS12 missiles into Port Stanley two days earlier, now back in the role of troop carrier.

I was puzzled by the description of our landing site given by the Gazelle pilot. Adrian Short had been clear in his brief that the final phase of assaults on the hills around Stanley was expected to take several days. A quick glance at my map told me that a landing on the southwest corner of Mount Harriet, as intended, would put us in full view of nearby enemy forces on Mount Tumbledown. As far as I was aware, our troops weren't due to have a go at Tumbledown until the following night.

Pulford radioed back to the Gazelle with our concerns. 'No probs, it's safe,' replied the Gazelle pilot.

'Confirm with him whether the next set of hills has been taken,' I asked Pulford, worried. The reply was again positive. We had no choice but to continue and hope that Tumbledown had indeed been taken.

After landing on Mount Wall, Jan Lomas loaded the back of the Wessex with as many bergens as he could cram in. It was an exhausting and time-consuming task. I could, and should, have climbed down to help. But I was completely focused on preparing a mental image of what the route and landing site might look like from the information on the map. *Junglie* pilots pride themselves on being the best navigators. We had to be. Operating so close to enemy forces, there was no scope for navigational error.

The Gazelle waited on the ground until we called that we were ready. We lifted off and followed closely behind the Gazelle at a few feet above the ground in the direction of Mount Harriet. As I had predicted from the map, there was little or no cover at the foot of Mount Harriet where the Gazelle indicated we should land. It was a wide-open area in full view of Mount Tumbledown. This time a couple of Royal Marines ran in to help Lomas throw the bergens out of the cabin.

Out in front of us, probably a mile or more away,

although it seemed like a matter of yards, we could see trenches dug into the side of the hill. Heads moved about and we could clearly see weapons. But the heads didn't stay up for long. Puffs of smoke revealed the result of artillery fire. Our soldiers were being fired on by the Argentines right in front of our eyes. We were probably on the ground for little more than a minute, but it seemed like an eternity. I felt incredibly exposed. It was with considerable relief when we heard Lomas's voice: 'Right, we're clear to go and, by the way, I've got you some Argie helmets as souvenirs.' Another over-the-shoulder take-off and we were soon exiting at low level just above the grass to collect our next load.

Back at Mount Wall we heard the Gazelle pilot ask another passing Wessex to help out. A familiar Irish tone filled the airwaves with a 'Hello there boys'. My 847 Squadron colleague Jerry Spence had been suckered in to help us out with his Royal Marine crewman Corporal Mark Brickell. Our two Wessex loaded up once again to complete our task and headed back at low level to the base of Mount Harriet. For the second time, the open position in flat ground felt horribly exposed as we watched the artillery shells exploding on Mount Tumbledown. It all seemed far too close.

The light was fading as we left Spence and Brickell to finish the final load. After the nerve-racking casevac under fire from Mount Longdon in the morning, the sorties to the base of Mount Harriet felt strangely subdued. By now, we were grateful to head back to Port San Carlos. Although the skies were clear, the complete absence of lighting throughout East Falkland meant that we could see little on the way back. We entered the San Carlos area from the north with our downward identification light switched on – code to inform the anchored warships that we were a friendly aircraft. As we approached our base at Port San Carlos we saw the vague outlines of several Wessex safely on the ground. Trying to land without lights was now extremely dangerous. We had no hesitation in switching on the bright landing light to make sure we were well clear of other aircraft and telegraph wires, and landed safely.

I looked across to Pulford and we shook hands. There was no one to meet us in the darkness so we traipsed back quietly through the grass and mud in our wellies to debrief. Back in the briefing tent, I told Mike Spencer how surprised I was that our troops were so far ahead of schedule. 'They're not,' came the shocking reply. We were stunned.

It wasn't our guys we'd been watching moving around in the trenches away to our front on the edge of Mount Tumbledown; it wasn't Argentine artillery fire raining down on them. Instead we'd been in full, unobstructed line of sight of the Argentine front-line soldiers. We'd been watching a British artillery bombardment, fired over the top of our heads from the mountain-top base we had just resupplied at Mount Kent. The teeny-weeny Gazelle and two much larger Wessex had spent several minutes right on the front line in full view of enemy soldiers. We were huge, prime, stationary targets. If it had been our guys, artillery or not, somebody could easily have had more than just a pot shot at us. We wondered if we'd ever get a chance to 'Rembrandt' the Gazelle pilot – to put him in the picture – for so badly misleading us.

Still out in the hills were Spence and Brickell. Just as we had been shifting bergens for the Royal Marines of 42 Commando, they were doing the same job for the Royal Marines of 45 Commando. Along with another Wessex, they were to take the bergens from 45 Commando's lying-up position on Mount Kent to the new forward dump on the slopes of Two Sisters, two miles north of Mount Harriet. Mark Brickell was not big but he was a tough and wiry Royal Marine. Somehow he managed to haul the huge dead weights up into the back of the Wessex cabin on his own.

The relationship between *junglie* pilots and aircrewmen was almost always thoroughly professional. But there were varying degrees of formality. Some of this boiled down to friendship and personal chemistry. First names were often used by pilots when talking to their crewmen, especially if of equivalent experience. If in doubt, the pilot would usually call the crewman by his surname and the crewmen called the pilot 'boss' or very occasionally 'sir'. A senior crewman might use first names with a junior pilot if they got along especially well. Because there was never an issue of competence to muddy the picture, rank was always respected. The exception to the rule was for Royal Marine aircrewmen, who were invariably – but by no means always – referred to by their rank. Somehow the formality seemed more appropriate.

From the slopes of Mount Kent, Spence raised the collective lever to maximum torque in order to ease the heavy Wessex off the ground and towards their destination of Two Sisters. Even for two excellent navigators, finding a six-figure grid reference in featureless terrain was not an exact science. Dusk was now falling, making the task even more difficult. Flying as low as he dared, just a few feet above the moorland, Spence manoeuvred his Wessex up over a ridgeline and along a flat saddle leading to a second higher ridge on the west face of Two Sisters. Unable to do much more than glance down at his map in the dull light, he started to wonder if this was where they should be going. 'Corporal Brickell, do you reckon we've got the right place?' he asked.

'Just a bit further boss,' replied Brickell. 'It's here.'

Spence flared the Wessex into a low hover above the rocky ground. There was nowhere to land and appeared to be nobody about. Just as Brickell started to manhandle the first few bergens out of the cabin, Spence watched three or four explosions of enemy mortar or artillery a few hundred yards in front of him beyond the ridgeline. 'Corporal Brickell, get them bloody out, let's get out of here.'

The prospect of a second run to the same drop-off point was becoming less appealing by the minute. By the time the Wessex was loaded up with more bergens, dusk had turned to near darkness. During the daytime, Spence had been using his green and red navigation lights to help avoid collisions with other aircraft. Now in darkness, flashing lights would simply make them a nice big target for enemy artillery spotters. Finally he resolved the dilemma. 'Fuck it, I'm switching them off.'

There were no explosions as they hovered over the Two Sisters peaks this time. But the darkness was fast becoming an even worse enemy. 'This is getting too dangerous,' said Spence. 'I've had enough.' Turning to the north-west and climbing slightly, to what would still have been considered low flying under normal conditions, Spence and Brickell headed back to Teal for the night.

'Being shot at, that's no problem!' said Spence to Brickell as they finally shut the Wessex down. 'Flying around the mountains in the dark, that's what's dangerous.'

As night fell at the southern forward operating base at Fitzroy, Lomas, Evans and some of the other aircrew had found a corner of a hayloft in which to try to rest after their own mammoth sorties. They had been tasked in support of the heroic medical teams of RAMC Field Ambulance who had been working at full tilt for days on end. The young medics had been faced with an appalling stream of burns victims from *Sir Galahad*. On top of that they were now treating horrifically injured British and Argentine soldiers from the battles in the hills just a few miles to the north-east. In the back of the casevac aircraft, Wessex and Sea King crewmen had done similarly heroic work keeping soldiers alive until they made it to the hospital ship SS *Uganda* in Falkland Sound.

Whilst casualties were being offloaded on deck of *Uganda*, a finger jabbed several times towards a mouth by a member of the aircrew would produce brown paper bags full of sandwiches, fruit, chocolate bars and occasionally a message of goodwill.

Back in their hayloft at FOB Fitzroy, Lomas and Evans were tucking in to their brown paper bags when a shattered young RAMC doctor walked in.

'I'm so knackered,' he told them, 'that if I were captured by the enemy, I'd tell them absolutely anything for an orange and a Mars bar.'

Evans and Lomas looked at each other. They each delved into their bags and handed over the named items. Overwhelmed, the young medic burst into sobs of uncontrollable tears. It was an appropriate reaction to a momentous day.

Chapter 16

White flags
13–15 June 1982

Even with the British forces poised for their final strike, the assault on Port Stanley, victory was far from a foregone conclusion.

While the troops on the ground were involved in acts of exceptional bravery, the helicopter crews were stretched to the limit in support of them. Flying in the mountains in darkness without modern navigation aids was especially challenging. On the front line, almost all helicopters came under mortar fire.

One question continued to dominate every moment of every mission. Where were the Pucaras? The Argentine air force may have been depleted, but they certainly weren't finished.

Now that 3 Brigade had captured the outer ring of hills around Stanley, it was vital to keep the momentum going. The Argentines were on the run but delays in the advance would give them time to regroup. Four-five Commando Royal Marines at Two Sisters were particularly keen to continue the advance through to Mount Tumbledown, just a few miles ahead of them to the south-east.

This Wessex has been taking underslung loads of ammunition in support of the British troops who are about to fight the last battles of the war. The end of the war may have seemed inevitable. It wasn't for the men on the ground.

It was important also to make use of the fresh troops of 5 Brigade. The initial plan had been to lift the Scots Guards, Welsh Guards and Gurkhas forward to holding areas on the outer ring by helicopter and attack the remaining hills late on Saturday 12 June. But the reality was that much of the helicopter force, Sea Kings and Wessex, were needed to ferry ammunition to the artillery positions. The big guns were not just running low on shells, artillery crews were also having to dig themselves out after continually sinking into the soft ground every time they fired. The problem would only get worse with the guns firing at longer range and the deteriorating weather conditions. The alternative was to move the guns forward. Either option required large amounts of helicopter lift.

The other problem was that 5 Brigade would have to be sent into battle without adequate artillery support or time for proper reconnaissance and briefing in position beforehand. Reluctantly, Brigadier Tony Wilson decided to delay the final phases of the attack by one day, until Sunday 13 June. It was not popular with the troops of 3 Brigade, exposed to worsening weather overnight on the hills and under artillery fire from the enemy. The Paras on Mount Longdon suffered especially badly from the extra wait. But it was the right decision.

Soon after making a shattered medic happy by sharing his orange and Mars bar, Mark Evans had been called out for another night casevac mission on the night of 12 June. Argentine shelling was targeting Two Sisters as well as Longdon. The night-vision capable Sea Kings were ideally suited to this sort of task, but command was deliberately keeping them aside for special operations. Once again, a Wessex crew was faced with the terrible dilemma: whether to try and fly out visually in the darkness and risk crashing, or refuse a task that might leave wounded soldiers dying in the field? Grabbing Noddy Morton and Kev Gleeson, Evans decided they would have a go.

The sky was clear and there was just the barest hint of ambient light. If they were careful, with the Wessex windows wide open, with all lights switched off, and with their eyesight fully adjusted to the darkness, they just might be able to see enough to find their way up into the hills and back.

Pulling in that first armful of collective lever is not much fun on a dark night. The ground is your friend while you're safely attached to it. But as the helicopter goes light on its wheels and begins to lift away, you realise the ground is trying to kill you. The temptation is to want to climb away as quickly as possible. On this night the two pilots would have to fight their instincts and stay low. That meant relying on their eyesight much more than their instruments. It would be like day-flying but with the daylight switched off.

Departing Fitzroy was straightforward enough. The two inlets of Port Pleasant to the south and Port Fitzroy to the north gave a distinctive outline between water and land. Morton used the first few minutes of the flight to get his eyes used to the conditions. While he flew the aircraft from the right-hand seat, Evans beside him in the left seat and Gleeson behind in the cabin focused on navigation.

'Right, you two,' said Gleeson, 'make sure you don't hit anything. Crashing out here will ruin my day.'

Passing the settlement at Bluff Cove, Morton made a cautious descent to low level and followed the track that would take them up towards the battle area. The mountainside of Mount Challenger loomed large to their left. Ahead of them, it was easy enough to make out the separate outlines of Two Sisters and Mount Harriet and the higher ground just before them. Approaching the grid reference they had been given, the track gave way to rough grass. They were now going so slowly that they were almost hover-taxiing. In the darkness, it became harder and harder to distinguish any features. 'Fuck this for a game of soldiers,' said Morton. 'We're no use to anyone if we don't get there. I'm going to need lights.'

There was just enough contrast between hillside and sky to keep the helicopter the right way up. But unable to distinguish anything closer in to the aircraft, there was a real risk of hitting the ground. By their reckoning, they only had a few hundred yards to go. The medics would identify the landing position with torches arranged in the shape of a 'T'. But without help, they weren't going to get there at all.

Morton switched on the landing light. It completely changed the perspective from the cockpit. Now he could only see the ground that was lit up immediately ahead of him. It was as if the land beyond ceased to exist. But the sudden blaze of light on a distant hillside also alerted the Argentine gunners to British activity. They were now a target. 'Someone's putting flares up for us,' said Morton.

Just outside of their bubble of light, a handful of dark splashes were visible in front of them.

'They're not flares, Noddy,' said Evans. 'We're being mortared.'

Morton switched off the light, pitching the Wessex back into blackness. The T-pattern of torchlight materialised out of the gloom in the nick of time. Landing at the first-aid post, two stretchers were quickly loaded into the back. With a thumbs-up and thanks mouthed from the medics, Morton lifted the Wessex into the air, accelerating for a few yards to gain speed before turning sharply back to the south-west and the surgeons at Fitzroy.

Soon after, the crew were back at Two Sisters for a second casevac. This time they kept the landing light off.

The twenty-five strong Wessex fleet was now operating from three different locations: the forward bases at Fitzroy on the south side and Teal on the north side, and Port San Carlos at the rear. Much the same was true for the twenty 846 and 825 Sea Kings. Only the Sea King night-flyers remained permanently based in the San Carlos area, along with the Chinook, lone representative of the RAF. A further handful of Wessex crews and aircraft were dotted around ships within the Total Exclusion Zone. Lieutenant Ralph Miles and his flight were sent to the damaged HMS *Glamorgan* to replace their Wessex 3, destroyed by the land-based Exocet launched from Stanley. But on their first night, one of their blades broke on the exposed deck during a severe storm, putting them out of action as well. Eight other aircraft of varying serviceability remained as a reserve on board *Atlantic Causeway*.

Throughout the morning of 13 June, the main role for the helicopters based at Fitzroy was to airlift 5 Brigade troops forward to their holding positions in the outer ring of hills. Between the Wessex, Sea Kings and Chinook, and the Scouts and Gazelles, there were now as many as forty helicopters operating between the forward operating bases and the front line. Air activity was frenetic.

Pete Manley was teamed up with Andy Berryman, another of Mike Tidd's new arrivals. They were flying Yankee Victor, one of several helicopters assigned to move the Gurkhas onto Goat Ridge, between Harriet and Two Sisters. The crew had already spent much of the previous day lifting troops and equipment forward. Their adrenalin levels were consistently high as the Wessex raced low over the grassland. The ground they covered in daytime was almost exactly the same as covered by Evans and Morton on the previous night.

It was as important to keep a good lookout for other friendly aircraft as it was to keep a constant search of the horizon for Pucaras. They were expecting to rendezvous with a Gazelle that would lead them into their exact drop-off point. The plan was to take several Wessex in at once, much as we had done on Longdon two days earlier. What

Manley was not expecting, as he moved the Gurkhas forward to the outer hills, was the distraction of something being waved around inside the cockpit down by his feet. 'What the bloody hell's going on?' he asked.

'I'm trying to give you this *kukri*, boss,' said the crewman. 'It's the first time they've been taken into battle in years. The Gurkha officer asked me to give it to the mission commander.'

The brief moment of pride wasn't to last long. Manley's concentration was soon back on the mission as the Gazelle appeared and turned to lead the formation of helicopters in to land. Once on the ground, the Gurkhas were quick to deploy outwards and begin digging themselves in. They would need to. Not for the first time, Manley found himself under artillery fire. Puffs of smoke marked the fall of shells a few hundred yards away. 'Have a nice time boys,' he mouthed to them as he pulled in power to leave. 'Right, we'd better leg it,' he said to co-pilot Berryman as he headed Yankee Victor back towards Fitzroy for another pick-up.

Out at sea to the south of Falkland Sound, Lieutenant Chris Clayton and his observer Lieutenant Peter Hullett were returning to their ship HMS *Cardiff* in a Lynx at around midday. They had been out looking for Argentine ships and were now flying at 1,000 feet above the sea. Suddenly vibrations rippled through their cockpit. It was like losing teeth off a gearbox. Clayton's immediate reaction was that there was something badly wrong with the aircraft. He instantly dumped the aircraft into autorotation and flared to reduce speed – it was the classic pilot's response to a potentially catastrophic failure.

At that moment an Argentine Dagger broke past on his port side, revealing its distinctive delta shape. 'Fuck me,

Mirage!' said Clayton, just as a second Dagger shot past on the starboard side. Realising the vibration had come from being strafed by cannon fire and not from his aircraft, Clayton pulled in full power and pushed the helicopter's nose down. The Lynx accelerated as they dived down to 150 feet above the sea.

Both Daggers were now trying to line themselves up for an attack. As the first Dagger turned, Clayton headed straight at him trying to keep inside the turn, making it impossible for the jet to get him in his sights. Splashes appeared in the water from cannon fire a hundred yards short of the Lynx. The plan was working. Clayton pulled up to see where the next attack was coming from as the second Dagger turned in. Again the jet overshot, missing the Lynx.

The jet pilots must have realised they were too close. One of the Daggers turned in the distance for a head-on attack. This time there was nowhere for the Lynx to run. Clayton could see the jet lined up and heading straight at them in a shallow dive. 'Let's go for it,' he said, tipping the aircraft nose down and pulling full power.

Hullett pressed the transmit button on his radio: '466, we've been bounced, two Mirage, we need help.'

The Dagger and the Lynx were now pointing directly at each other. It was a game of chicken which only the jet could win. Clayton accelerated to 140 knots, putting the Argentine jet in the middle of his windscreen. Keeping his Lynx just above sea level forced the attacking Dagger to steepen his dive. Cannon shells shot over the top of the helicopter as the Lynx managed to stay underneath the line of fire. The Dagger was barely a hundred yards away, almost filling Clayton's windscreen, when it broke.

A fourth attack followed the pattern of the first two, but the jet failed to get properly lined up and Clayton again managed to stay inside the turn. The two Daggers then disappeared as abruptly as they had arrived. Clayton and Hullett now turned back for their ship, *Cardiff*, giggling with adrenalin and excitement.

For his exceptional airmanship that day, which had saved both their lives, Clayton was awarded a Mention in Despatches.

Back in the relative safety of Port San Carlos, Al Doughty and I had been tasked as casevac helicopter at Ajax Bay for the day. Once again flying the unwanted battle-scarred Yankee Tango, we felt frustrated that we were to spend time away from the front line. But it still felt good that our superiors trusted a baby pilot and junior aircrewman enough to operate in a war zone on our own.

It was a beautiful clear and bright day as we passed between the handful of ships at anchor in the dark waters of San Carlos Bay. As we flew past the refuelling ship RFA *Olna*, with its huge gantries and high flight deck, neither of us had any idea that two more Wessex lay idle, locked away within *Olna*'s hangar. Our frustration was as nothing compared to that felt by Lieutenant Mark Salter, my main Wessex instructor from a few months previously. Despite a stream of increasingly heated requests to *Fearless*, and personal contact with two passing 847 Squadron pilots, his team of three pilots and two aircrewmen had been given no tasking whatsoever and told to keep their deck clear for refuelling. It was an inexplicable omission of two serviceable assets during the crucial last few stages of the war.

I set my Wessex on a long curving turn to bring us in to land next to the refrigeration plant that was the Ajax Bay field hospital. The words 'Welcome to the Red and Green Life Machine' stood out in red letters on the long sidewall. We were quickly greeted by the jovial figure of Surgeon Commander Rick 'Doc' Jolly. It wasn't often that a sub-lieutenant was addressed by a senior officer, especially in such polite and enthusiastic terms. Jolly was a huge fan of the many *junglie* crews, both Sea King and Wessex, who were consistently quick to offer their unofficial services as casevac helicopters throughout the war when official requests for helicopters had been turned down. We were unwitting recipients of this goodwill. Doughty and I were generously given a personalised tour of the impromptu operating theatres inside the plant. Jolly took special pleasure in taking us around a corner and pointing out his unexploded bomb. At this point I suggested it might be a good idea for him to tell us what flying he wanted us to do.

After parking my Wessex next to the main field hospital at Ajax Bay, nicknamed 'the red and green life machine', Surgeon Commander Rick Jolly took great pleasure in showing me the unexploded bomb that dangled next to his operating theatre. At this point, I thought it best to get airborne as quickly as possible.

After flashing up, we waved in the stretcher bearers to take our first patient out to SS *Uganda*, parked over the hill in Falkland Sound. As I pushed the nose of the Wessex over the top of the Sussex Mountain hillside and down towards the sea I suddenly became very aware that I wasn't wearing my goon suit. Combats and wellies wouldn't quite do the trick if I had to ditch in the freezing cold of the South Atlantic. We had no idea that we were passing over almost exactly the spot where Rick Jolly had voluntarily immersed himself twice, whilst going to the aid of survivors from the burning HMS *Ardent*.

The converted cruise ship *Uganda* stood out brightly against the very blue sea. My landing had to be at right angles to the deck, with the aircraft pointing out to the port side of the ship. So with *Uganda* sailing slowly into wind, I kicked the aircraft around to the left as we came to the hover just to the stern. It felt good to be capable of flying a non-standard approach. The deck landing didn't faze me.

On deck, Al Doughty asked me if I fancied anything to eat or drink. Definitely. A deckhand then ran in under the rotor disc clutching a cup of fresh coffee and a paper bag containing a sausage sandwich. It was the perfect gift to set me up for a long day's flying.

Ten miles to our north, a flight of seven Argentine A-4 Skyhawks from Grupo 5 swept low across Falkland Sound ignoring a British helicopter as they flashed past. An eighth Skyhawk had turned back soon after launch. The remaining aircraft continued on at low level over land towards the line of hills that led towards Port Stanley.

At 3 Commando Brigade headquarters near Mount Kent, Major General Jeremy Moore was in the middle of briefing his commanders. The first group of Skyhawks took the

British by surprise from the rear. Taking cover in trenches as the jets screamed overhead, the ground forces were quick to fire back, damaging at least one Skyhawk with small-arms fire and light rockets. Bombs exploded near two Army Air Corps helicopters, badly damaging both cockpit canopies and tail booms. There was nobody in the Scout and Gazelle helicopters; their crews were in at brigade headquarters being briefed on the next mission.

Further along the valley to the north-east, my colleague Lieutenant Paul McIntosh was gently easing X-Ray Bravo into the hover by 29 Commando's artillery position, with fresh supplies of ammunition for their guns. Dangling underneath his Wessex was a cargo net and pallet full of shells. McIntosh watched as the gunner on the ground marshalled them into position. The ridgeline of Mount Longdon lay ahead. He wasn't sure whether the ridge was occupied by British or Argentine forces. McIntosh was aware that the visibility was incredible and that the sun was probably glinting on his rotors, making them an easy target. But at least he was outside the range of small-arms fire.

As Petty Officer aircrewman Jed Clamp calmly gave a steady talk down to the landing point, McIntosh switched his gaze back to the gun emplacement out to his right. Suddenly the gunner pointed excitedly and grabbed his machine gun, swivelling it up towards the hills. Through the front of the cockpit windscreen, McIntosh saw a pair of Skyhawks just clearing the ridge, silhouetted against the skyline for a moment. The lead Skyhawk was heading straight at the Wessex. The number two was attacking to his left, flying in strike formation.

McIntosh knew instantly that he was personally marking the target for the Skyhawks. He also knew he was a sitting duck. Reacting quickly, but calmly, he told his crewman:

'We need to release the load. Now!' The urgency in his voice was obvious.

Clamp reacted quickly: 'All clear!'

McIntosh pressed the release button and the net fell away safely to the ground. His instinct now was to break right straight away, keeping the ground in view below him and putting the two big Gnome engines between him and the likely incoming blast. As he pushed the helicopters nose forward to accelerate directly across the firing line of the gunner, the gunner looked straight up at him even as he opened fire. 'Man the gimpy,' McIntosh shouted at Clamp, telling him to use the cabin machine gun. He already knew there would be little chance to fire it in the few moments available.

The Wessex and Skyhawks were now heading directly at each other. McIntosh watched their weapons release as two 1,000-pound bombs came off the rails. Now that the helicopter had begun to accelerate forwards, he yanked the cyclic control hard to the right. Achieving a crossing rate was standard fighter-evasion tactics. 'This is never going to work,' he thought as the Wessex rolled onto its side. The two jets roared past as they broke to their left, passing behind X-Ray Bravo and turning to the west.

The bombs landed the length of a cricket pitch away. There was no chance of escaping the blast. McIntosh braced himself. None came. There was no explosion. Both the artillery positions and the Wessex escaped wholly unscathed. The bombs had been dropped too close to their target and the fuses had failed to unwind. It wasn't just the ships that were being spared by the failure of Argentine bombs to arm.

As the first flight of Skyhawks completed their run over 3 Brigade headquarters, they turned to the west to escape.

This really captures the feel of what it was like flying near the front line during the last few days. It's the kind of view my colleague Paul McIntosh had just before two Skyhawks steamed over the ridgeline directly at him and dropped two 1,000-pound bombs right underneath his Wessex. Mercifully, they failed to detonate. Here, the hillside is smoking from enemy artillery fire as a Wessex comes in to land next to a regimental first aid post. A Scout helicopter waits with a stretcher strapped outside: the *teeny weenies* were far braver than us.

Right in front of them was a commando Sea King. Victor Alpha was on its way down from the top of Mount Kent where it had been dropping off ammunition. It was an opportunity target for the Skyhawks.

At the controls of Victor Alpha were Simon Thornewill and Dave Lord – both experienced instructors who had taught me on the Wessex training squadron just a few months earlier. Their senses were already heightened having just sat in the hover while the big guns next to them were still firing. The two aircrew in the rear cabin, Alfie Tupper and John Sheldon, spotted the Skyhawks through the bubble windows: 'Enemy A-4s astern of us!'

Thornewill was well versed in fighter-evasion techniques. He knew that the key was to change direction and height to make it as hard as possible for the jet pilot to get a clear shot. Making the break just as the pilot was ready to fire was crucial. Thornewill's response was automatic. Almost instantly, he had made up his mind to break down and to the left into the hillside. Going down was the only option because the Sea King doesn't have the power to climb rapidly. The narrow ravines running uphill might provide some sort of refuge. Thornewill now waited for one of his crewmen to make the call to break.

With the first pair of Skyhawks about 800 yards from them, Tupper gave the call: 'Break!'

It all happened in seconds. Thornewill rolled the Sea King into a tight left-hand turn and pushed the nose down to descend, snatching full power at the same time. The suddenness of the encounter and change of direction by the Sea King gave little time for the Skyhawks. As the two jets shot over the top, the second pair appeared behind them almost simultaneously.

The Sea King was now dropping fast into a ravine. But the tightness of the turn had also caused the big helicopter to slow down. They were a sitting duck for the lead Skyhawk. The crew heard the rattle of cannon fire from behind them and to their left as they disappeared into one of the ravines. There was no time to think. A mild thud came from somewhere on the Sea King's rotors. They had been hit.

As the second pair of jets sped on past, Thornewill continued manoeuvring the Sea King violently uphill through the narrow valley just feet above the ground. The aircraft was handling well. But watching the hillside flash past perilously close to his cabin doorway Tupper was convinced that the tail rotor was about to hit. It was

340

equally unnerving for Dave Lord, having to watch as a front-seat pilot but without his hands on the controls.

After continuing the evasion uphill, Thornewill soon found a Sea King-sized gulley in which to hide and shut down. The crew got out to find out what had been hit; it wasn't obvious at first. A cannon shell had passed through the main spar of one of the rotor blades. Otherwise they were undamaged. Within hours, Victor Alpha was repaired with a new blade and back on task. It was another astonishing escape.

A beautiful day for war. I was flying just about the only helicopter back at San Carlos while this *junglie* Sea King was unloading 5 Brigade troops thirty-five miles away on the front line ready for the final assault. Later this morning, a flight of Argentine Skyhawks attacked our nearby gun positions, damaged a couple of *teeny weenies* with bombs, and put a bullet through a Sea King blade. It was the last air raid of the war.

As the Skyhawks sped off across East Falkland, the same way they had come, the fleeing Argentine pilots jettisoned their empty external fuel tanks. Whether deliberate or not, two of the jets appeared to lob theirs directly into the line of two Wessex helicopters beneath them. In one of the Wessex, Willie Harrower watched the drop tanks fall harmlessly nearby as the jets sped past him. In the other, Paul McIntosh had his second escape of the day. He could see the jets approaching fast from eight o'clock. There was no need for violent manoeuvre as the falling drop tanks were clearly going to miss by a matter of fifty yards. McIntosh and his aircrewman Jed Clamp kept a wary eye on the Skyhawks as they passed low overhead and on into the distance. He felt frustrated at being so defenceless: a pod of rockets would have been very handy for fighter evasion.

Nonchalantly recounting his calmness under pressure later that evening, another pilot told him: 'Mackers, you are such a steely bastard.' It was one of his proudest moments of the war.

My own encounter with the Skyhawks definitely disqualified me for the steely bastard award. Sitting on the deck of *Uganda*, after depositing further casualties from Ajax Bay, I was waiting for Al Doughty to finish talking to the deck crew. Facing south, I could see the Sussex Mountains off to my left gently sloping away down to the flat landscape of Goose Green and down into Lafonia. Directly ahead was dark blue sea and light blue sky.

I saw the two jets straight away as they skylined from behind the Sussex Mountains. My recognition was pretty good. But at about five miles away I couldn't tell for sure whether they were Harriers or Skyhawks. Nor was I completely sure whether the Geneva Convention would provide the same protection for my large green combat helicopter as it did for the large white hospital ship underneath me. I wasn't about to hang around and find out. 'Are we clear?' I asked Doughty.

'Yes boss,' he replied.

I called 'Lifting' as I pulled in power and cleared the deck with urgency. The two jets were now coasting out over Falkland Sound right in front of me. I hauled the Wessex round in a sharp turn to the left and came to a low hover over the sea directly behind the ship. If the jets happened to turn north, they would no longer be able to see me. I was using the hospital ship as a shield. There was nowhere else to go. I had rather mixed feelings about this game of hide and seek, feeling clever, stupid, brave, and cowardly all at the same time. Anything but steely.

I was sitting in the cockpit of my Wessex on the deck of the hospital ship SS *Uganda* out in Falkland Sound. I had just been handed a sausage sarnie and a cup of delicious fresh coffee when I saw the two Skyhawks crossing the coastline a couple of miles ahead of me. I quickly lifted off the deck and hovered behind the ship to hide from them, feeling both clever and stupid at the same time.

The Skyhawk attack on Mount Kent turned out to be the final Argentine mission of the war from the mainland. Grupo 5 had been the most impressive of the Argentine air units. They had accounted for the losses of *Ardent*, *Coventry* and *Sir Galahad* and inflicted serious damage to *Argonaut*, *Tristram* and the supply depot at Ajax Bay. Their final mission could have been spectacularly successful, destroying British headquarters and an artillery position. All they achieved this time was to put a couple of Army

Air Corps helicopters out of action for a few days and a Sea King for just a few hours.

It had been a harrowing day for Jerry Spence and Mark Brickell also, flying what seemed like a constant stream of wounded soldiers back to Ajax Bay. There was a brief pause in the day's activity as the crew shut down their aircraft and joined the Paras in burying their dead from the battle at Mount Longdon. A digger had prepared the ground. Body bag after body bag was lowered into the grave with as much dignity as could be mustered. The commanding officer of 3 Para said a few words and that was that. Back to business, boys. There would be time to mourn later.

Coming face to face with the wounded men who had been lifted out of battle also made a big impression on Rob Flexman as he took the opportunity to wander around the field hospital set up at Fitzroy. Moving from bed to bed, being introduced by the doctor, explaining each patient's injuries, and chatting with the soldiers, it was a moving experience.

So when he was asked to fly three seriously wounded men to Ajax Bay in the dark – not an appealing prospect – he had all the motivation he needed for the risky transit. Flying with Mike Crabtree with navigation lights switched off, it was hard to make out anything at all outside the aircraft. It was certainly impossible to estimate their height by eye. The temptation to stay low to the ground was huge. British air defences might easily assume an aircraft popping up on radar flying east to west was an Argentine Hercules flying re-supply missions in and out of Stanley. Indeed later that evening, an Argentine Canberra bomber escorted by Mirage jets, bombed British positions in the hills from high level. HMS *Exeter*'s formidable Sea Dart claimed its fourth victim of the war. The Canberra navigator was killed. The pilot ejected into the sea near Fitzroy and scrambled ashore.

For Flexman and Crabtree, the Sussex Mountains were still invisible somewhere off to the right in the pitch-blackness. If they flew low, they would almost certainly fly into the ground. There was no real choice but to fly at 1,500 feet, their height above sea level shown on the barometric altimeter. The radio altimeter, measuring their actual height above ground, told them they had chosen wisely. The radalt needle dipped dramatically to a few hundred feet as they crossed the unseen ridgeline and headed north into San Carlos.

Landing in the darkness was going to be a problem. Within the bay area, there was just enough contrast with the shoreline below them to allow a descent. They could only hope that the warships *Plymouth* and *Andromeda* would gamble on them being a British helicopter. As their height reduced, Flexman and Crabtree began to make out the outline of ships in the water and buildings dotted around the shore. They moved their eyes constantly to make use of their peripheral vision. Not wishing to illuminate the entire field hospital with their bright landing lights – unlike us who had no such inhibitions on the previous night, or the Chinook a few nights previously – they cautiously switched on the much less bright downward identification light for the final landing. It was enough. The wounded soldiers were offloaded to Ajax Bay, and Flipper Hughes and Chris Eke took them on to the SS *Uganda* the next morning in X-Ray Bravo.

With 5 Brigade troops now settled in and artillery support resupplied, the Scots Guards set off from Goat Ridge on the evening of Sunday 13 June. Earlier, ground-attack Harriers had bombed and destroyed what they thought was the Argentine headquarters on Mount Tumbledown.

The open slopes to the south of Mount Tumbledown contained Argentine defensive positions, some of which I had gazed at unknowingly the previous day. This was the target of the diversionary attack. The diversion group comprised a twelve-man assault team and support that included Scorpion and Scimitar light tanks. With only minutes to go before the main force set off from Goat Ridge, the assault team engaged the Argentine defences, fighting from position to position for two hours. Leaving two dead men behind, they eventually withdrew through a minefield under enemy mortar fire.

The Scots Guards were lucky to get to the action at all. They were very nearly wiped out in their landing craft by naval gunfire as they approached Fitzroy. Here they are about to get their chance as they prepare to attack Mount Tumbledown, supported by a *junglie* Sea King.

The diversion was a success. Advancing across the high ground, the Scots Guards captured the abandoned western end of Tumbledown without a shot being fired. Argentine flares announced the beginning of the battle proper. The first assault by the Guards was repulsed with losses on both sides. For the next three hours, there was stalemate with neither side able to gain the advantage. The slow attrition of wounded men hit the Argentines hardest. But it was another act of individual bravery that broke the deadlock. After salvoes of artillery fire, Major John Kiszely took the initiative and led a solo charge up the hill. His men followed and in the following hour skirmished their way to the top, fighting hand-to-hand. For this action Kiszely was awarded the Military Cross.

With the summit of Mount Tumbledown held by just four soldiers, the British were vulnerable to counterattack. A sustained assault through fierce but sporadic resistance completed the advance to the eastern end of Tumbledown. Eight Scots Guards and one Royal Engineer were killed and forty-three Guardsmen wounded. In early light the next morning, an Army Air Corps Scout helicopter piloted by Captain Sam Drennan flew back and forth across the hillside of Mount Tumbledown, taking out casualties under sniper and artillery fire. For his rescue of sixteen wounded soldiers under fire Drennan received the Distinguished Flying Cross.

A heavily laden SAS soldier watches as an Army Scout, fitted for missile firing, prepares for a casevac mission. The Scout crews were extraordinarily brave, coming in again and again under fire to pick up the wounded.

* * *

While the battle for Tumbledown was coming to an end, Gurkha soldiers made their way towards Mount William. As they edged their way around a minefield, underneath the northern cliff face of Tumbledown, they came under artillery fire that wounded eight of their men. They found themselves thwarted in their attempt to engage the enemy. Maybe it was their fearsome reputation, willingly exaggerated by the British; maybe it was simply the state of the battle. But by the time the Gurkhas had rounded the eastern end of Tumbledown and turned south for their attack on Mount William, the Argentine defenders had fled. Mount William was captured unopposed.

Overnight, two further battles had taken place to secure the hills to their north. The special forces, keen not to miss out, had been given approval to attack Cortley Hill, the ridgeline immediately opposite Stanley on the north side of the harbour. The attack began from the sea, with four rigid raiding craft crossing to Port William. Using the Argentine hospital ship *Almirante Irizar* to screen their approach turned out to be an expensive strategy. A soldier on board turned a searchlight on the raiders as they motored past. When the raiders beached, the soldiers came under heavy fire from the ridgeline, wounding three SBS and SAS soldiers. Under covering artillery fire that diverted assets from the main assaults, the British force withdrew onto their boats under heavy fire. It was an adventure that could easily have ended in disaster.

After their expensive victory at Goose Green, 2 Para made relatively light work of their series of assaults on Wireless Ridge, also from the north. In the face of withering fire from four accompanying Scorpion and Scimitar light tanks, the Argentines fled from their defensive positions. However, resistance was fierce on the eastern edge of the ridge, delaying completion of the battle until dawn on 14 June. A brief and brave counterattack was repulsed. An Army Scout helicopter fired four SS11 anti-tank missiles into a gun position at Moody Brook. The battle left three British and twenty-five Argentines dead.

For most of us, Port Stanley, the Falklands capital, had acquired almost mythical status. Nobody quite knew what it looked like. But we were all extremely keen for our first aerial view of the place. It was after all the goal, our ultimate destination. A few had already had a brief look from the air. Pete Manley and Arthur Balls had fired their missiles at distant lights four days earlier. The visibility may have been limited but their view was at least officially sanctioned. Two days after that, Jack Lomas, Oily Knight and Smudge Smyth had a rather better view, albeit an unofficial one.

Yankee Bravo was bringing Gurkhas up to their holding position just behind Goat Ridge. It was early evening on 12 June, at about the same time Jerry Spence and I were shifting bergens for 42 and 45 Commando. The hills in front of them, Two Sisters and Harriet, were in British hands. The Gurkhas were digging in as shells were coming over the ridge. After a couple of trips to bring in more troops, Knight turned to Lomas and said: 'We're here now, Jack, shall we go and have a look at Stanley?' Lomas was quick to agree to the idea.

Occasional shells were exploding, but not near enough to threaten them. After the last of the troops had disembarked, Lomas lifted Yankee Bravo away from the drop-off point and hover-taxied up the hill onto the ridgeline. They passed a huddle of soldiers: probably a headquarters group having a briefing. They seemed none too impressed to see a Wessex tip-toeing noisily past them.

Yankee Bravo edged forward over a lip of rock near

the summit of the ridge. Suddenly a few miles out in the distance, there it was, Port Stanley. It wasn't as if they were expecting skyscrapers, but the ramshackle collection of red and green corrugated-iron roofs stretching out towards the airport was a bit of an anti-climax.

There was an empty pause. 'God that's disappointing,' said Lomas.

The moment was shattered by the blast of a shell landing in front of them. 'We'd better get the hell out of here.'

My first view of Port Stanley on the day after the surrender. We weren't exactly expecting skyscrapers but, having built up the capital of the Falklands in our minds, the reality was still pretty disappointing.

Dawn on Monday 14 June, Wessex Yankee Charlie was refuelling at Fitzroy. In the right seat sat Mike Booth; in the left was Paul McIntosh, flying as co-pilot. A runner signalled to approach the Wessex under the rotor disc and handed a briefing note up to Booth in the cockpit. His face went white as he read it. A company of Welsh Guardsmen and Royal Marines were trapped in a minefield. Casualties had already been reported. They needed to be moved forward to a new position urgently.

The Welsh Guards again, thought Booth. He could only imagine the hell they had been through. First *Sir Galahad*. Now this.

He passed the note across to his co-pilot. 'Check the grid ref, Mac. We're going to need help for this.' He then squeezed the radio transmit button on the cyclic stick. 'All callsigns, this is Yankee Charlie, report availability for urgent task.'

With the disaster at nearby Port Pleasant still very much on aircrew minds, it didn't take much to generate an immediate response to the call for help. Within a couple of minutes, Booth had acquired an impromptu flight of six or seven aircraft, mostly Wessex and at least one Sea King. Normally, a mission briefing would take place on the ground, either face to face or by a MAOT charging from aircraft to aircraft and plugging into the intercom. For obvious reasons, tactical information such as grid references couldn't be passed over the radio. But because of the need to brief en route whilst airborne, the radio was the only way to conduct a brief. It was a rare occasion where the *junglie* crews had to remember how to use the day's crypto code to encode and decode the pick-up and drop-off points.

The pick-up location was easy to see. Clusters of men huddled next to one another on the frozen bog. An Army Scout helicopter was already on site, presumably to collect two of the wounded Guardsmen. As Booth led the formation of Wessex and Sea King into a line-astern approach, he told his crewman to step away from the door: 'If they're anti-personnel mines, they shouldn't do much more than take the tyres off and damage the oleos.' He landed the big Wessex gingerly, just feet away from the first huddle of very frightened soldiers.

* * *

Meanwhile, on the north side of Tumbledown, several Wessex were moving mortar troops forward in support of the Gurkha advance through Mount William. Moving a mortar troop forward usually took three loads. The first lift was the heavy mortar baseplate and two or three of the crew. The second lift was the rest of the crew and equipment. The final lift was an underslung load of ammunition.

Puffs of smoke from Argentine artillery shells dotted the landscape as the Wessex moved the mortar crews forward. But now that British troops held the last major high ground around Stanley, Argentine troops were in full retreat. The Gurkhas were increasingly frustrated. No sooner had the crew set up their position ready to fire than they were told to move forward again as the target was now out of range.

Jack Lomas had just dropped his second load when the troop leader ran in saying: 'They're running too fast. Can you take me another mile further.'

This was now uncharted territory, beyond the front line of even an hour earlier. Again on the second load, the troop leader said: 'I'm still out of range. Take me forward again. This time, don't bother about getting the rest of the boys, just bring my ammunition.'

Lomas went all the way back to the original position for the underslung load of ammunition. The firing position was now within range of the outskirts of Stanley.

As some of the Welsh Guards piled gratefully into the back of Yankee Charlie from the minefield, McIntosh looked to where he was supposed to take them. He pointed at the map. 'This grid reference doesn't look right,' he said to Booth. It was much too close to the summit of Sapper Hill. They would be well within firing range of Argentine troops dug in on the summit.

'Best we land a few clicks short then, on the track here, just to make sure.'

The likelihood was that 5 Brigade command had given them a grid reference for the start line for the troops. The start line was the worst possible place to insert a group of large commando helicopters, in range of the enemy and in full view. It wasn't the first time that such an oversight had been made, as I'd learnt myself two days earlier.

Booth gave enough time for the other helicopters to load before calling 'Lifting, follow me'. The drop-off point was just a few miles to the east along the track. It was an easy transit at low level, flying just a few feet above the terrain. The loose formation of aircraft passed to the south of Mount William. It would have been an impressive sight to the Gurkhas above them, who had taken the hill unopposed. Just after a small quarry, Booth raised the nose of the Wessex slightly to bleed off speed and bring the helicopter smoothly down onto the track. The new grid reference was well short of Sapper Hill.

The crews of all the helicopters had noticed that this was not the expected drop-off point. But since the boss was in charge, most followed as they thought he must know what he was doing. In any case, the new landing point was safe from enemy view. It wouldn't take much to overshoot and end up crossing enemy lines. Although the other Wessex followed Yankee Charlie in to land on the track, an 825 Sea King decided that the original grid reference was correct and raced on ahead.

In the back of the Sea King were Royal Marines of 9 Troop 40 Commando. As the big aircraft flared just short of the summit, Argentine troops opened fire with machine guns and mortars. The aircraft shook from damage to the port side as the wheels hit the ground. The noise from the aircraft and fire was deafening as the troops spilled out, not entirely clear where they were but well aware that they were in contact with the enemy. In seconds, the Sea King lifted away and cleared to the south.

The ensuing firefight lasted just ten minutes before it became clear to the Marines that the Argentine defences had withdrawn. It was to be the final action of the Falklands war. Even if completely accidental, 825 Squadron's 'ridge too far' was also the only opposed heliborne assault of the war. By good fortune, the action probably accelerated the decision by the Argentine command to surrender. If the British were willing to push on through like this right on the edge of Stanley, they thought, they weren't likely to stop once they entered the capital.

After my day on casevac duty at San Carlos, I was back up on the front line again flying out of FOB Teal, this time in X-Ray Delta with Norman Lees and Jock McKie. We were carrying a load of ammunition up towards 3 Brigade Headquarters at Estancia House when we heard the news: 'All stations. White flags are flying over Stanley. Do not fire unless fired upon.'

Lees and I looked at each other. It was over.

I knew I should have felt a surge of relief, but that just wasn't my immediate reaction. After setting off late from the UK, enduring the excruciatingly slow plod 8,000 miles through the North and South Atlantic on *Engadine*, and arriving late in the war, I felt I'd just got started. I hadn't had enough. My first reaction was disappointment, even if I knew that it was fabulous news for everyone else.

For the vast majority who had definitely had quite enough, there was an overwhelming sense of both victory and relief. Paras and Marines scrambled for the honour of reaching Stanley first. Streaming in from Moody Brook, the Paras claimed the glory.

Back in the command tent at San Carlos, Lieutenant Commander Bill Pollock was asked to supply a helicopter to fly Major General Jeremy Moore into Stanley. With fading light and snowstorms, it could have been done in a *jungle* Sea King with night goggles. But it made so much more sense to offer the job to one of the radar-fitted Sea Kings. Pollock was very aware that the squadron had already lost two aircrew. All of the rest of his guys were still alive. He wanted to keep it that way. 'But you'll miss the credit,' commented a staff officer.

'Of killing the General and my crew? No thanks,' replied Pollock.

The job fell to an anti-submarine Sea King of 820 Squadron which had been detached to San Carlos from the carrier HMS *Invincible*. Flown by Lieutenant Commander Keith Dudley, the Sea King landed safely in Port Stanley. The formal surrender itself took place well after dark between Moore and the Argentine General Mario Menéndez.

Even with victory in the bag, huge practical hurdles remained. There were still over 10,000 Argentine soldiers to repatriate. Meanwhile, thousands of British soldiers lay in the hills surrounding Port Stanley, exposed to freezing snow showers.

For the *jungle* helicopter crews, Monday 14 and Tuesday 15 June saw the highest number of flying hours during the entire deployment. On these two days, my own contribution was over sixteen hours in the cockpit. On the last day of the war, my squadron's Wessex crews alone flew fourteen sorties averaging six hours and forty minutes each.

Up in the hills it was a race to reunite soldiers with their equipment or get them off the exposed hillsides altogether. Rob Flexman had been involved with the final push with the Welsh Guards. Although, like me, he hadn't wanted to miss out on the action, he was delighted by the news of the Argentine surrender. 'We've done it. It's over,' he told his crewman.

But his delight turned to concern as the expectations of the soldiers on the ground began to exceed the capabilities of the aircrew. Troops who had spent long weeks out in the field were understandably keen to get extracted now that the war was over. Royal Marines were very familiar with helicopter operations and knew what could and could not be achieved. Army units were less familiar. From the ground, it all looked pretty easy. Fly in. Load up. Fly out. The evening gloom made it extremely taxing.

Having already taken several loads of troops off the hills, Flexman returned to collect what would necessarily be his final load of the day. Daylight was fading and the situation was becoming dangerous with half a dozen helicopters groping around in the darkness. As the troops were clambering into the cabin, an Army major climbed up the side of the aircraft. He leaned into the cockpit, shouting to make himself heard above the noise of the hot exhaust below and whirling gearbox above: 'I need thirty more men out of here.'

'I'll take what I can, but this will have to be my last trip,' Flexman shouted back at him.

It was not what the frustrated and exhausted major wanted to hear. 'I demand that you get us all out of here,' he replied testily.

'I'll do what I can.'

It was simply not safe to come back for another load. Most of the thirty men would have to spend another night out in the open. As Flexman lifted off into the half-light, over the radio came the unmistakeable voice of Jack Lomas. 'This isn't in the script.'

A couple of miles to their west, his namesake Aircrewman Jan Lomas was on the ground hauling what seemed like an endless pile of bergens up into the cabin of Yankee Bravo. Above him in the cockpit, Hector Heathcote could hear the breathlessness in his voice through the distortion of the throat mike: 'Bloody hell, there are dozens of these things. I'm sweating like a pig.' They were both well aware of the importance of their task, of reuniting kit, equipment and men. Soldiers who had survived the war might easily not survive another freezing night out in the hills. Getting their sleeping bags to them was vital.

The Wessex had a spare lift capacity of some 3,000 pounds. The urgency of the task meant that Lomas crammed in far more than he should. He had counted seventy-eight bergens into the cabin weighing around 5,000 pounds. The Wessex was now horribly overweight. Even if they could achieve enough power to get off the ground, the gearbox might quite simply crack up under the excess load. 'Oh well,' thought Heathcote, 'let's suck it and see.'

Amazingly, with full power applied, the Wessex rose gingerly upwards and wallowed uncomfortably off the edge of the mountainside, helped by the cold air and light breeze. The helicopter felt unstable and vulnerable. Heathcote hung onto the cyclic stick with an unnecessarily strong grip, as if letting go would cause the aircraft to topple over. He could just about see where he needed to go, having already completed several runs to the drop-off point in daylight. But it was now almost pitch black. He still had to get the aircraft down safely in one piece. With such an overweight aircraft, there was not enough power for an overshoot if they got it wrong. Once the aircraft was in the descent and slowing down, that was it. They would have one shot.

The landing, as it turned out, was fine. But Heathcote and Lomas both knew they had seriously overstepped their own and their aircraft's capabilities. 'That was frightening,' said Heathcote.

'Too right,' echoed Lomas. 'Best we go home. I've had enough now, thank you very much.'

For the first time since leaving Yeovilton ten weeks earlier, the decision about whether to use navigation lights was an easy one. With all their lights flashing, Yankee Bravo headed back to find FOB Fitzroy. 'Mountain flying in an overweight Wessex,' a very relieved Heathcote said as they shut down. 'That was ridiculously, stupidly dangerous.'

It was still dark on Tuesday 15 June, the first morning after the surrender, when Ric Fox flashed up X-Ray Yankee at FOB Teal. His brief was to get himself back to Port San Carlos as soon as possible and report to the ops tent. Half an hour later he was at his second briefing of the morning. He was to go with Dave Greet, a handful of Royal Marines and medics, and take the Argentine surrender at Pebble Island.

Fox and Greet grinned nervously at one another, hiding their apprehension. It was an extraordinary responsibility for a young sub-lieutenant. The war was over. But would the Argentine troops out on West Falkland know?

The thirty-mile transit across Falkland Sound towards Pebble Island seemed painfully slow because of a stiff breeze blowing in from the west. The settlement houses were clearly visible from a long way off. A few miles short of the houses two Argentine soldiers stood by a parked Mercedes jeep.

'Let's get those guys first,' said Greet. 'We're quite a target.'

As Fox began his approach towards them, the two soldiers dropped to their knees behind the Mercedes.

'Shit they don't know about the surrender,' warned Fox.

It felt like a Mexican stand-off. Fox brought the big helicopter into a hover fifty yards away, with the nose skewed off to the left so that Greet could train his cabin machine gun on to the soldiers. The Argentines remained hidden, crouching down behind the vehicle. After a couple of very tense minutes, one of them stood up with his hands in the air. 'Phew,' said a relieved Fox, side-slipping the Wessex closer in to pick up the Argentines.

The Marines escorted the two soldiers on board. Soon afterwards, Greet casually told Fox what they had been doing: 'We'd better not hang around here. They were picking up mines.'

Fox needed no further encouragement to get airborne with the two prisoners. Quickly covering the short distance at low level, he put the aircraft down on the ground within the settlement itself. The grassy Pebble Island airstrip, scene of the SAS raid just a month earlier, lay beyond them beneath a skyline of rocky hills. Damaged Argentine aircraft, mostly Mentors and Pucaras, were dotted around the strip with their cockpits open, exposed to the recent snow flurries.

'Shit,' said Fox again as he shut the aircraft down. From the cockpit of X-Ray Bravo, his attention was drawn back from the aircraft to a huge number of soldiers. It was quite a sight: the eight Royal Marines and medics were hugely outnumbered as they walked forward to take the surrender of over a hundred Argentines.

The Argentines had imprisoned the islanders since occupying Pebble Island in April. Now their roles were reversed. East and West Falkland were back in British hands.

Epilogue

Over the next few days, the Sea King crews returned home to the UK as squadrons on aircraft carriers and the larger ships. My Wessex colleagues of 845 Squadron returned in dribs and drabs, with some flights sailing back on supply ships and others flying back via Ascension Island in a C-130 Hercules.

The fragmented nature of the Wessex squadrons meant that few received an organised welcome. Ric Fox arrived back exhausted at Yeovilton wearing a mix of combats and Argentine clothing, only to receive a reprimand from the duty officer for being in the wrong rig. He told the duty officer what to do with his reprimand.

Hector Heathcote found himself wandering around Tesco in Yeovil in a daze. Just hours earlier he had been in a war zone. A few short weeks later, he was posted back down to Ascension Island for three months to relieve his commanding officer. It seemed a huge injustice to be sent away so soon.

The rest of us – the 847 Squadron Wessex crews – having arrived late in the war, became garrison squadron. We moved our base from Port San Carlos to Navy Point, just across the harbour from Port Stanley. The flying was sensational. Over the next three months I flew 220 hours, rarely venturing more than thirty feet above the ground.

This is my colleague Jerry Spence refuelling his Wessex on the runway at Stanley airport soon after the war ended. Mount Kent and the other infamous final hills are out in the distance to the west. The runway looks in pretty good condition considering the overblown claims of the Vulcan missions.

Most of the work was the big clean up from the war: moving people and equipment, stores and ammunition. We flew bomb squad and mine clearers out into the surrounding hills to deal with unexploded ordnance, and burial parties to deal with unburied bodies. Much of it was pretty gruesome. We also provided search-and-rescue cover for all of the British forces on the islands.

Having a dozen or so helicopters gave us extraordinary bartering power. My lovely late mentor Ray Colborne quickly became known as the squadron grocer. Like a character out of the novel *Catch-22*, he used his contacts on the RFA supply ships to acquire all manner of stores.

He cornered the entire Falklands market in eggs. Our squadron maintenance area was piled high with boxes and boxes of them. Somebody calculated that we had 96,000 eggs. We also acquired 100,000 Duracell batteries, this time through administrative error. The engineers had ordered 100 batteries for our torches. I remember lifting the 3,000-pound load marked for our squadron from a nearby supply ship and wondering what on earth it was.

We used our good fortune to be especially sympathetic to the Rapier air defence crews, still dug in on the hilltops, and to the generous islanders with whom we occasionally stayed overnight. We ate well and slept well on these trips. There was even the occasional bath. We did as much for them as we could in return. I remember one of our Wessex flying out to a remote settlement, known locally as 'camp', with a cow dangling underneath in a net. It was a classic British hearts and minds campaign.

I visited the Falklands capital just once. Hector gave me a lift there in his Wessex three days after the Argentine surrender. I wandered around Port Stanley as a naval sub-lieutenant in my wellies, green combats and blue beret, armed with a 9mm Browning pistol, but not much of a clue otherwise. The place was a mess. There were Argentine gun emplacements, wrecked helicopters and battered vehicles lying open to the elements, as well as all sorts of debris – endless rounds of ammunition, helmets, clothing, ration packs and boxes – scattered everywhere.

I spent a while looking around an abandoned Puma helicopter parked on Port Stanley seafront. I should have been wary of booby-traps but I didn't think. I walked brazenly into Government House, amongst the Paras and Royal Marines who were milling around. I was amused to bump into one of our own MAOT Marines unashamedly heating up a mess tin of food on the floor of one of the colonial rooms. In the backstreets further into the capital, I passed hundreds of Argentine prisoners and giant piles of discarded rifles and other weaponry.

With the war over, I was able to enjoy the remote beauty of the Falkland Islands. I flew a group of us out to look at a colony of over a thousand king penguins at Volunteer Point. We were able to walk right up to them and their grey fluffy offspring. The noise and smell was overwhelming: it was an extraordinary experience. In between ferrying people and stores, I also messed around, nearly overdoing it one day at Goose Green chasing a rabbit in my Wessex. Startled by the prospect of a vast aerial aggressor, the rabbit fled across the grassy strip until suddenly it stopped and backtracked underneath the helicopter. I flared rather too sharply, suddenly realising that I was now pointing up towards the sky at zero speed and was about to slide backwards into the ground. It wouldn't have looked good on the accident form. Luckily I got away with it.

Failing to heed my near miss, I then hovered over the top of a nearby damaged Argentine Pucara. Looking down from the open cockpit window, I eased my right wheel neatly onto the tail of the enemy aircraft. A little downward pressure and I was pushing the Pucara's tail down, rotating the nose nicely upwards. I then realised I was stuck. Worrying how to get out of the situation, I decided to move the Wessex sideways as quickly I could. The Pucara tail sprang back up, releasing the Wessex but missing the explosive flotation canister on my wheel by a whisker.

So what did happen to all those Pucaras? Altogether twenty-four made it to the Falklands. The Sea Harriers destroyed three in their first attack on Goose Green; the SAS blew up six in their raid on Pebble Island; three more were shot down, one by Sea Harrier and two by ground fire; and another crashed into the mountains. Of the remaining eleven only three were flyable by the end of the war. Bombing runs by Sea Harriers and ground-attack Harriers did some of the damage. The damp weather also played its part making it hard to keep the aircraft electrics working.

After the battle of Goose Green, the Pucaras flew three more sorties. All of them happened in the last few days while I was there. Thank God I never saw them, nor did any of my colleagues. Seeing a formation of three Pucaras would have been the most frightening experience imaginable for a helicopter pilot. I remain forever grateful to our Sea Harrier pilots who proved an even more frightening threat to the Pucara pilots, as well as being a whole lot more effective. The Sea Harriers were spectacularly successful in air-to-air combat, shooting down eighteen Mirage and Skyhawks and three other aircraft, whilst not being beaten once. Why did we ever get rid of them?

Interestingly, one of the Pucaras was shipped back from the Falklands to the test pilot school at Boscombe Down. The following summer, Simon Thornewill managed to fly the Pucara twice, discovering a little secret that dispelled some – but only some – of its mystique. At slow speed (below ninety knots) the Pucara handling was not half as manoeuvrable as we'd feared. It would have been nice to have known this during the war.

I have three emotional memories of life at Navy Point. The first was the Falklands wind. It blew through my ears and knocked me off balance so much that I felt physically sick. The second was the showers on board the RFA *Sir Tristram*. After the attack at Port Pleasant a few weeks earlier, the half-burnt, half-intact ship was towed around to Navy Point. I had mixed feelings every time I walked on board. I would come out clean on the outside but with the terrible smell of burning seared inside my head. The smell still lingers with me today, decades later.

After the war, we moved our base from Port San Carlos to Navy Point, opposite Port Stanley. I spent three months there. The bombed-out ship *Sir Tristram* had been towed around from Port Pleasant. Wandering onboard for a shower posed a real dilemma. The showers were brilliant but the smell of burning was sickening.

The third and worst memory concerned an appalling accident at Port Stanley airport a month after the war. A group of Welsh Guards were clearing snow from the airfield when a taxiing Harrier inadvertently released two Sidewinder air-to-air missiles. Sidewinder has only a small explosive charge in its head; it's the expanding wire, designed to cut through the controls of the target aircraft, that does the damage. The missile flew straight at the Guardsmen, causing terrible injuries to eleven. Within minutes my colleagues were casevacing the dreadfully wounded soldiers to field hospitals and hospital ships, our aircrewmen trying to staunch the flow of blood en route.

The following day I was sitting in my cockpit on the deck of SS *Uganda*. A stretcher was brought out with one of the casualties, a healthy-looking Welsh Guardsman, wrapped under a silver survival blanket. I was about to take him to the airport to be flown home in a Hercules. The downdraft from my Wessex lifted his blanket to reveal that both his legs had been amputated. The war had finished and I had relaxed my guard. I simply wasn't ready for the shock. I retched.

On my final day in the Falklands, I flew gratefully out to the troopship MV *Norland*, which had brought my 845 Squadron colleagues to relieve us. As I sat in the hover alongside the ship in San Carlos Water, my air-speed indicator read fifty-five knots of wind. I was very pleased indeed to be going home. Three months after the war ended, I flew the 8,000 miles back to UK via Hercules to Ascension and VC-10 to Brize Norton and a wonderful but small family reception.

After a few weeks leave, most of my colleagues rejoined 845 Squadron, having discovered that 847 Squadron had been disbanded. We were promptly despatched to Northern Norway for Arctic training. It would be my third winter in a row. At least Hector had returned to the warmth of Ascension. But if you can't take a joke, went the well-known military refrain, you shouldn't have joined.

June 2007. A bunch of us arranged to meet up in a Whitehall pub the night before the twenty-fifth anniversary parade down the Mall. I was looking forward to it but also felt apprehensive. I had been out of the *junglie* loop since completing my first tour on 845 and 847 Squadrons at the end of 1983. I'd spent my second tour as flight commander of the frigate HMS *Apollo* flying an 829 Squadron Wasp. It was a responsible job for a young pilot. But it put me totally out of contact with the rest of the Fleet Air Arm.

After flying a Wessex, my second job was flying this Wasp helicopter from the frigate *HMS Apollo*. The Wasp is the naval version of the Army Scout. During the Falklands War, three Wasps like this one fired several AS12 missiles in a vain effort to sink the Argentine submarine *Santa Fe* in South Georgia. Unfortunately the fin of a submarine is hollow.

After these two tours, I left the Royal Navy altogether to pursue a career in business in the Far East. Now I was back in the UK running a charity. I'd only kept in touch with a few former *junglies* who told me about the parade and the meet. I felt a little unsure of my welcome. As I walked in, I could see someone at the far side of the pub wearing a baseball cap. 'Sparky?'

'Harry!'

It was bloody brilliant to see an old friend. He'd been even more apprehensive than I was about meeting up again. Having been court-martialled and kicked out of the Navy after his crash in Norway, he thought he might be shunned. No chance.

In walked some of the other guys. I wasn't sure if anyone recognised him. 'Do you know who this is, Hector?' He shook his head. 'It's Sparky.' Tears welled up for all of us. The three of us had been in the same house at Dartmouth together. It was a great moment. Then the beer flowed and we were off, sharing an extraordinary array of war stories.

I suddenly realised that between us we'd been involved with almost every major incident of the war, barring the *Belgrano* sinking. Pete Manley told us about his AS12 strike on the police station with Arthur Balls. Whatever happened to Arthur, we asked? Another lovely man. No one knew. I was astonished to hear Hector's amazing story about his Mirage strafing and *Ardent* rescue on D-Day. I had no idea. Jack Lomas reminisced about the FOB at San Carlos and Oily Knight's brush with two Tigercat missiles and a bullet through the windscreen. So that was what happened to Yankee Tango, I thought. We laughed until it hurt when we heard that Oily had got his come-uppance just before going home. He lost the very last game of 'spoof' at Port San Carlos and was made to eat a giant ration pack tin of greasy cold steak-and-kidney pudding, charmingly known to all as 'baby's heads'.

I told my own story about coming under fire on Mount Longdon with Andy Pulford. I learnt that he was now Air Vice-Marshal Pulford RAF – Wow! Everyone agreed with Jerry Spence when he admitted he had found flying in the hills at night far worse than being shot at. And Mike Tidd talked about his amazing crash and rescue on Fortuna Glacier.

The war seems to have affected us all in different ways. Most of us are fine about it. I think either the long journey home by sea or the long stint as garrison in the Falklands gave us time to process what we had seen and done. Several found it harder than they expected being interviewed for this book.

A few colleagues still feel aggrieved about management. Even if Jack Lomas did a great job as senior flight commander, there was no Wessex squadron commanding officer or senior pilot on the ground in the Falklands until a week from the end, when *Engadine* turned up. Even if we did a huge amount of useful work, Wessex tasking was impromptu to non-existent at times. We often arrived for an assigned task only to discover some other cab was already on it. On occasion, valuable crews and aircraft sat unused and frustrated in San Carlos Water. Some of the early operating practices, such as routinely exceeding power limits, were questionable. Had the burnt-out remains of a Wessex and its crew been found some distance from its rotors and gearbox, these practices would not have seemed so wise.

Amongst the *jungle* Wessex crews, Jack Lomas and Mike Booth were each awarded the Distinguished Service Cross for their leadership of 845 and 847 Squadrons respectively, to a large extent on our behalf. Apart from

Pete Manley and Arthur Balls, who especially deserved their Mentions in Despatches – an oak leaf to go on top of their Falklands campaign medal and rosette – no other Wessex crews or maintainers received bravery awards.

The *Sir Galahad* incident still sparks discussion. Flipper Hughes and Bill Tuttey missed out where other helicopter crews who did near-enough identical work were recognised for their courage. I and most other Wessex colleagues are pretty sanguine about this and unreservedly congratulate the 825 and 846 Squadron Sea King aircrews, who did receive awards. The prevailing view at the time was that we were just doing our job. Frankly the troops on the ground were vastly more heroic.

I wear my own Falklands campaign medal and rosette with great pride. My award ceremony was unexpectedly informal. It was a shout down the corridor from the 845 Squadron staff office at Yeovilton. 'Oi, Benson! Come and get your gong. It's in your pigeon hole.' I awarded my medal to myself.

After satisfying the immediate interest in the war when I returned home, I found I didn't want to talk about it to anyone again for many years. I buried the whole subject away until the twentieth anniversary, when I suddenly felt compelled to revisit it all. I watched TV documentaries and read books. I cried a few times, all in private. What was that all about? I really don't know. Maybe it was what I'd done: the strange paradox of the exhilaration of flying in a war as a young man, doing a job I was really good at, and the shocking fact of facilitating violence between my fellow men. Maybe it was what I'd seen, the explosions and bodies and wounds. Loud bangs still scare the living daylights out of me. Others experienced far worse. I rang up a former colleague to talk it all through because he would understand. He didn't at first. He told me years later he felt bemused about the whole thing. Five years later, he rang me in a flood of tears himself, desperately needing to talk. It had finally hit him.

After almost all of the forty-five interviews I did for this book, I heard similar views expressed. Telling the story felt cathartic. For many it was the first time they had let it all out. As I arrived at one colleague's house, his wife told me she would leave us alone; after all she'd heard all his war stories before. After three hours of being interviewed, he told me this was the first time he'd ever told anyone the whole story. Some of the individual stories have never been told to anyone at all. I felt privileged to hear them for the first time.

My job today is far removed from flying a Royal Navy *junglie* helicopter. I teach couples and new parents how to stay together. I've run hundreds of relationship courses. I get to read a great many research papers. One of the most striking findings from research into military families is that it's not the long periods of separation that make couples more likely to split up. It's the experience of combat. If you've been in battle, you're far more likely to split up than other comparable families. I can well understand why.

It makes me wonder how the troops on the ground have coped. They experienced battle at close quarters. Our aircrewmen also came face to face with appalling wounds and human suffering. But we pilots just acted as glorified taxi-drivers. I wonder what kind of mental health time-bombs we have in store from our vastly more shocking forays into Iraq and Afghanistan. They used to be called honourable wounds.

Nobody talks. That's why I wanted to tell our story.

List of Illustrations

P 294 Port Stanley raid © Jerry Spence

P 313 Wessex on Two Sisters © Imperial War Museum (FKD 117)

P 319 Gazelle and Wessex, Crown Copyright © 1982 / Soldier Magazine / Paul Haley

P 327 Wessex, Crown Copyright © 1982 / Soldier Magazine / Paul Haley

P 335 Ajax Bay © John Ryall

P 339 Wessex coming in to land © Imperial War Museum (FKD 362)

P341 Sea King unloading troops, Crown Copyright © 1982 / Soldier Magazine / Paul Haley

P 343 SS *Uganda* © Harry Benson

P 346 Scots Guards, Crown Copyright © 1982 / Soldier Magazine / Paul Haley

P 347 SAS soldier and Scout crew, Crown Copyright © 1982 / Soldier Magazine / Paul Haley

P 350 Port Stanley © Harry Benson

P 362 Wessex refuelling © Jerry Spence

P 366 *Sir Tristram* © Harry Benson

P 368 Wasp © Harry Benson

Plate Section 1

On my way to the Falklands © Harry Benson
RFA *Engadine* © Harry Benson
Night flyers © Simon Thornewill
HMS *Sheffield* © John Ryall
San Carlos water © Simon Thornewill
D-Day landings © Rick Jolly
Sea Kings on SS *Canberra* © Simon Thornewill
Sea King © Simon Thornewill
Sea King refuelling © Harry Benson

Harry Benson

HMS *Antelope* © Press Association Images
HMS *Coventry* © John Ryall

Plate Section 2

847 Squadron rescue © Press Association Images
Sea King and RFA *Sir Galahad* © Press Association Images
RFA *Sir Galahad* © Tim Stanning
HMS *Plymouth* © Rick Jolly
Forward Operating Base at San Carlos © John Ryall
End of the war © Harry Benson
Pucara © Harry Benson
Formation fly past © Harry Benson
Arriving home © Jamie Guise
Lieutenant Benson RN © Harry Benson

Acknowledgements

Writing this book has been a real labour of love. I started interviewing former colleagues in the summer of 2009. I am indebted to all who put up with my digging into ancient memories that many may have preferred to be left alone. Most said they would remember little. All remembered a lot. I am grateful for their cooperation and hope they will be proud of the end product. It's our story.

Thank you so much to my *junglie* and other aircrew friends and colleagues for generously allowing me to interview you and revisit 1982 together: Splash Ashdown, Arthur Balls, David Baston, Andy Berryman, Mike Booth, Mark Brickell, Chris Clayton, Stewart Cooper, Al Doughty, Mark Evans, Rob Flexman, Nick Foster, Ric Fox, Ian Georgeson, Sparky Harden, Willie Harrower, Paul Heathcote, Tim Hughes, Trevor Jackson, Dave Knight, Steve Larsen, Jack Lomas, Jan Lomas, Pete Manley, Paul McIntosh, Ralph Miles, Richard Morton, Nigel North, Dave Ockleton, Bill Pollock, Mark Salter, Reg Sharland, Pete Skinner, Jerry Spence, Ian Stanley, Tim Stanning, Simon Thornewill, Mike Tidd, Bill Tuttey, Ian Tyrrell, Peter Vowles, Roger Warden. Also a huge thank you to some key characters who gave me their valuable insights: Ed

Featherstone, Rick Jolly, Julian Thompson. Thank you too to Georgina Reed for transcribing many hours of recordings.

I spent ages trying to work out how to take a load of interviews and make a story out of it. I am very grateful to Rowland White, author of *Vulcan*, who allowed me to grill him for an afternoon on the technical side of writing. I also had to work out how to organise telling my own first-person story alongside the third-person stories of my colleagues. What I hope I have produced is a book with the personal feel of what it was like to be a young Royal Navy *junglie* pilot at war.

Without a war diary to work with, and with very fallible memories of events nearly thirty years ago, I've had to assemble a jigsaw puzzle of individual stories and reconcile them with the available records. Oddly, the least useful have been the official squadron records, only some of which were available, but which provided only the barest outline of events. Perhaps this was because they were written by squadron junior officers like me. I am grateful to Anna Clark at the Fleet Air Arm Museum, Yeovilton, for providing me with a great starting point. More accurate and interesting were the few official reports of proceedings submitted by commanding officers. These gave a good flavour and some fascinating details. Thank you especially to Mike Booth for lending me his report of Wessex squadron activities and to Bill Pollock for his report of the incredible Sea King night-flying missions. And to those who dusted off their old action photos for the book, especially Arthur Balls, Mark Brickell, Stewart Cooper, Rick Jolly, Pete Manley, Jerry Spence, Tim Stanning and Simon Thornewill.

Pilots' log books were generally a very accurate source for dating particular sorties. Yet even these had inconsistencies. Two pilots flew their first sortie together in the Falklands but recorded it on different days. Another pilot managed to record the wrong airframe number for much of the war. By far the best written record is the extraordinary book *The Falklands Air War* by Rodney Burden et al (1986). It is dripping with details of the squadrons and individual aircraft on both sides. Without this resource I would have found it much harder to put together a timeline of events. By comparing this secondary source, official records and log books, I have been able to turn forty-five interviews and literally hundreds of vignettes into the story of the helicopter war in the Falklands.

I've also drawn from the following excellent works: Max Hastings and Simon Jenkins's still fresh and gripping *Battle for the Falklands;* Richard Hutchings's highly recommended personal account of the 846 Squadron night-flyers *Special Forces Pilot*; Rick Jolly's story of the *Red and Green Life Machine*; Nick van der Bijl's insightful view of the land campaign, *Victory in the Falklands*; Max Arthur's collection of heroic deeds, *Above All Courage*; and Roger Perkins's detailed account of *Operation Paraquat: The Battle for South Georgia.*

There are many more terrific *junglie* stories in John Beattie's wonderful collection *The View from a Junglie Cockpit*, published by and available from the Fleet Air Arm Museum. All of the interviews, records, spreadsheets, timelines, aircraft and combat details used for this book are now preserved in the Fleet Air Arm Museum's archives. If you visit the Museum – and you should – you will see half of the Wessex that I flew in the war (painted Zulu Mike on the side, it was coded X-Ray Lima in the Falklands). Pete Manley, Ric Fox and Dave Greet's Wessex, Yankee Sierra, is still intact and gets wheeled out on display at the Museum from time to time. It was the second Wessex to arrive in the Falklands.

A few final but crucial thankyous: to my agent Annabel Merullo for finding me a publisher; to Trevor Dolby at Random House who thought it good enough and then covered it in post-it notes telling me how to do it better; to Kate Johnson who edited the manuscript; to Nicola Taplin for putting it all together and finally to my family, for putting up with my erratic moods. It's been emotionally exhausting spending so much time with half of my brain stuck in 1982 revisiting my own and everybody else's experiences. I hope you enjoy reading our stories.

Harry Benson, March 2012

Index

(the initials HB refer to Harry Benson;
page numbers in italic type refer to photographs)

Index

Index

Index

Index

Index

Index

Index

Soviet Union 69
Special Air Service (SAS) 49, 77–8, 190, 245
  D Squadron 121, 190, 206–9
  deaths among, in Sea King crash 119
  and Fortuna Glacier 5–17, *11*, *54*, *56–62*
  insertion in inflatables attempted by 62
  mainland Argentina mission of 113, 114
  Mount Kent mission of 206–9
  Pebble Island mission of 108–12
  and Port Stanley operation 290
  Pucaras blown up by 363
  San Carlos mission of 120, 121, 127, 134
  and *Santa Fe* 64
Special Boat Service (SBS) 49, 77, 105–6, 118, 154
  and San Carlos landing mission 121, 122, 124, 126, 133, 134
  and *Santa Fe* 64
Spence, Sub-Lt Jerry 277, 286, 321, 322–4, 344, 349, *361*
  at reunion 369
Spencer, Lt Cdr Mike 39–40, 41, 103, 286, 300, 322
Spens-Black, Lt Peter 116
  and Mount Kent mission 208
Stanley, Lt Cdr Ian 62–3
  and Fortuna Glacier 7, 9–11, 15–17, *57–9 passim*, 61
  on San Carlos landing mission 125, 132, 133
  and SAS inflatables mission 62
  shrapnel injures 133
Stanning, Lt Cdr Tim 40, 52, 70, 94, 129, 184, 185–6, 231, 255
  recceing of forward bases by 253–4
  and *Sir Galahad* 263, 264, 270
stovies 20–1
Stromness, RFA 128, 143–4
Super Etendard 88, 113, 149, 172, 211
Super Frelon 102
Sussex Mountains 128, 140, 143, 155, 190, 195, 196, 249, 307, 342, 345
Swan Inlet 240

Sycamore helicopters, in Suez crisis 19

Task Force HQ, Northwood 250
tasking 192
Tattersall, Petty Officer Aircrewman Colin 78
Taylor, Lt Nick 90
Teal 190, 213, 238, 240, 242, 243, 249, 254, 277, 289, 293, 300, 301, 307, 318, 319
teeny-weenies xxvi, 257, 322
Thatcher, Margaret 37, 65
Thomas, Sub-Lt Jerry 235, 277, 290
Thompson, Brig. Julian 183, 184, 190, 198, 257
Thornewill, Lt Cdr Simon 39–40, 40–1, 72, 210, 269, 339–41
  and *Coventry* 166
  Pucara flown by 364
  on San Carlos landing mission 132
thunderflash 28
Tidd, Lt Mike 41, 56, 94, 226–7, 277
  Falklands-bound *55–6*
  and Fortuna Glacier 6–13 *passim*, 15, *56–62 passim*
  prisoner management by 66–7
  at reunion 369
  and *Santa Fe* 64
Tidepool, RFA 96, 121, 159, 161
Tidespring, RFA 56, 60, 64, 66, 94, 226
Top Malo House 213–14
Trims (maintainer) 300
Tupper, Chief Aircrewman Alf 167, 339–40
Tuttey, Ch. Petty Officer Bill 229–30, 236, 255–6, 260–1
  and *Sir Galahad* 262–3, 263–4, 264–5, 370
Tyrrell, Cpl Ian 'Gus' 171, 174–5, 176–7, 181, 182
  recorded missing in action 181

Uganda, SS 192, 215–16, 219, 325, 336, 342–3, *343*

Veinticinco de Mayo, ARA 87–8
vessels, see individual ships' names
Vowles, Lt Cdr Peter 38, 41

Index

Wallace, Lt George 278, 301
Ward, Lt Cdr Nigel 'Sharkey' 134, 162, 235
Warden, Lt Cdr Roger 38, 42, 186
Wasp 63–4, 139, 153, 367
  firing on *Santa Fe* 63
  and hospital-ship inspections 219
Wells, Lt David 63
Wessex:
  almost continuous flying of 317
  ammunition transfer facilitated by 74
  Ascension Island preparation of first of 43
  and *Atlantic Conveyor 100*, 176–8
  boarding, knack to 274
  casevac work for 215
  control fault in 132
  and *Coventry* 167, 168–9
  'dead reckoning' navigation method on 73
  downwind fast stop of 244, 284
  Engadine boosts contingent of 272
  expectation of more of 161
  flotation canisters on 51–2
  Fortuna Glacier mission of, *see* Fortuna Glacier
  Gazelle compared with 26
  and ground resonance 47–8
  in gunship role 144
  HU Mk 5, HB learns to fly 26
  HU Mk 5, service entered by 19
  hydraulic systems in 146
  in-flight refuelling considered for 87
  machine gun in *156*
  maximum speed of 140
  Mirage attack fails to destroy 136–7
  missile launched at 84–6
  missing 182
  nighttime closeness of 237
  normal maximum power of 124

operating from three locations 330
operating without coordination 185
in Operational Flying Training 28
pictured on *Antrim* 82
at Port San Carlos *234*
rocket capability of 196–7
rocket pods on 28–9
and San Carlos landing mission 121–6 *passim*, 128, 129
Sea Kings more powerful than 70
single-engine capability of 233, 238, 268
and *Sir Galahad* 262
South Georgia crashes of 9–12, *11*, 72, 119
swapping seats in 282–3
and tasking 192
thermal image camera on 122, 197
turning point for operations of 231
typical flight of 51
underused 143
West Falkland 1, 108, 118, 137, 149, 152, 154, 160, 162, 203, 258
Weston, Simon 265
Whale, FOB, on 153, 154, 192, 210, 223, 231
  move for 231
Whirlwind, in Suez crisis 19
Wilson, Brig. Tony 239, 240, 328
Wilson, Ldg Aircrewman Tug:
  and Fortuna Glacier 6–8, 10, 13–14, 60, 61–2
Wilson, Petty Officer Aircrewman Tug:
  and *Sir Galahad* 263, 265
Wireless Ridge 348
Woodward, Admiral Sandy 76

Yarmouth, HMS 89, 90, 140, 251, 305
Young, Capt. Brian 13, 65